MUSICAL
STRUCTURE
and
PERFORMANCE

MUSICAL

STRUCTURE

and

PERFORMANCE

Wallace Berry

YALE UNIVERSITY PRESS

New Haven and London

Published with assistance from
the Louis Stern Memorial Fund.

Designed by Kaelin Chappell
and set in Sabon type.
Printed in the United States of America by
Vail-Ballou Press, Binghamton, New York.

Library of Congress Cataloging-in-Publication Data
Berry, Wallace.
Musical structure and performance.
Bibliography: p.
Includes index.
1. Musical analysis. 2. Music—Performance.
3. Brahms, Johannes, 1833-1897. Stücke, piano, op 76.
Intermezzo, B♭ major. 4. Berg, Alban, 1885-1935.
Stücke, clarinet, piano, op. 5. Nr. 3. 5. Debussy,
Claude, 1862-1918. Ariettes oubliées. C'est l'extase.
I. Title.
MT6.B465M9 1989   781   88-27958
ISBN 0-300-04327-9 (alk. paper)

The paper in this book meets the guidelines for permanence
and durability of the Committee on Production Guidelines for
Book Longevity of the Council on Library Resources.

10 9 8 7 6 5 4 3 2 1

Again,

to Maxine

The musical act of converting a string of note signs into a sequence of tones is by no means a simple one-to-one translation. If this task is left to a computer, the result is generally very poor from a musical point of view.
   —*J. Sundberg, A. Askenfelt, and L. Frydén,*
     "Musical Performance: A Synthesis-by-Rule Approach,"
     Computer Music Journal

The dialectic between feeling and understanding is seen, then, as a process of checks and balances, with feeling appealing to and illuminating the path of reflection, while reflection enhances, sustains, and ratifies feeling. This reciprocity is never ending, and it is for this reason that . . . we never have certain knowledge of when feeling is authentic. To try to provide a "moment of arrival" is to imply that the meanings in a piece are finite and exhaustible. . . . In any case, the failure to attain certainty . . . is to be seen not as a failure of method, but as an acknowledgment of the ongoing life of a composition.
   —*Thomas Clifton,* Music as Heard

Certainly, one cannot read this poem without effort. The page is often corrupt and mud-stained, and torn and stuck together with faded leaves, with scraps of verbena or geranium. To read this poem one must have myriad eyes, like one of those lamps that turn on slabs of racing water at midnight. . . . One must put aside antipathies and jealousies and not interrupt. One must have patience and infinite care and let the light sound.
   —*Virginia Woolf,* The Waves

Contents

Preface

Among life's few authentic sublimities, moving and stimulating musical performance ranks very high. A profound musical experience is not truly describable in words, but we may think of it variously, even as music is infinitely varied in its potential expressive scope: affecting, rousing, intimately engrossing, intellectually engaging. And musical performance is at its best marked by apparent ease, spontaneity, and supremacy of control over sweep and detail. Just as words fail to describe the depth and virtual transcendence of the intense musical experience of performer and listener, the secrets of interpretation often seem intractably resistant to articulate revelations. Indeed, it is likely that performers more often than not act intuitively. And their intuitions, however hard to fathom, are assuredly not ex nihilo, but rather a product of deep experience, ultimately toward a motivating, evaluating consciousness.

The concept of intuition as deriving from experience, yet lacking the corroboration of analysis and articulate reason, dismisses any metaphysical basis of knowing and puts aside as irrelevant to the complexities of interesting musical structure any human responses which may be neurologically programmed. Intuition is of course applicable to musical analysis as well as performance, although no self-respecting analyst would settle for it; pure intuition is in analysis no less unreliable than in performance.

These studies are not concerned with those elusive intuitive insights which, with technical mastery, can fortuitously enflame great musical performance; they do not attempt to explore the typically undefined impulses of imagination, absorbed experience, and consequent recreativity by which satisfying musical realization can at times be characterized. Musicians frequently refer to such qualities of intuitive grasp as incommunicable in teaching, unless through active example. And the record shows the psychology of acquired intuitive understanding to be acutely problematic, elusive of objective understanding.

This book is, rather, about the systematic, rational examination of music toward demonstrable insights into structure as immanent meaning, and thence to concrete, pragmatic issues of tempo and articulation reflected in the myriad, subtle details of execution. With the intuitive cognitions of experience assumed, this book asks how, in very precise terms and carefully defined circumstances, a structural relation exposed in analysis can be illuminated in the inflections of edifying performance. That the relations between discerned structural elements and interpretive choices are exceedingly complex may be judged from, for example, the extensive discussion of formal significance in seven bars (measures 13–19) of Brahms's Intermezzo, Op. 76, No. 4, or that concerning multifarious implications of a single chord (measure 13) in Berg's Op. 5, No. 3, to mention two cases involving especially problematic questions of functional significance in the musical content, and consequently of interpretive attitude and detail.

Moreover, analysis as a basis for decisions about interpretation often leads to the conclusion that a particular interpretive intent is subject to fulfillment in more ways than one. It may also suggest that, once such a basic condition as tempo has been decided, details of evident musical content are best projected in a relatively neutral realization, without interposed modulations of tempo and articulation in performance. (I refer to acts of the performer beyond the strict representation of notated elements as interpretive "interventions.") In fact, the determination that an impartial realization is warranted is no less founded in analysis than is a decision to *do* something beyond playing the notes clearly and accurately.

Implicitly at the root of a study such as this is the rhetorical question: Does it matter whether the performer is consciously aware of the elements and processes of form and structure? In an important sense, the entire content of this book can be summarized as an effort to justify my answer to that question: yes. But allowing that analysis is a necessary basis for enlightened, illuminating interpretation, a point that may seem almost ironically platitudinous, why do performers so rarely give time and thought to the problems of probing inquiry into musical structure, and theorists to the practical measures of performance? One factor of explanation may well be the intense difficulties of pinpointing specific, plausible connections between the findings of analysis and consequent outlets in performance, and the resultant temptation to depend instead on the fallible dictates of intuited feeling. I should be less than candid if I failed to grant at the outset that these difficulties are much in evidence in this volume.

One is aware too of the hazard of an overloaded consciousness in musical performance, when analysis has pointed to multifarious possibilities out of which a coherent whole, comprising compatible, chosen elements, must be derived and conveyed. The awareness of a network of complex relations (multileveled, explicit and implicit, registrally conjunct and disjunct) reasonably conceivable in most interesting pieces can induce a paralyzing, bewildering set of conflicting impulses in which the vital illusion of spontaneity is manifestly out of the question. That is why in each of this book's major analyses, probing many of music's structural dimensions, I often suggest divergent views, emphasizing that any thoughtful performance is an individual portrayal arising out of searching scrutiny *and* justifiable selection.

The analytical comprehension of structure is usually assimilated to a submerged level of consciousness, with the details of performance—elements to project, underscore, or subdue—ideally falling into place in a motivated stream of action and reaction shaped by exhaustive prior thought and conditioning experiment. This is not to say that once the preparation is secure an artist's conceptualization is set forever into a determined mold: as we all know, the life of an interpretation is marked by further discovery, and even by radical conceptual transformations. It may also be that an interpretation will vary—not of course capriciously—according to differing circumstances of time and place. As long as performance is shored up and sustained by cogent considerations, such variance can have positive value and fascination for both interpreter and listener.

My procedure of dwelling in extenso on just a few pieces may well be disputed; but historical context and development are also not what this book is about, nor does it inquire into the undeniably vital considerations of historical-stylistic appropriateness in performance. These are of course imperative, and the resources for looking into historical performance practice are abundant. One overviewing essay which I particularly admire is "The Historical Performance Movement," in Joseph Kerman's *Contemplating Music* (Cambridge: Harvard University Press, 1985), which comments wisely on the thorny problems of documentation and authenticity, on the complications of defining and resolving many attendant questions (including that of intuitive performance), and on certain items of the pertinent literature.

Most music theory affirms the conviction that much of general import can be learned about musical structure, realization, and experience in intense examination of the particular workings of almost any challenging piece, however the piece may reflect the broad terms of a particular style or system. To have dwelled at length on three compositions, each of them in its special way elegantly and eminently expressive, has been enlightening for me, as I hope it may prove for readers. But while it is monumentally rewarding to discover what and how an individual work communicates, and how its elements interact to expressive ends, the essential point of probing a few provocative musical examples in such prodigious detail is the quest for broad principles by which musical structure is meaningful, and by which structure and content can be understood, and illuminated in performance. This book is thus a testimony to the conviction—one without which much, probably most, analytical music theory would have only dubious utility—that however specific its individuated terms, any piece that embodies systemic procedures reveals principles of structure (and hence of realization in performance) that are analogously evident in other pieces. Indeed, I believe, as is borne out in much of my writing, that there runs through all of music, except that of recent date in which alignments of concurrent elements are random or in all details of association prescribed (and in either case adventitious in result), a pervasive unity of many common principles of function and expression. And to illustrate principles of musical structure and performance by thorough penetration of a few short compositions, often by way of changing angles of view respecting a number of structural dimensions, has the important advantage of vividly exposing derived principles in total contexts, where overreaching conclusions and constructions can often emerge.

In that each of my three primary subjects is treated in investigation of various elements regarded in different perspectives, this book is about analytical approaches as well as about the issues of performance to which the analysis leads. Attention is given to: continuities of line deemed important to interpretation; interactions of textural components; tonal and harmonic functions; motivic terms and relations requiring deliberate awareness; rhythmic properties; processes by which forms are articulated and structural lines of progression and recession delineated; the reflections of text in music (especially in the Debussy song); and particular, special problems of performance, such as the ambiguity of the fermata, and decisions of tempo. Practical questions of interpretation are posed and addressed at every stage, often with suggestions of alternative possibilities of interpretive intervention which follow from and are consistent with particular structural concepts presented.

My purpose is, then, to pose critical questions of performance in selected, particular contexts representing important genera of tonal music, and to ask how the analysis of formal and structural elements can be responsive to such questions, establishing a perspective for rational approaches to resolving them.

Looking over this book's layout—its central expanse of detailed analysis and commentary lying between relatively brief introductory and concluding segments—brings to mind S. J. Gould's apt characterization of a certain volume as, if I remember correctly, a huge sandwich. My first chapter briefly develops a statement of fundamental problems to which the study as a whole is addressed, setting forth certain premises. Chapter 2 is a compendious summary of underlying, essential issues in the relations of analysis to performance, outlined in general terms, with examples drawn from various sources in which these issues arise. This broad survey leaves detailed investigations for subsequent chapters, where complete pieces, in which basic and essential questions recur in radically disparate stylistic idioms, are subjected to deliberately multifaceted analyses of structural and interpretive possibilities. Finally, important observations and findings are briefly recalled.

While relying wherever possible on conventional signs and terms generally understood, I have in some of the illustrations devised or adopted special indications of performance interventions. These include conventional verbal instructions (such as ritardando, come sopra, and the like) and established symbols of articulation as well as a few which I have contrived. The latter are, where not self-evident, set forth in the Notes on Usage at the front of the book. Of course, the inescapable imprecisions of interpretive signs and directions are a constant dilemma, usually requiring supplementary comment in the text.

There are, as always, many whose help should be acknowledged. I owe deep appreciation to Allen Forte, my distinguished colleague and valued friend; he has given generous and supportive encouragement of many kinds and of inestimable significance to me in and beyond our shared professional concerns.

Ruth White of the University of British Columbia graciously listened and responded to some of my developing thoughts about the Verlaine poem, in addition to clarifying certain points of translation; I thank her even as I must emphatically relieve her of accountability for any questionable conclusions drawn in my analysis.

Some of the issues discussed in chapter 2 were brought to my attention by graduate students; for example, those concerning Beethoven's Op. 106 arose in connection with a fruitful study by Barrie Barrington. Constructive and invigorating discussions with Dr. Charles Morrison, in the course of his important research into Bartók's tonal structures, contributed to my own thinking about late tonality. And the investigations represented in this book, reflecting and incorporating ideas that have emerged gradually over many years, have been greatly served by useful exchanges with many other students and colleagues.

The musical illustrations were prepared by John and Kimberley Roeder, using a resourceful new computer program developed by Keith Hamel. I am grateful to copyright holders who have granted permission for me to reprint excerpts from restricted publications: European American Music, agents for Universal Edition, for the Berg; Theodore Presser Company, agents for Editions Jobert, for the Debussy; and Belmont Music Publishers for the excerpts from Schoenberg's Op. 19. John Clough, editor of *Music Theory Spectrum*, has allowed me to appropriate from an article I contributed to the journal's volume 10 a number of paragraphs of commentary and two illustrations, the present examples 2.11 and 2.12.

Jeanne Ferris and Fred Kameny of Yale University Press have rendered sympathetic and invariably useful advice and guidance. And I owe thanks also to an anonymous prepublication reader whose suggestions led to some important clarifications and changes of organization.

It is my hope that the concepts laid out in this book will elicit interest among musicians of varying professional commitments, inevitable differences of approach and conclusion notwithstanding. I have sought, by explanation and illustration, to make these concepts clearly accessible to the reader who is experienced in musical analysis and performance.

Musical Structure and Performance incorporates some work presented in lectures, seminars, and papers of recent years, none of it previously published, and all submitted to rigorous reexamination and reformulation in 1986 and 1987. In an important sense, this work's origins may be traced to courses offered at the University of Michigan in the early 1970s and at the University of British Columbia in 1984. Chapter 2 evolved from a paper presented at McGill University, Montréal, in March 1986. The actual writing of the book has by no means been marked by a consistent line of progress from start to finish; indeed, a considerable output of five years ago was more or less abandoned in favor of more clearly directed, concentrated work during a year's leave in 1986–87, spent in and around Vancouver and in Carmel, California.

While the present effort represents a culmination, the perplexing questions of structure and interpretation in music have of course been with me through all of my professional life, not least in connection with my own extensive activities in performance. It seems to me best, in fact, that this book be read as the weighed and reweighed analytical impressions and reflections of a practicing musician— composer and pianist—more than as systematic theory. No doubt the issues raised here will be treated by many other scholars in the coming years, which are certain to see a continued, burgeoning interest in the relations of analysis to performance. I hope to have contributed to that effort, eliciting constructive— corroborative or divergent—responses concerning the music, and the ideas, into which this book inquires.

Notes on Usage

Pitch-class names are given as underlined uppercase letters except with reference to a tonic in such expressions as D-major Prelude, or C:V. Names of specific pitches are identified as C (two octaves below middle C̱—the lowest pitch of the cello); c for the octave above C; c_1 (middle C̱); c_2 (the octave above middle C̱); and so forth, with corresponding symbols and subscripts for pitches lying within the octave above each.

The expression "c–e" denotes a succession, whereas in the expression "c, e" the elements c and e are associated in some indicated sense not necessarily of succession. Where a group of pitches or pitch classes has in some stated significance an integral structural unity, it is often given within braces: {c,e}. And I use the solidus to conjoin, in noncommittal references, enharmonically equivalent members of a pitch class, as in E̱-flat/Ḏ-sharp.

In the music examples, the abbreviation "m(m)." denotes "measure(s)." Wherever illustration requires indication of an interpretive act or tendency of tempo or articulation beyond those notated in the score itself I give it in square brackets, except in a few cases where such interpolations are self-evidently mine. Many extreme refinements of inflection are suggested only in the descriptive commentary accompanying the examples, rather than in the musical notation. And throughout the text I use Italian terms and phrases of usual currency without italicization or translation, and such participles as "ritardando" and "sforzato" are at times employed, according to common usage, as nouns.

I have coined a small number of symbols to represent interventions, especially of articulation, for which conventional notation is inadequate. These are given below:

slightly held (un poco tenuto)

slightly emphasized, by intensity or duration; most pronounced impulse denoted by the symbol at the left, least by that at the right

[>]   [–]   [∪]

punctuation; most pronounced denoted by the symbol at the left, least by the vertical slash through staff line, leger line, or beam

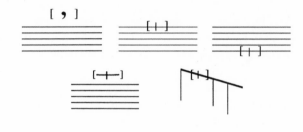

directed line of action to, from a cited event

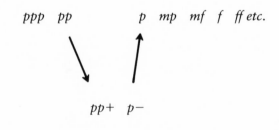

marked for attention as discussed, not necessarily by intensity or duration; one or more notes

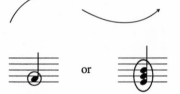

or

moved deliberately

[⟶]

the scale of dynamic intensities:

ppp pp   p mp mf f ff etc.

the symbols + and − denote greater and lesser intensity, respectively, in relations of the immediate context

pp+ p−

Chapter One

POINTS OF DEPARTURE

The consideration of bases for interpretive decision in cogent musical realizations would appear to be of fundamental significance to theorist and performer alike. Yet music theory has, by and large, surprisingly little to say about issues of interpretation as these might reasonably derive from observations and hypotheses about musical form, structure, and process.

References to issues of interpretive realization following from theoretical constructs occur of course in historical music theory: one has but to think of Riemann and Schenker, not to mention more distant theorists who set forth technical principles (such as those of ornamentation) in particular stylistic idioms. And despite considerable inattention in recent theory to matters of analysis and performance, there has emerged a distinct theoretical subdiscipline that is increasingly comprehensive in addressing the concerns of interpretation. I mention a few cases in passing.

An early milestone was Edward Cone's monograph of 1968,[1] some facets of which he reconsidered in 1985.[2] And some contemporary writers (Meyer, Epstein, Cogan, to mention a few) refer significantly and productively to issues of performance pursuant to theory, as do some basic texts in music theory (of which Joel Lester's is a worthy example).[3] Moreover, conferences on music theory now include presentations on issues of performance, too rarely bringing together theorists (ideally, theorist-performers) and interpretive artists; an insightful and engaging paper by Janet Schmalfeldt in the format of a dialogue on two Bagatelles of Beethoven was heard initially at a conference of the Society for Music Theory and later appeared in print.[4] So important and challenging are the problems to be considered that the current surge of interest will likely continue, resulting in major symposia and special issues of journals.

The growing literature on analysis and performance notwithstanding, even the most thoughtful interpreter commonly acts on purely intuitive inference and judgment rarely of articulate substance. This is not to deny that intuitively informed performance is often convincing, as for example when a gifted interpreter, out of long and profound experience, relatively spontaneously finds the "right" tempo or dynamic inflection. But we all know how frequently and how deeply musical realization can suffer from the performer's failure, whether out of inability or impatient denial, to explore in probing analysis those problems of interpretive choice which every artist faces in encounters with challenging works. This is a fact of professional life in spite of special problems in the relatively ambiguous notation of earlier tonal music, where even fundamental tempi may be unspecified, and formidable difficulties of other kinds in the literatures of conventional tonality, late tonality, and post-tonal styles, however the details of realization may be stipulated in notation. Indeed, no notational system—other than those requiring of human participation only the switching on of tape or other programmed "performance" medium—is without significant margins of latitude within which interpretive choices have to be made.

Thus an interpreter's involvement with the many recurring issues of choice is inescapable, in pedagogy (in which most performers are engaged) as in performance itself, even though the path from analysis to interpretive decision is anything but straight and narrow, and fraught with often harrowing complexities owing to the network of structural content and process commonly functional in interesting music. If the performer does anything beyond mere execution, the doing must not be merely intuitive or mimetic; it must result from informed discretion and deliberate control. Analysis tempers the purely subjective impulse, resolves unavoidable dilemmas, and offers means by which the teacher can articulate ideas persuasively and rationally.

The central issue of interpretation can be summarized in two questions: In a particular unit of musical structure, to and from what points (and states) can directed motions be said to lead? And what is the performer's role in projecting and illuminating essential elements of direction and continuity? With these questions, embracing many difficult, subsidiary issues, it is vital that any discussion of theory and practice in performance resist pretensions of dogmatic instruction; I repeat that for virtually any given line of reasoning, from analytical finding to interpretive decision, there are defensible alternatives within the necessary perspective of comprehended structure and process. Moreover, every structure is unique in its particulars of functioning elements, balances, unities, and identifiable processive tendencies, whatever broad stylistic-generic parallels may pertain among related compositions of some given class.

What are the domains of expressive latitude in which a performer can intervene, where it is appropriate and desirable to project and expose some conceptual image of a piece? What beyond mere verbatim execution can a performer do in the exercise of interpretive discretion?

These questions bring to mind first the element of tempo—not only the setting of an underlying rate, as might be stipulated in a metronomic value or frequency for the referential pulse, but also adjustments of acceleration and deceleration in the course of a piece, at times minute in degree. The deliberate control and modulation of tempo is surely one of the more telling kinds of interpretive intervention in musical performance.

A second realm of interpretive activity is that of articulation, the calculated control of the discrete musical impulse itself, in an infinite range of possibilities. Here are included all tempering adjustments of individual events: in intensity, in duration, in consistencies of legato by which events may in one sense be grouped, and in punctuations by which they are, however slightly, separated. Like the choice of tempo articulation often suggests expressive character, especially in its broad tendencies but also in modulations of the surface.

If tempo and articulation are the essential categories of interpretive intervention, the choices applied within each can be understood to denote an interpreter's attitude, projected as appropriate in the portrayed realization of a given structure. Presumably, the general attitudinal approach—conditioned by the best possible comprehension of structural functions and processes—governs and is reflected in the specific acts of interpretation by which cofunctional elements are realized and overtly related in performance.

That these two broad categories of interpretive choice are not absolutely distinct does not compromise their validity as broadly applicable domains of expressive action in which a performer intervenes. And although it is perhaps paradoxical that a truly infinite range of potential expressive interventions should be subject to so simple a classification, the fact is that the things a performer can do in interpretation are indeed essentially matters of tempo and articulation.

I have observed that the literature on analysis and performance is sparse. Yet, there are a few important resources that require mention with regard to my own thinking; these are acknowledged at appropriate points in the text.

As every reader will appreciate, it is inevitable that particular concepts which have been engendered, forged, and tried in personal experience and cultivated in my published studies will constitute a recurring, basic perspective in this book. I give here and at various points to follow a certain amount of summary comment regarding these ideas, but cannot of course repeat to any substantial degree what is treated exhaustively elsewhere, notably in my *Structural Functions in Music*.[5]

It is useful to think of traditional musical form in terms of certain consistently relevant processes by which it is expressed: that of *preparation* or *introduction,* commonly of relatively simple texture and tentative, dissonant tonal content; that of *expository statement,* often in a context of relatively stable tonal conditions and direct motivic display (or *expository restatement,* a further manifestation of the process of basic exposition, yet often involving variation in one or more elements); that of *transitional bridging,* often modestly developmental—substance and activity contrived to lead from here to there or there to here; that in which the active *development* of previously exposed materials is a primary concern; and that of *closure,* in which prevailing element-processes are directed into relatively resolutive conditions. Of course, these processes are not rigidly discrete: any particular composed segment is likely to reflect more than one in a context of a singular essential tendency, the content of which depends on position in the broad formal narrative. In traditional form, applicable well into twentieth-century literatures, the study of thematic design is often best considered with reference to such processes, articulated in line, rhythm, harmony, and other elements the particulars of which are often a basis for the classification of style and idiom. An understanding of functional process is often the key to enlightened performance decisions, as is emphasized in the studies that follow.

I have conceived of function in musical structure as the place and processive role of any given event in an identifiable directed tendency. The function (or role) of the particular event is thus heard in relation to preceding and subsequent events, immediate or overreaching—more or less, farther or nearer along assessed linear streams, and at levels of or "under" the surface. Such a concept of function has been well demonstrated as applicable to all structural elements. But its significance in music is perhaps most powerfully appreciable within the realm of conventional tonality, where harmonic and melodic degrees stand at calculable distances from the tonic, along some line of inferred relations, in a palpable system of mobility. I have traced comparable streams of directed events to and from relatively normative, resolutive states discernible within other elements—texture and meter, for example—cofunctioning complementarily or counteractively in relation to tonality.

A state of stasis is presumably conceivable except at the most immediate surface of a structure. But in general a succession of events is regarded as at some level of structure *receding* toward resolution or *progressing* toward conditions away from the resolutive focus of reference. Events cofunction in a network of directed activity between immediately contiguous events or between temporally separated events having overreaching spans of implication and, in this sense, consequent hierarchic superiority. The structural network may reflect a relatively simple, primary governing tendency, or, in intricate, expansive works, may be of a truly challenging complexity. At the same time, music's form (as process) and structure (as the interactions of progressive and recessive tendencies) are of course materially interconnected: any particular formal process is, again, likely to involve a particular, predominant structural inclination.

For example, that of closure embodies prevalent recessions toward resolutive states, and that of introduction is usually characterized by progressions into relatively dissonant, active conditions.

The foregoing, too terse account of certain essential points of departure must serve as a preliminary, general explanation of structural tendencies and processes explored, along with other pertinent factors of structural content, in examples investigated in this book.

It appears likely to me that there is a direct correlation between an event's nearer-foreground manifestation and its susceptibility to interpretive intervention and control in performance. That is, any deliberate interpretive projection of theoretically asserted overreaching associations must surely be relatively problematic of realization, as well as potentially (and ironically) disruptive of surface lines, directed processes, and details of content by which expressive effect is most potently engendered, which are most accessible to experience, and in which a composition's special distinctiveness is embodied.

My analyses thus pay close attention to surface and near-surface detail—a piece's individuating, comparatively dense network of foreground and middleground lines. Where a discernible background of pitch relations is as in much recent music comparatively individual and particular rather than conventional, it is presumably more likely to want some manner of deliberate assertion in performance, commonly in relatively brief works.

As many of my examples demonstrate, it is nonetheless imperative that any interpretive decision respecting immediate events and their interrelations be informed and illuminated by an articulate concept of the whole, and of the place of immediate events in a larger frame. Further, although I tend to regard conventional background tonal structures as largely inert entities, systemic and hence lacking in distinctiveness, it is fundamental to my sense of structure that there is often manifest in the musical structure an underlying dynamic course of events, to and from points—even at times one central, focal point—of primary expressive orientation. Such a "background," the content and course of which may constitute a kinetic, all-embracing gesture, is decidedly amenable to explicit awareness and projection in performance, as opposed to the common and essentially referential structure of farthest-spanning pitch events. The concept of a dynamic, expressive, gestural whole, applicable to many compositions, figures prominently in the examples treated in this book.

Musicians often observe that all serious musical activity—of composition, research, and rehearsal—has its ideal fruition in the act of performance. Apart from the mental imagery of the specialist and variously dim memories of others, music's only reality (unless it is electronically preserved) is in the passing moment of its performance—its direct experience in an intimate sharing between interpreter and listener, the composer and scholar manifest but unseen.

How ironic then that the disciplined study of relations between structure and performance is so neglected, with interpretive realization and resolution of those quandaries which arise inescapably in the performance of challenging, intricate works left to impulsive reaction, to mimicry, to ambiguous (if at times fortuitously apposite) instructions emanating from the intuitive reflections of experience.

In this study I hope to suggest rational principles by which the critical moment of realization may be informed, and to expose thoughtful approaches to specific problems of decision in performance. The underlying conviction is simple: that the musical experience is richest when functional elements of shape, continuity, vitality, and direction have been sharply discerned in analysis, and construed as a basis for the intellectual awareness which must underlie truly illuminating interpretation. In that sense, a good performance is a portrayal, a critical discourse on the conceived meaning of a work, and a fruit of inquiry and evaluative reflection. Such an interpretation makes for that transcendent moment in which creative, theoretical, and practical efforts are fulfilled. The ideal musical performance, at once moving and enlightening, mirrors the noblest impulses in human endeavor: that of rational examination, that of powerfully significative abstract imagery, and that of fervent commitment.

Chapter Two

QUESTIONS ARISING IN THE RELATIONS OF ANALYSIS TO PERFORMANCE

Pianists, singers, conductors, and other performers make choices, and to deny that these ought to have reasoned bases would seem to negate the imperative of rationality itself, a value by which at least in more civilized moments we like to think ourselves guided. A performer's awareness of music's structure is a valuable, indeed requisite, basis for doing—and not doing—particular things in realizations of particular pieces.

Music theorists give necessary attention to deep, under-surface lines of continuity, but do not thereby underestimate the vital import of surface detail in the musical experience: it is at the surface that we hear most of the distinctively expressive elements of any musical organism. Yet theorists are likely to hold that attention in performance to matters of immediate detail must not be at the expense of deeper lines of continuity and indirect relations. Interpretive focus must be on the functions of rich detail in the context of a grasp of broad continuities, however problematic the projection of such continuities. In stating so obvious a caveat, I acknowledge that we are at times content with absorption in lavish surface color and nuance, which may well be affecting; and it may be doubted that genuinely convincing balance between detail and the organic whole is commonly achieved in performance.

The Intuitive Factor in Performance

Despite a number of seminal explorations, the study of how interpretive decision follows the analysis of form and structure remains subsidiary to other interests of music theorists and performers. This is due in part, I believe, to the wide acceptance of intuitive bases for interpretive choices, as opposed to articulate justifications derived from serious analysis.

As performers work out the technical problems of a piece, they often rely on what "feels" right in matters of tempo and articulation. Related to this tendency is the pedagogical method of demonstration, as distinct from efforts at logical reasoning and articulate explanation. This all too common pattern, with the student's assimilation of interpretive concepts by mimicry, is often indicative of intuitive rather than inductive or deductive decision. (My reference here is to the creatively interpretive aspect of performance, rather than to those matters of mere fidelity to score and style which of course preempt a certain amount of pedagogical attention.)

Doing as a means of instruction is not necessarily unsound; in many circumstances it is no doubt the best way to make a point. Nor is there any question that the intuitions of sensitive performers are often valid, as the long-range outcome of deeply assimilated experience conducive to spontaneous responses which indeed may be virtually unerring. But intuition can also be a capricious guide, and it is clearly inadequate in solving problems, as when a performer faces a dilemma respecting tempo or articulation, and where an interpretive choice needs to be underscored with explanation and substantiation, as in teaching.

Specificity and the Lack of It

Those who look to music theory for guidance in performance are right to expect more than generality. Given a reasoned view of structure, to what *particular* interpretive decisions might it be said to lead? What, for example, might the performer *do* in recognition and portrayal of an accepted analytical construct, allowing that any particular structural continuity or function can usually be served in a number of ways? Such questions are all too often neglected in studies of structure and interpretation; or they are treated with broad pronouncements whose utility comes into serious doubt in particular circumstances.[1]

The following statement by Edward Cone has such a ring of validity that one might be inclined to post it prominently in the performance studio: "We must first discover the rhythmic shape of a piece . . . and then try to make it as clear as possible to our listeners."[2]

But if a piece's "rhythmic shape" is indeed somehow inferred, what does a performer do to "make it as clear as possible?"[3]

A theorist may of course choose merely to point out a particular structural factor, posing pursuant issues without specific suggestions of practical interpretive consequences. Yet this is less than we must ask of studies explicitly devoted to analysis and performance, and the theorist's stated conclusions about performance must go beyond gratuitous generality. Interpreters whom we address may well ask not only to exactly what choices and procedures an analytical construct reasonably leads, but also whether any stated suggestions of performance decision follow logically and persuasively from such a construct, serving to elucidate the analysis.

I shall cite two examples from Schenker, both occurring in analytical studies of Bach's music for unaccompanied strings, and both followed by typically brief comment concerning implications for performance. In an essay on the Largo of the Sonata, BWV 1005, for violin, Schenker makes the point that "a sforzato is necessitated by the chromatic tones";[4] and in his study of the Sarabande of the Suite, BWV 1009, for cello, he refers to "the immutable rule that chromatic alterations be emphasized."[5] Here are instances in which interpretive "necessities" are affirmed very precisely indeed; yet such claimed precepts are clearly far too sweeping in implication. They are in fact potentially obtrusive, not least with respect to Schenker's portrayals of encompassing lines of continuity in these pieces.

Obviously any probing analysis reveals many important elements, not all of which can be expressed overtly. Indeed many inferred, comprehensive lines of structure may be incapable of interpretive realization, just as a gratuitous interpretive stroke intended to project some analytical construct may intrude on and distort lines of structure inferred within other elements, or at other levels. Overt emphasis on a chromatic alteration simply because it is there may impair a vital middleground continuity, diminish some essential proximate event, or exaggerate the occurrence with regard to its formal context. Moreover, arising in such a perspective is an allied, crucial question: Is the particular factor exposed in analysis and deemed vital in the structure self-evident, requiring no intervention on the part of the performer? To raise these questions is a way of calling attention to the necessity for delineating priorities among elements made apparent in analysis, and of setting a perspective for many problems of analysis and performance identified in the following pages.

Diverse Conclusions of Analysis and Practice

That there can be divergent, reasonable concepts of structure in any given piece is a fundamental rule of existence for the analyst unfettered by bias. That unalterable fact of life accounts in part for the sometimes bewildering complications of relating analysis to performance. Another reason for such complications follows inescapably: a particular analytical construct by no means points to a singular, pursuant direction of realization.[6]

In 1985 I wrote that most analyses by music theorists deal with "nonfacts," that is, that they reveal plausible opinions rather than incontrovertible truths, and that this is evident "in the invigorating circumstances of . . . analytical theory . . . [and in] the disparity among satisfying performances of any piece."[7] Schmalfeldt makes this point, noting that three recorded performances of a Bagatelle by Beethoven achieve a particular (in her view desirable) result in three different ways: "*There is no single, one-and-only performance decision that can be dictated by an analytic observation* [italics in original]."[8] Although one may be unprepared to apply this to all analytical findings, the general truth of the statement is scarcely disputable.

To put this into the terms of a specific realm of interpretive decision: no general guidelines can be said to apply to all instances of any cited formal process—all retransitional preparations, all consequent phrases, all motivic correspondences, all sequential developments. Nor can general guidelines be adduced with respect to all instances of any given structural process—register transfers, descending protolines, compound melodies. Each piece demands its own argument, its uniquely apposite possibilities of realization, whatever its commonalities of form and structure in relation to other pieces. And while performances can indeed distort and suppress essential elements, divergent interpretations can satisfyingly illuminate different things.[9]

Because there may be diverse reasonable analyses of any piece, and because any structural element may be interpreted in different ways, the path from analysis to performance is one of great complexity. The challenge to theorist and performer is to decide which specific conclusions about tempo and articulation may reasonably be drawn from analytical observations about place, process, and function in musical events. And if, as commonly conceded, there is no "best" or "correct" interpretation of a piece, there are nonetheless infinite possibilities of misrepresenting, and of interpretive intrusion; analysis must often tell the performer what should not be done. And multiple meanings of an event may suggest that the execution be as neutral as possible and that the notes be allowed to speak for themselves; this is especially true in the area of dynamics, where the performer's intervention can be particularly blunt.

Examples of Interpretive Questions

The examples that follow illustrate twelve challenging interpretive issues. These examples concern not only a variety of issues, but also a broad range of structural elements in which interpretive intervention is conceivable.

Some of the examples illustrate more issues than one, and the questions of interpretation that are raised only briefly and tentatively in this chapter are left for fuller consideration in the extensive, detailed studies that follow in chapters 3, 4, and 5.

1. The first question is easy to state, harder to resolve: What note do I play?

Ex. 2.1ab
Chopin, Prelude in C minor, Op. 28, No. 20

Documentary evidence concerning the third measure of Chopin's Prelude in C minor (ex. 2.1) is ambiguous: the final note of the upper voice may be either E-natural or E-flat. The pianist's choice has implication for direction in the melody, which descends locally within a context of ascent at the level of the phrase (ex. 2.1b). Choosing E-flat allows the pianist to have it both ways: the earlier, undisputed E-natural is consistent with the broader ascending motion, and the later E-flat, of relatively local import, is in accord with the momentarily digressive, elaborating descent. It may conceivably be subordinated in performance as a parenthetical motion within a general line of ascent and crescendo.

Ex. 2.2ab
Beethoven, Sonata in B-flat, Op. 106,
first movement

In the example from the "Hammerklavier" Sonata (ex. 2.2), where early sources again reflect notational uncertainty, I should argue that the vital function of chromatic voice leading (ex. 2.2b) in a powerfully directed retransition to the B-flat tonic requires A-natural rather than A-sharp.

2. Assuming I do not get in its way, is the motive self-evident, or does it require some deliberate projection?

A representative problem of motivic articulation is discussed by Schmalfeldt: it is what she calls a "turn motive" in the second Bagatelle of Beethoven's Op. 126—an elaboration of the fifth degree of the scale by upper and lower neighbors (E-flat–D–C-sharp–D). The motive is explicit early in the piece, a necessary basis for the assertion of its inferred, relatively covert appearance later. Schmalfeldt suggests that it is to be "made more prominent by . . . 'finger-pedaling'" (even though the notes to which she refers occur variously as the first, second, and fourth in sixteenth-note groups) and by holding the tempo so that the motive is not lost in a rush of sixteenth-notes.[10]

Example 2.3 is from the Sarabande of Bach's Cello Suite No. 6, in a medium in which texture (and hence motivic occurrence) can be problematic, often bewilderingly so. The initiating motive (marked "a" in ex. 2.3b) is plain enough, but subsequently it has a number of inferrable, texturally covert manifestations. The second segment of the motive (marked "b") can be heard as a source for much of the bass, as bracketed in the illustration. Perhaps this requires slight tenuto articulations of key components, notably the lowest pitches of measures 5, 6, and 7; or these notes would at any rate not be sacrificed in performance to more overt motivic elements of the upper voice.

Ex. 2.3a
Bach, Suite No. 6 in D for unaccompanied cello, Sarabande

Ex. 2.3b

In Schoenberg's Piano Piece Op. 19, No. 3 (ex. 2.4), there is an inferrable motivic unity defined primarily by directional and rhythmic affinities, as well as dynamic shape, in a pattern of imitation. In measure 4 the motive ("b" in ex. 2.4*b*) concludes a progression of systematically enlarged interval components (the interval-class succession 3-1, then 4-2), which affects the sense and quality of cadence; so of course does Schoenberg's forte-pianissimo relation of the two

Ex. 2.4ab
Schoenberg, Piano Pieces, Op. 19 (No. 3)

occurrences, the second of which must be distinct as imitation. The beamed grouping designated "a" (ex. 2.4*b*) may well be more problematic than "b" despite a precise identity of interval-class content.

Example 2.5 is motivic in another sense: it is the characteristic descending third that is vital to the compact unity of the introduction to Beethoven's Symphony No. 4.[11]

Ex. 2.5a
Beethoven, Symphony No. 4 in B-flat, first movement

m. 8

m. 13

Ex. 2.5b

mm. 1-5, 13-24   32-35   36-42

The motivic third exists at three levels: that of the immediate foreground; that which overreaches the initiating, repeated motion from B-flat to G-flat; and that which constitutes a sequence underlying the entire introduction's broadly elaborated I-V (ex. 2.5b). The immediate third-relations are exposed so nakedly that there seems little if any needed intervention. Moreover, the overreaching B-flat and G-flat that constitute the middleground occurrence are emphasized by dynamic inflections and duration. And the crescendo and diminuendo accorded the G-flat in measures 5 and 17 (ex. 2.5a), and the bass recurrence of the G-flat at measure 9, are important not only to motivic function, but also in view of the G-flat's crucial enharmonic role as a springboard for tonal divergences that follow. The sequence of related thirds spanning the entire introduction is the most problematic of interpretive expression. But if the conductor has carefully delineated the initiating motivic elements, their ultimate role in elaborating an overall descent linking the first and fifth scale degrees comes through, especially in light of Beethoven's durational emphasis on the A (measures 32–35), a critical point at which sequential fluctuation is halted, and of the dramatic, chromatic intrusion at measure 36 of F as the root of the primary dominant seventh. The performer's business here is scrupulously to follow Beethoven's lead.

3. What about dynamic inflection where none is indicated?

Ex. 2.6
Bach, Sonata No. 3 for unaccompanied violin, Largo

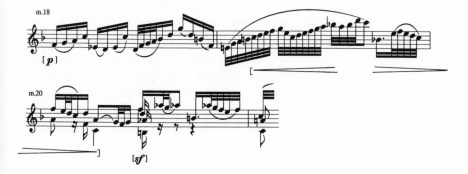

This issue arises in comments by Schenker, characteristic in the analytical essays, concerning certain affirmed principles of performance. The illustration given here (ex. 2.6) comes from a study in which Schenker prescribes, within a primary dynamic level of piano appropriate to the movement's conclusion, a superficial crescendo toward and diminuendo from the B-flat of measure 19, noting that such "inner dynamic shading serves to unify the progression of a 3rd, b-flat¹ [measure 18]-a¹ [measure 21]-g¹."[12] Whatever one may make of this stated basis for "dynamic shading," there seems indeed a natural tendency of (discreet) crescendo at the dramatic, accelerated octave shift of the fourth scale degree, and a consequent diminuendo in the descent from this registral apex. The substance of one's justification for dynamic inflection is critical.

Ex. 2.7
Bach, Suite No. 3 for unaccompanied cello, Sarabande

In analyzing Bach's Sarabande cited as my ex. 2.7, Schenker prescribes diminuendo for all three cadences, which is consistent with resolution as well as with the articulative emphasis indicated by Schenker for the immediately preceding dissonances. With reference to the quoted excerpt, Schenker states that "the chromatic tone [C-sharp], neighboring tone [B-flat], and cadence in bars 13–16 are subject to . . . dynamic motion ($\overbrace{}$ $\overbrace{}$)."[13]

Schenker's instructions do not have a clear, consistent basis, although they may be deemed understandable in light of such processes as melodic ascent and descent (ex. 2.6), cadential ebbing motions (ex. 2.7), and cadential function within Schenker's prevailing piano dynamic level of the Largo's concluding bars. Here too Schenker invokes an "immutable rule that chromatic alterations be emphasized" (to justify the interventions noted in connection with ex. 2.7), and views "tensions created by the raised third of the applied dominants" as "principal determinants" of "dynamic motion."[14] One may dispute these claimed general principles, which embrace dynamic projection of inferred voice leading, important tonal events such as modulation, cadential occurrence, dissonance, and chromaticism.

4. Are there not times when deliberate effort is needed to convey the sense of a significant, not necessarily explicit, voice-leading connection?

Ex. 2.8a
Wolf, "Anakreons Grab"

Ex. 2.8b

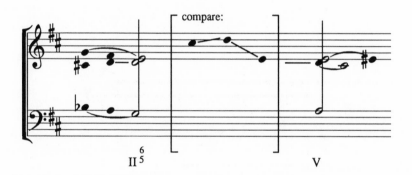

Example 2.8 is from a song of Hugo Wolf; the tenderly beautiful introduction that sets the scene is represented (ex. 2.8*b*) in terms of voice leading by step, which is often inferred in octave transfers disguising an inherent unity. The pianist who is aware of this may decide to express it, for example in the descent from G to F-sharp to E (ex. 2.8*b*). But if the downward leap of a seventh is integral, the inferrable motion from F-sharp to E must yield to this distinctive gesture.

In ex. 2.9, an active texture must be assessed in the bare notation of string passage-work, so that voice leading, particularly of the surface, can be as perplexing as it is critical. Represented is the point at which tonal action really begins after a typical, tonic-centered opening segment (measures 1–7). It seems likely that the middle-voice suspensions will require subtle tenuto articulations at each preparation (a, g, and so on) to convey the sense depicted by the dotted tie in ex. 2.9*b*. One can imagine too a slight minimizing of the passing notes toward the bass B, and of the parallel groups that follow, by a discreet acceleration toward the bass note and a modest lengthening of it.

Ex. 2.9a
Bach, Suite No. 3 for unaccompanied cello, Prelude

Ex. 2.9b

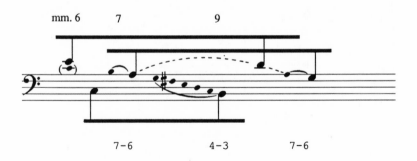

In the piece from Schoenberg's Op. 19 (ex. 2.10) I suggest an instance of deliberate, perhaps tonally implicative, semitonal voice leading that the pianist will appropriately articulate by persuasive legato connections, directed to an appreciable cadential goal in which the {G,E-flat} third is integral (ex. 2.10*b*).

Ex. 2.10ab
Schoenberg, Piano Pieces, Op. 19 (No. 3)

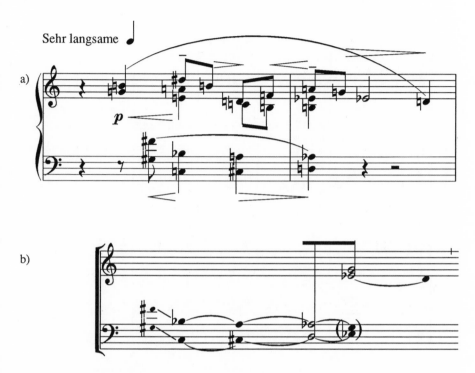

Used by permission of Belmont Music Publishers.
Copyright 1913 by Universal Edition; renewed 1940 by Arnold Schoenberg.

5. My fifth point is central to Schmalfeldt's discussion of Beethoven's Op. 126, No. 5: Performance decisions are elucidated at critical times by analytical awareness of place in a formal process. (Schmalfeldt arrives at a realization of the problematic concluding bars of Beethoven's piece by identifying them as "a coda that is badly needed" and "that substitutes for a reprise.")[15] The analysis of functions of particular events as to place in the formal narrative is indeed often the most direct path to purposeful thinking about interpretive conduct.[16]

An example of interpretation according to formal process is convenient in Bach's Cello Suite No. 3 (ex. 2.9), where I characterize the opening seven measures as relatively stable (and tonic-centered) and followed by comparatively active development, although here the expository and developmental contexts are assuredly not identified on any basis of thematic differentiation. The example is typical of many of Bach's preludes.

Ex. 2.11a
Beethoven, Symphony No. 2 in D, fourth movement

m. 139

m. 144

m. 150

m.156

Ex. 2.11b

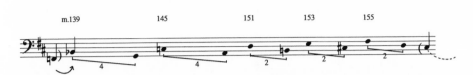

One of Beethoven's surging developments is the source of ex. 2.11:[17] a driving acceleration corroborated in proportions of sequential grouping (ex. 2.11*b*) and by motivic fragmentation and imitation in stretto (ex. 2.11*c*). The characterization of the development as accelerative must refer also to complementary factors of expansion in sonority and timbre, especially with the entry of the horns.[18]

Such passages pose urgent, difficult questions of interpretive conduct: Does the conductor go along, discreetly accelerating the metronomic tempo? Or should intrinsic musical processes speak for themselves, while performance clearly enunciates and accommodates—at least does not contradict—the overt tendencies of musical elements? Or is it conceivably appropriate to resist inherent tendencies of acceleration, very subtly counteracting them in tempo? I should find it hard to imagine performance doing other than yielding to the accelerative drive, confirming rather than enforcing or exaggerating it, by a tightly controlled acceleration in metronomic tempo. But it seems doubtful that general answers to such questions are attainable; this issue will arise again in connection with Beethoven's Op. 2, No. 1, in a context of exposition (ex. 2.16), and in the major examples treated in later chapters.

Ex. 2.11c

Ex. 2.12a
Bach, Little Prelude, BWV 926, mm. 42–48

In the Bach Little Prelude in D minor (ex. 2.12), there are functional changes in the rhythms of harmony and of step descent spanning much of the structure;[19] accelerations in these rhythms probably signify for the performer firmly controlled supportive accelerations in real tempo.

At the end of the Prelude, however (see ex. 2.12a), following a cadential hemiola, Bach introduces marked acceleration (ex. 2.12b) in renewed step descent from the register in which the primary melodic motion had originated. This final plunge of course takes place in a much shorter time than that of its broader precedent, and the context of closure involving harmonic recession and stability dictates a bracing tempo and final ritardando toward the fermata.

Here an awareness of formal context and direction is crucial to the performer's interpretive decision. Articulate interconnections and delineations among phrases and other associated formal units are further germane to the problems of illuminating musical form in performance, and this is one factor in my next point of inquiry.

6. What decisions concerning groupings of events may reasonably follow from the analysis of form and structure?

I have suggested that a fundamental property of rhythm is evident in the groupings within cofunctioning elements (form, meter, harmony, timbre, and others),[20] such grouping modes often, but not necessarily, concurring in any particular structure. The performer must decide which should prevail in effect, and the fact is that interpretive realization often favors motivic and other formal groupings. The listener may feel otherwise that something is unnatural, as when a singer sings through a formal dividing point to enforce semantic continuity in a line of text.

Ex. 2.12b

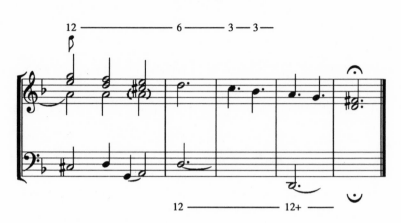

In his discussion of Chopin's Prelude, Op. 28, No. 20, Cone observes that measures 1–5 can be heard "as an expansion of the I-IV-V-I of the opening measure. . . . Which of the two relationships [that of two four-bar units and that in which measures 1–5 are conceived as a unit reflecting the harmony of measure 1 in augmentation] is to be brought out? Whatever decision one makes, one gains something, but one also loses something".[21] That the harmony of measure 1 (ex. 2.13b) is reflected over the larger span is tenable, but what can one do with that conception in performance? Is it imaginable that the formal delineation between measures 4 and 5 might be overtly compromised in realizing such a broader continuity? If so, by what particular means?

Ex. 2.13a
Chopin, Prelude, Op. 28, No. 20, mm. 1–5

Ex. 2.13b

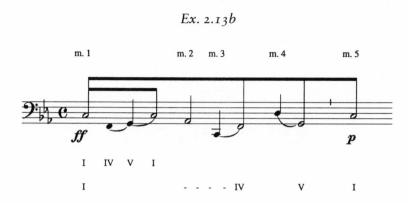

To raise a further question of grouping, I refer to the much-discussed chorale adapted by Brahms as a theme for variations (ex. 2.14). The five-bar phrase is construed by Schenker as 3 + 2 (ex. 2.14*b*) in view of two descents of a third (D–C–B-flat, E-flat–D–C), and two basic harmonic events: a "tonic" in measures 1–3 and the cadential II-V of measures 4–5.[22]

Ex. 2.14a
Haydn?, Chorale St. Antonii, mm. 1–5

Ex. 2.14b
(See footnote 22 for source.)

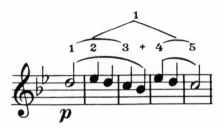

Ex. 2.14c

Ex. 2.14d

According to a contrary view (see ex. 2.14c) the structure is 2 + 3, with respect to essential harmonic content consisting of I, then V (both elaborated by neighbors), and a vital textural departure in measure 3 (shown in ex. 2.14d). I suggest that the textural activity and chromaticism of measures 3–5 adumbrate the ternary's midsection (ex. 2.17). My grouping might be realized by slight punctuation, by a very modest difference in dynamic intensity at measure 3 (un poco più piano), by articulation più legato in the second segment, or by some combination of the three. The performer's justified conception of intraphrase grouping is clearly of the essence in interpretation.

7. Where a texture may be interestingly complicated by an implicit, relatively disguised imitation, is it possible and desirable for the performer to communicate this?

Ex. 2.15a
Mozart, Sonata in G, K. 283, first movement

m. 6

Ex. 2.15b

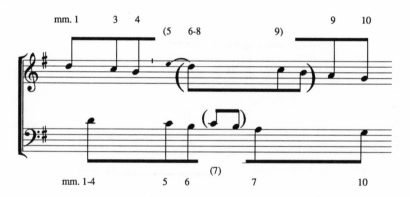

Ex. 2.15c

Ex. 2.16a

Beethoven, Sonata in F minor, Op. 2, No. 1, first movement

Ex. 2.16b

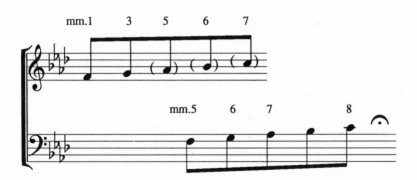

In answering this question, each case must be addressed on its own terms. In exx. 2.15 and 2.16 the analyst might well claim significance for underlying lower-voice imitations, in the first instance responding to the upper voice's essential descent from the fifth scale degree to the first, in the second to an essential ascent from the first to the fifth; these relations are shown in exx. 2.15*b* and 2.16*b*. What can this mean for performance? A possible slight articulative intervention is posited in ex. 2.15*c*, drawing attention to the beginning of the inferred, imitative lower voice, the continuation of which becomes plainer in the bass from measure 5, where an assurance of clarity is probably all that is needed.

Beethoven's imitation is more important. Because it takes place in a shorter time than the upper-voice ascent, it contributes to a deliberate, composed acceleration toward the apex of the phrase at measure 7. The pianist, aware through analysis of this vital relation, could well bring it out judiciously yet with some urgency, or would at least avoid any obscuring or nullifying distractions. And performance probably requires a cautiously supportive acceleration in tempo complementing that which Beethoven has composed.

A further case of functional textural activity is evident in Bach's Cello Suite No. 3 (ex. 2.9), where after the initiating, comparatively uncomplicated, tonic elaboration, texture complements tonal action as the Prelude gets under way. How vital it is that the cellist understand the nature, content, and significance of these factors in a medium in which only calculated interventions will bring them out!

In the theme cited again as ex. 2.17, deliberate textural diversification in the ternary's midsection (foreseen, as noted above, in relations within the initiating period) functions with tonal factors to delineate form, and is to be expressed in opposing voices within the protracted V. Of commensurate importance is a "recession" in the textural element in the second phrase of section (B), where contradirectional motions are largely abandoned, textural parallelism complementing melodic descent. These actions suggest a complementary, regulated, modest crescendo in measures 11–14 and a diminuendo in measures 15–18.

Ex. 2.17a
Haydn?, Chorale St. Antonii, mm. 11–18

Ex. 2.17b

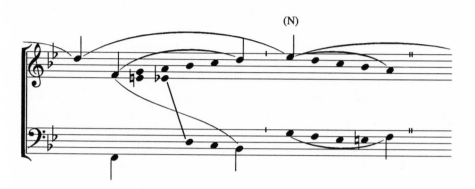

A further textural factor vital to interpretive awareness is the scale of functions and values among lines and voices. Is a particular component accompanimental, coequal in a dialogue or imitation, elaborative and subsidiary, or
thematically prevalent? We have but to think of this kind of assessment in
chamber music or in the concerto to appreciate how crucial is the performer's
consciousness of the place of each event in a total sonorous perspective.

I mention in passing the common problem of apparent textural simplicity
masking actual diversity, as when a compound melody functions discernibly at
two or three registral strata, borne out in performance by calculated consistencies of quality and intensity within each inferred continuity. Could anything be
more critical to the relations of analysis to performance, perplexing as it may at
times be? A case in point is the opening theme of Mozart's K. 283 (see ex. 2.15):
Is the upper-voice melody a complex of three strata? Or does it consist of two,
one of which undergoes registral shifts? And what exactly does the interpreter
do to project such potentially interesting interactions?

8. I proceed to the critical issue of tempo in its fundamental, "metronomic"
aspect. Apart from putative formulaic schemes such as those of simply proportionate whole-number relations (i.e., 1:2, 2:3, and the like), or circumstances in
which the composer's intent is presumably explicit, we commonly assume that
metronomic tempo is best decided in relation to pace and content within
pertinent structural elements. But is tempo to be complementary or compensatory in relation to these elements?

Ex. 2.18
Brahms, Intermezzo in E-flat, Op. 117, No. 1, mm. 1–4

What a precarious balance must be struck in the enchanting opening phrases of Brahms's Intermezzo in E-flat! Here the inertness of harmony, activated only in changes of position by which the tonic triad is linearized in the bass (ex. 2.18), suggests a complementary, poised tempo (and stillness of physical deportment), lest the calm to which we are summoned by the first notes be corrupted by some gratuitous distraction. But this is far from the end of the matter, for the languid rhythm of harmony, the confinement of melodic motion, and the regularity of surface rhythms accommodate a gently moving, cautiously compensatory tempo: Brahms's andante moderato, perhaps un pochissimo vivendo. This is the challenge of the precarious balance referred to above, which takes into account the analysis of pace and content in relevant structural elements. Examples 2.11 and 2.12, cited in connection with formal processes governing interpretation, pose comparable questions of appropriate inflections within an established tempo, and the relation of tempo to the intrinsic actions of other critical elements.

9. The next point—two issues, really—concerns concepts of surface metric fluctuation and primary metric downbeat which I have developed elsewhere (or these concepts may be regarded in some other terms).[23] Does the performer underscore by judicious articulative stresses or durations palpable metric fluctuation at the surface? Assuming a comprehensive metric whole applicable to some—I should say many—pieces, around a primary, accentual point of orientation documented in this book's Brahms and Debussy studies, what does the

performer do with it? Should there be an intensifying approach to the climactic event and an emphatic projection of it?

In the matter of surface fluctuation, I have discussed a metric irregularity in Chopin's Prelude in D major, Op. 28, No. 6—an irregularity in which all textural components concur;[24] and I have pointed to examples from Stravinsky, Josquin, and Brahms with respect to metric fluctuation in which textural components do not concur.[25] Also relevant are a number of studies of pieces regarded as to overall metric structure or gesture, to and from a dynamically focal event: these include a study of Bach's Little Prelude cited earlier (see note 19), and more recently published studies of C-major Preludes of Bach and Chopin.[26]

Where metric organization is deemed at variance with a meter signature or with metric precedent, the performer must often yield to compositional intent through the sort of prudent enforcement of accents that arises naturally out of mere awareness. But this depends on context, perhaps more than anything cited in this survey of interpretive problems. It seems clear, for example, that Stravinsky requires more overt interpretive accentuation than do composers in tonal and pretonal idioms; and in many instances accents, notably of duration, speak without intervention by the performer, by virtue of their intrinsic properties. What is imperative is that the performer, aware of fluctuant meters, do nothing to violate them, imposing a gratuitous regularity where mobility is intended.

As for the conception of an overall metric structure directed to and receding from a central, primary accent at the deepest level, I have no doubt that interpretive realization is ideally shaped in correspondent pointing and receding lines of action. This is a critical issue of performance, manifest in the detailed studies that follow; it calls on the performer's command of shape, direction, and control. This is the kind of conceptualization by which I should characterize Cone's "rhythmic shape of a piece."[27]

There are of course many ways of conceiving wholeness in pieces, and musical structures differ markedly in aspects of wholeness. Yet the idea of a dynamic structure disposed around a primary accent can be vital in guiding a performer's conduct through a piece, and circumspect interventions in tempo, in dynamic intensity, and in the timing of functional events can serve an encompassing design.

Ex. 2.19a
Chopin, Prelude in A, Op. 28, No. 7, mm. 9–12

Ex. 2.19b

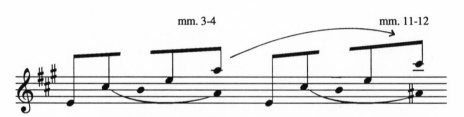

An especially guileless specimen is Chopin's Prelude in A (ex. 2.19), in which no very sophisticated penetration is needed to see something special in measure 12. Whatever one's views of essential under-surface tonal structure in the piece, there seems no question that measure 12 is focal in senses that may be critical for performance.

Measure 12 functions in at least five dimensions as an apex of development:[28] in tonal distance (as a dominant thrice removed, the springboard for cadential descent in fifths toward the tonic); in register; in textural density; in dynamic intensity; and in dissonance. Moreover, its approach is by way of crescendo and harmonic-rhythmic acceleration. By all these counts, it seems to me a central focus for interpretive orientation, subject to slight tenuto and little else, as so much is already explicit in the event itself. Further, one can imagine a guarded, very slight modulation of metronomic tempo at the direct approach—paradoxically either a modest acceleration or a holding back.

The Sarabande of Bach's Cello Suite No. 3 (ex. 2.20) poses provocatively conflicting claims along the lines I am considering. Few would disagree with the premise of a tonal structure of which the overreaching upper voice traces an octave descent from c_1 (ex. 2.20a). Does this imply an essential dynamic shape—an overall metric or gestural image—configured as a broad recession in relation to an initiating "point from which"? Or is there some other key point, "to which and from which," determined by the dynamic confluence of elements?

Ex. 2.20a
Bach, Suite No. 3 for unaccompanied cello, Sarabande

Ex. 2.20b

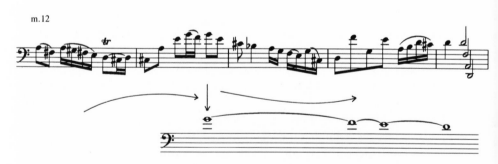

My illustration considers a dynamic focus at the approach to measure 16, one of the trisecting cadences. Bach's interior development points to this moment (measure 13), to which the performer's progress can persuasively be directed by calculated, mounting intensity (and often is, perhaps intuitively). Measure 13 has special properties with respect to register, dissonance, and tonal distance (the V of the supertonic, which prepares the ultimate primary V of C); it is a turning point toward the final cadential recession. I should argue that a view of the pitch g_2 as the registrally displaced extension of the fifth scale degree in an overall octave descent does not mitigate against its attributions in the present sense,[29] since tonal and metric structures are different things, the latter more amenable to interpretive control. Indeed, the cellist preoccupied with tonal structure and broad octave descent could well overlook, undervalue, and under-play the vital approaches to measure 13, a critical perspective for the final cadence.

10. This issue is severely difficult and clearly important. It concerns the interpretively problematic structural element of tonal background.[30] Is there anything the performer can or should do about a piece's broadest tonal struc-ture, however one may conceive it? If not, does the awareness of such a structure matter? And how does the performer convey a distinction between essential and auxiliary tonal events, especially where the latter are vital in processes other than tonal ones? Examples 2.21 and 2.22 pose different questions of broad tonal associations.

Ex. 2.21
Beethoven, Sonata in B-flat, Op. 106, first movement

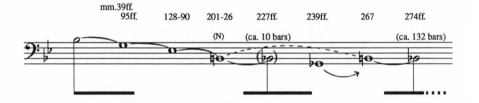

In the first movement of Beethoven's great "Hammerklavier" Sonata, much has been made of strong, startling references to an apparently deviant B minor. My simple sketch (ex. 2.21) portrays the B minor in two aspects: as an expan-sive linear upper auxiliary to the primary tonic; and as a factor in an overall tonal succession in thirds. Both aspects are obvious, yet neither mitigates a sense of anomaly in Beethoven's assertive thematic statements in B minor. Moreover, these two functions appear to imply contrary claims of interpretation: accord-ing to the latter, B̲ emerges as the logical, essential outcome of prior tonal events; according to the former, it is clearly tentative and subsidiary. Does subsidiary tonal status imply understatement in performance? My inclination is to underscore Beethoven's irony and allow these dramatically divergent tonal references the full prominence implied by their dynamic setting, recognizing that B minor's auxiliary relation to B-flat is quite vivid in Beethoven's final durational amplification of the primary tonic. (B-flat prevails unmolested for some 132 bars of recapitulation and coda.) And the position of B minor in the overall plan of descending thirds is clear if the pianist etches each interim arrival point markedly, though not brutally. These conditions argue against any apologetic understating of the anomalous B minor.

Ex. 2.22a
Brahms, Intermezzo in A minor, Op. 118, No. 1

Ex. 2.22b

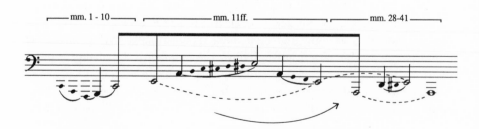

In Brahms's Op. 118, No. 1 (ex. 2.22), one can trace a comprehensive linear expression of the elusive A-minor triad through the bass viewed synoptically: the C̲ of the first cadence, the E̲ on which so much of the subsequent harmony is rooted; and the final cadential goal, A̲. This overall tonal design is shown in ex. 2.22*b*.

What interpretive choices might an analysis of these factors imply? And what about the many surface manifestations of A minor—suggestive augmented sixth chords, for example? Are these to be exposed in some special way? Or are all these things self-evident, requiring only that the pianist not contravene or diminish them? Or is the chief point of Brahms's tonal design inherently ambiguous, so that elements of potential clarification should be interpreted somewhat indifferently? I leave these questions unanswered, noting again however that analysis is the inescapable basis for interpretive doing and not doing.

A further sense in which synoptic wholeness may be conceived, and may yield interpretive insight, is discussed as a fundamental "thematic essence" in the extended analyses in chapters 3, 4, and 5: this is the encapsulated, midlevel expressive substance of a piece, derived by probing through elaboration and repetition to an underlying gist comprising the prevailing thematic and other structural currents. Such a synopsis embodies in summary the piece's distinctive motivic components, governing tonal directions, and other individuating elements; it is a generalized "recomposition" that can be read, played, and heard as representing the piece's expressive substance in essence. This concept is explored extensively in connection with exx. 3.5, 4.30, and 5.24.

11. This issue touches everything, from general interpretive deportment to the smallest detail of nuance. Where music is used descriptively, as often in text settings, how do analytical findings concerning descriptive elements condition interpretation?

Ex. 2.23a
Wolf, "Anakreons Grab"

m. 7

welch ein Grab ist hier, das al -

m. 8

m. 10

Ex. 2.23b

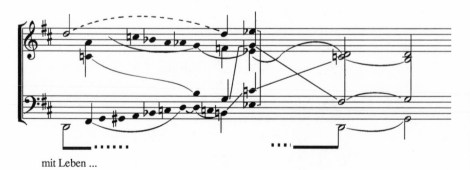

In Hugo Wolf's matchless homage to Goethe, the song "Anakreons Grab" (ex. 2.23), there are two crowning instances of clearly descriptive musical imagery, neither materially accessible to singer or pianist without searching analytical study.

The composer's masterfully apt expressions of the key words *Leben* and *Ruh* rest more than anything on contrasts of tonal mobility and immobility, with other elements compatibly directed. The setting of "mit Leben schön bepflanzt und geziert"—Wolf's and Goethe's depiction of the poet's grave, bedecked with life—emphasizes *Leben* agogically, and is reflected as well in other elements of the music's structure: the tonal fluctuation to subdominant and its subdominant, crescendo, active surface rhythms, and heightened chromaticism and dissonance.

The setting of the contrary image (*Ruh,* the grave's other aspect) starkly outlines the G-major triad, interim goal of preceding tonal motions. The vocal melody descends, dissonances resolve, all rhythms slow in a lengthening of durational values, and there is a complementary diminuendo. Without analytical insights into these factors, how do the performers even begin to make appropriate modulations of tempo and dynamic intensity, while evoking by calculated sonorous inflections and qualities an atmosphere appropriate to Goethe's text and Wolf's commentary on the text? In chapter 5, an extensive study of a song by Debussy, I shall probe many details of text setting and its implications for performance.

12. The final issue is of very general implication: Does not a probing, just analysis reveal to the performer an attitude appropriate to the character of a piece, and is this not in itself compelling justification for analysis informing interpretation? Brahms's Intermezzo, Op. 117, No. 1 (ex. 2.18) offers a striking example of how expressive structure can condition interpretive deportment. Here the elements of content suggest a concordant calm, a minimum of physical involvement, and care that tempo not violate the music's character by overaction (especially in the precarious first measures, where tempo is ideally conceived in an easy, leisurely two pulses to the bar). The performer's general attitude and physical approach to a piece are as much governed by the findings of analysis as are details of nuance and inflection.

Perhaps this prefatory survey of issues has revealed something of the volume and complexity of relations between analysis and performance, and shed light on some specific instances of interpretive latitude and choice. The area is indeed enormously complex, given that there are many plausible analyses of any piece and that each may point to any number of reasonable choices of tempo and articulation. As was stated at the outset, musical performance cannot be left altogether to capricious intuition, which does not solve problems. Yet the theoretical study of performance decisions and their articulate, rational bases is like analysis itself an interpretive art, telling the performer what not to do as much as what to do in bringing music to life.

Every analytical finding has an implication for performance, even when it suggests a relatively neutral execution that projects explicit, self-evident factors of structure. Far more commonly, analysis suggests to the performer specific, practical measures that will illuminate the less obvious relations of discerned elements cofunctioning to expressive ends.

The following series of exhaustive analytical essays treats three disparate musical idioms with the objective of gleaning some vital general principles respecting structure and interpretation. In each of the studies, detailed concepts of musical organization are set forth as a basis for pragmatic inquiry into the particulars of decision in performance.

Chapter Three

FIRST CASE
Brahms, Intermezzo in B-flat,
Op. 76, No. 4

To be considered in this essay are many details of Brahms's Intermezzo, Op. 76, No. 4, as well as a number of broad analytical constructs, and many concomitant questions of interpretation. The piece, reproduced as ex. 3.1, is a work of consummate mastery—elegantly, warmly expressive, typically economical in substance, tightly ordered.

The first part of this chapter deals with some general observations respecting the music's intrinsic properties of form and character, after which there is extensive analysis of elements of structure, process, and continuity.

Ex. 3.1

The Intermezzo's Form and Character

The Intermezzo is characteristically ternary. There is decisively contrasting tonal content at and following measure 21, section (B), where a freely inverted variant of the primary motive of section (A) is used (ex. 3.2); this is followed by reprise (A') of the initiating material. One might ask: What implications for performance follow from such prefatory observations of broad formal outlines, as a general and provisional framework for further detail?

Ex. 3.2

An obvious factor of performance is that the pianist, recognizing the hazard of redundancy, must carry out the literal repeat of (A) relatively straightforwardly, as a "paler" reflection of material already exposed. Direct repetition thus underscores basic materials and relations—motivic, tonal, and other—in relatively neutral articulations. But it offers at the same time a challenging opportunity to bring out some further dimension of substance, for example a motivic variant compatible with adopted interpretive premises and appreciable now that basic exposition has taken place. I return to this point in a later discussion of motives in the Intermezzo (see below, and ex. 3.20).

The (B) section starting at measure 21 requires no particular interpretive assertion at its inception, which is exposed as a result of certain inherent factors: a renewal of the prevalent dynamic level of piano following a diminuendo; the return to a relatively explicit form of the primary motive after the digressive variant heard at measures 13–20 (ex. 3.3); marked tonal contrast; restoration of the original register after descent; recurrence of the precise surface rhythms of the opening, in all voices; and return of the original tempo after stringendo modulations in the preceding bars.

Ex. 3.3

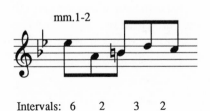

mm.1-2

Intervals: 6   2   3   2

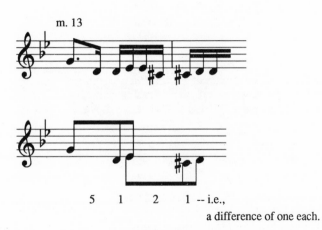

m. 13

5   1   2   1 -- i.e.,

a difference of one each.

Also: m.14*   16   17-18

A permutation derived from the permutation in m. 13.

The reentry of the material from (A), explicit yet in interesting ways covert, requires deliberate awareness and control in performance. For example, the upper-voice e-flat$_2$ of measure 31, ostensibly cadential, wants slight projection, especially as the object of crescendo in its repetition (measure 31, second beat); there should be just enough to extend its sonority into measure 32—a delicate urging is all that is indicated—followed by a comparable projection of the a$_1$ of measure 32, also to sound into the next bar. These two somewhat concealed events are of crucial import in the reprise (ex. 3.4), where they are embedded into the cadential process of section (B), after which the recapitulation is for a time literal, and accordingly relaxed.

Ex. 3.4

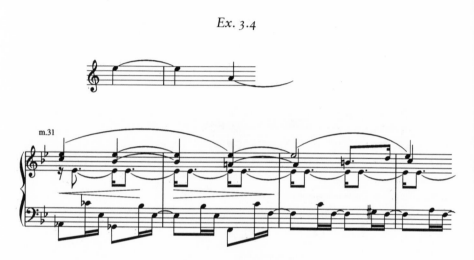

On the other hand, the articulations to which ex. 3.4 draws attention take place in an elided context of essentially cadential and retransitional process, of which the chief indicators are the settling of the upper voice on a sustained pitch (that which initiates the thematic return) and the arrival on the primary dominant. These overlapping processes suggest restraint befitting the music's functional ambivalence and the composer's clear intent of evasive thematic entry.

Adjustments of tempo can clarify form in the Intermezzo. Such adjustments would include, for example, a modestly accelerated and subsequently held back (B) section, the content of which will be seen to justify these modulations in tempo; another would be playing un poco ritenuto such vital cadences as those of measures 4–6 (ending the first phrase) and, more critically, measures 19–20, which introduce the transitional, structural G-flat of the approaching contrasting segment. At such points tempo is typically slackened almost imperceptibly, to set a subtle basis for its later resumption. A slight deceleration may also be used to underline the important thematic articulations at the approach to the reprise (ex. 3.4), followed by a delicately controlled restoration of tempo as the thematic return gets under way unambiguously at the second half of measure 33. The same slight holding back serves formal delineations at measures 12, 44, and 51, and establishes a perspective for the subsequent, controlled renewal of tempo, scaled to the context of closure.

In all the cited instances of modulation of tempo there is adjustment too of dynamic intensity, explicit in the composer's notation. And the suggested cadential inflections (poco ritardando), typical and in performance no doubt irresistible, are extremely restrained, in keeping with an overall character of graceful fluency that must be maintained until the final, decisively conclusive attacks of measures 54–55.

In the truest sense, the piece's character is the sum of all its structural elements. Yet even the most preliminary inquiry can yield important general conclusions about performance. Obvious "grazioso" characteristics are the restricted dynamic range and the restrained almost steady sixteenth-note rhythm of the surface.

In the latter context, Brahms's inner voices are at the same time hesitant and quietly impulsive as a result of the prevalent suspension into each half-measure, a rhythmic factor discontinued at the activated cadential segment with which each of the outer segments concludes (measures 13 and 45).[1] Against an accompanimental fabric made up almost entirely of harmonic components in this distinctive rhythmic setting, the upper voice gently leads, with changes of bass subtly marked in performance, and inner-voice attacks like those of the right-hand thumb just audible. The tempo (allegretto—moderately moving yet restrained) is appropriately hesitant in accord with expressive, grazioso character.

Two Synoptic Views of the Upper-Voice Melody

Here, and in a later discussion of two views of harmonic structure, I shall trace four different yet compatible concepts of comprehensive structure in the Intermezzo.

As one guide to interpretive possibilities, the distinctive upper-voice melody, which stands in constant relief in the Intermezzo's homophonic texture, is examined in two of its broad aspects: that of its most essential course and directions, and that of its orientation to, from, and around a focal peak almost exactly at the middle of the piece's temporal span. It will be seen that both views give rise to questions of, and are suggestive of approaches to, interpretive realization.

The first view (ex. 3.5) evaluates the piece's relatively fundamental material as distinct from that which is subsidiary and parenthetically elaborative, and derives from this evaluation a thematic essence embracing in synopsis melodic and harmonic elements in characteristic, literal, motivic aspects. This reduction is a conceptual digest of content in which essential, thematically distinctive events are represented in actual pitches from the piece. One can hear in it the governing melody's broad course as well as its specific gestures, and the piece's fundamental harmonic directions.

In the example, measure numbers are circled; some component elements are represented once only to show a precedent elaborative technique or recurrent motivic factor, and many measures, embodying repetitions or tentative divergent motions, are overlooked. The result is a generalized impression of the total melodic and thematic continuity and its distinctive, individuating constituents. Because such constituents are germane to this derived image, the sketch falls far short of ultimately abstracting the tonal degrees B-flat and F, to which the melody is in another sense finally reducible.

Ex. 3.5

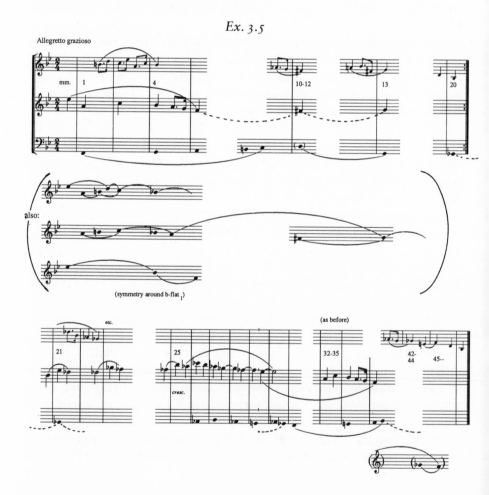

The analysis portrays the melody, the first two notes of which clearly imply the V that is to be prolonged, as directed initially to c_2 and then to the tonic (as b-flat$_1$). Both these key points are elaborated by encircling upper and lower neighbors. Later the melody of section (A) follows an essential course of descent to the dominant degree (as f_1) and then (here the representation includes motivic interpolations) through the chromatic F-sharp to the upper neighbor G (the g_1 of the cadence). (The enharmonic relation of F-sharp to G-flat will emerge as one of the piece's predominant chromatic features.)

The melodic basis of section (B) is, over G-flat, one of arpeggiation of the E-flat-minor triad (the modally altered IV of the primary tonic—ultimately functional in setting up the primary V for retransition). The broad outline in this melodic segment is thus one of departure from and return to a critically functional e-flat$_2$, tracing a path through the subdominant triad and reaching an elaborative melodic apex, c-flat$_2$. The melody of the reprise is as before, except for its decisive echoing of the midsection's bass succession from G-flat to F, cadentially reversing the earlier precedent of melodic and tonal direction. Again, the sketch depicts these essential motions with elements of the surface that are distinctive, that is, by which this particular realization of the generic tonal structure V-I is identifiable in content and effect. The fundamental gestures shown in ex. 3.5 reveal in an important sense the piece's individuating thematic framework, as well as its midlevel tonal basis.

Some important comments regarding interpretive possibilities arising from broad concepts of structure come later, especially after analysis of the Intermezzo's harmony; those (pp. 65–69) should be viewed as complementary to the following observations.

In general, a basic thematic frame consists of relatively active points oriented toward objects of motion, interim and cadential. In the melodic reduction shown in ex. 3.5, there is a preliminary encircling embellishment toward c_2, then motion toward b-flat$_1$ at measure 4, which is felt as a provisional goal of parenthetical actions; the c_2 is its upper neighbor. An awareness of the melodic phrase's essential course can motivate modest attention at key points that falls short of disrupting the melody. There can be for example a slight hesitation at the point of tentative arrival, a hint of articulative import of the sort a string player induces by the barest pressure of the bow.

Similarly, the A-flat and F-sharp, as chromatic inflections at measures 8–9 and 10, substitute respectively for the A and cadential F in the melody's redescent following the further elaborations of its second phrase. Perhaps the pianist may shape the melody to some degree by giving the impression of the first phrase's C reaching toward B-flat, and the later F-sharp toward G; indeed these four notes, in the register in which they occur here, are themselves a further melodic summation of the initial thirteen bars. (See other possible interpretations of melodic association shown parenthetically below ex. 3.5.) These melodic components are at the same time active elements, as compared to the cadential f_1 of measure 4 (object of the melody's first descent) and the g_1 of measure 13 (the first trisecting cadence, on the deceptive sixth degree).

Toward measure 13, a diminuendo complements the cadential process, whereas the composer's late, slight crescendo toward measure 14, followed by its reversal, is an overt impulse of motion through the subsidiary, interim cadence, as are elements of texture to be examined later. The performer's awareness that at measure 13 the first principal melodic actions have taken their course will induce in the eight measures preceding the double bar an interpretation of actions "aside," where the salient pitch class G̲, essentially pianissimo, is inherently emphasized by duration and reiteration in an environment of quickened but superficial activity.

It was stated above that in the immediate repeat of section (A) a paler version of the material is likely, yet one that might project some new element, exploit some new angle of hearing consistent with the derived sense of structural whole. What ensues following the double bar has significance for melodic structure in the resurgent rise, in altered tonal conditions, that is represented in its fundamental motions in ex. 3.5. The pianist moves circumspectly but expansively, directing the upper-voice line toward b-flat$_2$ and its dramatically exposed upper neighbor, after which melodic structure descends toward the cadential (and at the same time ongoing) e-flat$_2$ sustained after measure 31. In this pivotal phase for the piece as a whole, the composer's dynamic inflections are unmistakable in their import and complement the melodic directions. The analysis shown in ex. 3.7 deals specifically with this segment as a dynamic apex in which melodic structure parallels those of a number of other elements yet to be considered.

A preliminary view of the intriguingly veiled entry of the reprise was shown in ex. 3.4. Once launched, its prevailing melody, now in its third hearing, is subject to interpretive understatement, perhaps a somewhat more affirmative tempo, relatively unmodulated, and a slightly more subdued dynamic level in an atmosphere of easy recollection.

From measure 41 everything is of course functionally transformed. Here an enharmonic shift, first evident in the bass, is to be given importance: the progression B̲–C̲–C̲-flat–B-flat is the basis for a redirected harmonic structure. A further manifestation of enharmonic change is the melodic G-flat at measure 42, which descends immediately in the tenor and over a longer range in the upper voice, thus reversing the earlier implication of F̲-sharp. The active, crucial g-flat$_1$ underlying measures 42–44 must be an object of interpretive attention especially at its first articulation, and the crescendo extending through its retention is an aspect of this.

Resolution of the melody to the prolonged f_1 entering at measure 45 calls for a correlative diminuendo as before, and the following, closing material is again interpreted as an aside, in acknowledgment of melodic and harmonic actions now consummated. From here the essential melodic course is down, in staged movements from the prolonged f_1 through the notes of the tonic triad. In a complementary relation to the conclusive melodic descent, textural and rhythmic elements also recede. All this is in the perspective of a broad melodic course spilling over the point of essential cadential articulation (measure 45).

For the performer, there is one guiding sense of whole in this conception of the melody as a succession of focal and subordinate, functional movements heard and interpreted in relation to the fundamental thematic essence portrayed in ex. 3.5.

Another way of viewing the Intermezzo's melodic structure, consistent with that of ex. 3.5 but different in emphasis, is to regard measures 21–31 as a potently active phase for the melody as a whole (ex. 3.7) and accordingly as an area of orientation in relation to which all surrounding events may be interpreted.

As a basis for exploring the melody of section (B) in this light, ex. 3.6 looks at the essential course of that of section (A) as fundamentally one of descents: to f_1, to f-sharp$_1$, and to the cadential diatonic neighbor, g_1. The upper-voice of (A), so conceived, is then essentially of descending gestures, with surface undulations in melody as in other elements. The initiating structure embodies in this sense an expressive attribute of restraint, setting a basis for developmental events to follow. The developmental process is traced, again with respect to basic directions of the upper-voice melody, in ex. 3.7.

Ex. 3.6

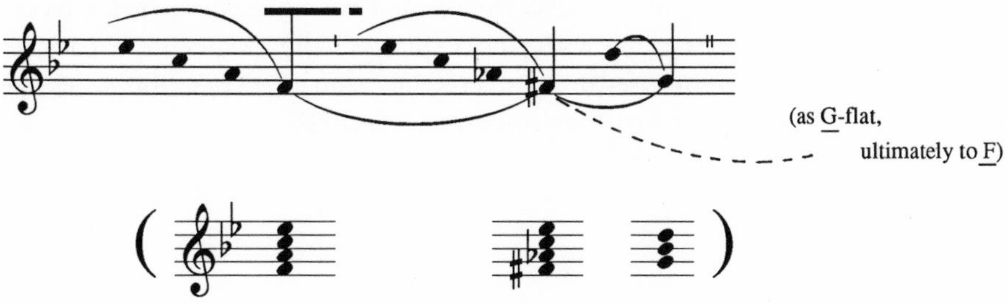

(as G-flat,
ultimately to F)

Ex. 3.7

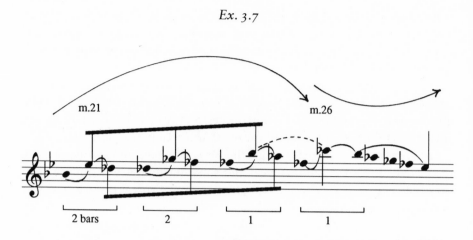

A sweeping, expansive progression rises to the climactic pitch c-flat$_2$ (the only higher pitches are in the context of recessive closure at the piece's end). In this melodic progression, interim points arpeggiate a fundamentally functional minor subdominant, which is the foreground harmony of section (B)'s extremities, measures 21 and 31–32.[2] In relation to this underlying triad the climactic c-flat$_2$ is an upper auxiliary. In this context of active dissonance and registral prominence it is also a point of dramatic, dynamic orientation in relation to which progressive and then recessive actions are oriented. The melodic apex, which is also an object of rhythmic drive, is thus pivotal in the piece's dynamic, organic, broadly expressive shape. From measure 26 the line descends to e-flat$_2$ (exx. 3.5, 3.7), the pitch of the Intermezzo's inception and of course of the beginning of ternary restatement within a restored, broadly prevalent V.

Acceleration is vital in the progress toward the melodic apex (see ex. 3.7). Subsidiary peaks occur at progressively smaller intervals (two bars, then one) and there is an impulsive, local sixteenth-note anacrusis preceding the climactic attack, a device occurring elsewhere as a quarter note. A further aspect of acceleration is a kind of stretto: an overlap in sequential repetitions of the descending melodic motive with its resumption (ex. 3.8).

Ex. 3.8

m. 21

A sense of dynamic shape is imperative in performance of this passage: each event in each applicable element must have a discernible place. Brahm's crescendo (arguably to mezzo forte) progresses into measure 27, the goal of the segment's first bass movement, which interestingly does not coincide with the goal of the ascending upper voice; it is a crescendo to be scaled precisely. As the bass of measures 26–27 makes its contribution of ascent through the point of the principal melody's apex, there are complementary elements—the abrupt doubling of the upper-voice melody and the enrichment of texture by addition of a further, motivic voice—and these conditions prevail to the end of the consequent descent to measure 31. The right hand is suddenly fully preoccupied at measure 27, the expanded textural substance of which requires clear delineation in modest relief.

Sensitive interpretation of this central progression requires a knowingly measured realization in an atmosphere of urgency. The metronomic tempo is prudently motivated (poco a poco pressando) in support of composed accelerations. At the same time, Brahms's dolce is an inhibiting direction that accords with the prevailing grazioso character. In keeping with the provocative noncoincidence of outer-voice peaks of ascent, the bass's A-flat and B-flat of measures 26–27 are articulated with importance in the scaled crescendo: they are sustained by pedal and subtly stressed, yet not so as to impede motivic clarity, especially in measure 27.

Some Factors of Rhythmic Process in Section (B)

Meter is of vital relevance to properties of intense development in the passage discussed above. (For the present purpose meter is regarded simply as a punctuation of the musical surface by relatively exposed accents. The acute problems of levels of metric structure, and of degrees and hierarchic values of accents, arise only limitedly in the present discussion.)[3]

In the Intermezzo metric articulation is by and large unequivocal with respect to the notated barline. The melody's initial descent might in itself be ambiguous with respect to the accentual relation between the first two pitches, but a bass accent (of register, duration, and anacrusis) is unmistakable. Afterward the upper-voice melody usually has an accent at the barline (especially of duration) and at the half-bar a quite consistent subordinate accent, also largely of duration. These accentual punctuations assert a general and clearly appreciable metric field of reference for other events, and at the same time offer a perspective for such activating subtleties as the accompanimental ties into each quarter-note beat.

Clearly the interpreter accedes to this metric state of affairs, doing nothing to underscore the recurrent accents that sustain two surface levels of metric structure. Indeed, as commonly in tonal music, these must be rather understated to avert a gratuitous, exaggerated regularity—except where barline events function critically in a vital structural process (such as that surrounding measures 26–27) and the judicious urging of the metric impulse will reinforce that process.

In the more active, developmental section (B), metric process of the barline level is moderately variable, and decidedly substantive. At measure 21 the motivic inversion (ex. 3.2) results in a patently stronger barline accent than that of the motive's genesis at measure 1, because of the leaping ascent in pitch, which like the tonal situation foreshadows a relatively active content. In the process initiated here, the modest change in accentual values brings about metric punctuation appreciable at a level slightly deeper than that of the barline, which has an important function in the emerging progression.

Thus although the accent at measure 21 is decisive, enhanced as it is by leaped anacrusis and pitch superiority, that of measure 22, which embodies only the recurring durational value, is subordinate especially with regard to pitch. (It is represented by a broken barline in ex. 3.9a.) The effect is to reinforce the sense of two-measure units often implicit in the Intermezzo's bass articulations, now supported by the altered contour of the motive and resulting subordination of the melodic accent of the second measure. In ex. 3.9, accents assessed as of subordinate value because of pitch repetition or inferiority, or the absence of an anacrustic leap, are represented by broken barlines and broken brackets.

Ex. 3.9a

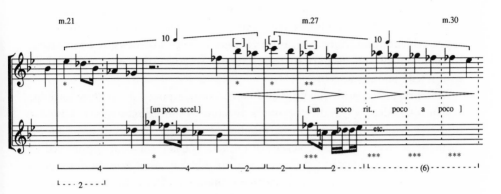

*Points of pitch superiority, leaped approach.
**Peak of crescendo.
***Interjection of motive's agogic accent in context of descent; textural enrichment at m. 27.

Ex. 3.9b

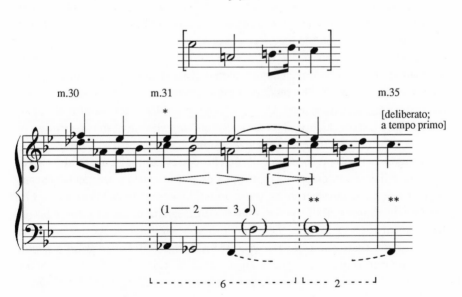

*Point of (phased) cadential arrival, and of subordinate agogic accent; syncopations articulate a low-level retardation in the durational succession 1–2–3 as indicated.
**Motive's agogic accent of thematic renewal: hesitant, then deliberate, in a phased reentry.

Measure 27, the peak of crescendo and a point of textural enrichment, reasserts the characteristic agogic accent of motivic interpolation; these factors counteract the decline in upper-voice pitch now under way. Brahms's markings suggest dynamic intensity at measure 28, inferior to that of measure 27 by virtue of redundancy and as part of the generally recessive process confirmed by continued melodic descent.

Measure 31 is plainly the goal of this recession, a point of tentative settling; accent is less decisive, and this point is thus one of subordinate metric articulation and pronounced change in a number of elements (see ex. 3.9*b*).[4] In the thematic reprise, the agogic accent of measure 34 is somewhat suppressed in conditions of fixed accompanimental texture and harmony, and the stationary upper-voice e-flat$_2$ (presumably scarcely audible). These are the considerations—unequivocal at the most critical phase of accentual acceleration—adduced in the rhythmic segmentations shown in ex. 3.9.

Example 3.9, into which some performance indications have been introduced, depicts an acceleration in accent frequency until measure 27, and consequent deceleration from that point, such metric processes complementing those of a number of elements, including pitch movements, dynamic change, and harmonic dissonance. Inferred changes in the accentually articulated units are in the relations 4-4-2-2-(2)—the parentheses denoting intervals of subordinate accentuation. From measure 27 to measure 35, the relations 2 + 6 and 6 + 2 contribute to unmistakable recessive process.

The two (6)-units comprise balancing, steadying areas of retardation that complement other receding elements, with consistent surface rhythmic activity sustained through both. The second of these (measures 31–33) is decidedly less active than the first (measures 28–30). Its chief unifier is the sustained upper-voice e-flat$_2$, goal of the broad melodic descent and vehicle of the absorption of thematic reprise in a context of formal elision.

The significance in performance of such processes cannot be overemphasized. An easy, judicious underscoring of primary accents is called for, especially at the stage of heightened acceleration (the 2-units), by controlled (dolce) stresses or tenuto articulations. It is crucial that measure 27 be treated as the peak of dynamic intensity, and that there be clear motivic interjection in the inner fingers of the right hand. To the end of the composed acceleration a slight, gradual hastening of real tempo, as suggested in ex. 3.9, can be made convincing if this and other interventions take place within a prevailing attitude of inward fervor appropriate to the Intermezzo's character. It follows that dynamic changes following measure 27 are accordingly restricted (piano to mezzo piano), with all activity diminishing in keeping with the recession that prevails.

The treatment of measures 31–35 is conditioned by its conception as an object of receding elements, an arrival phased in two elided states: that of the upper voice at measure 31, and that of the bass, on the V root, at the second beat of measure 32. (Compare the noncoincidence of outer-voice movements at measures 26–27.) Subtle projection of the covert thematic entry (ex. 3.4) has to be controlled on many counts, not least to avoid disruption of the extended cadential unit functioning within a retarded process. With a noticeable thematic a_1 in measure 32, there is ideally enough e-flat$_2$ to sound (barely) into measure 34, in a very precarious balance of textural components.

A further item of continuity is the bass F o͞f measure 32, understated as the object of diminuendo yet sustained by pedal to the middle of measure 33 or even the end of it. This note supports the sense of a broadened cadential unit but without mitigating the renewal of the bass register at measure 35, where thematic resumption is unambiguously under way.

A somewhat guarded motivic entry at the middle of measure 33 also heightens continuity in the cadential unit, and is in keeping with Brahms's muting of thematic reprise. Yet it is a further sign of the precarious balance of relations here that at the same time the motivic entry denotes resurgence: its subdued agogic accent, unimpeded as the sole impulse at the barline of measure 34, clearly sets up the 2-unit represented in ex. 3.9*b,* and is thus functional in reestablishing relatively stable, downscaled reexposition. And even as the surreptitious motivic entry of measures 33–34 is hesitantly understated in a context of tentative withdrawal, so measure 35 calls for a restored tempo deliberato (ma sempre grazioso e delicato).

Harmonic Basis and Continuity in a Compact System

The Intermezzo's harmony will be examined in two lights (exx. 3.10, 3.11), as was its melodic structure.[5] Certain characteristics are at once evident (ex. 3.11*a*): evasion of the primary tonic harmony until the final close, resulting in extreme harmonic mobility through most of the structure; prevalence of the V, chiefly in the outer sections of the ternary, denoting mobility in one sense, immobility in another; important, pivotal enharmonic relations: G-sharp/A-flat, B/C-flat, and especially F-sharp/G-flat; into measure 13, what may be described as an inflated deceptive cadence on the strongly tonicized VI, emphasized by the direct repeat of (A), the VI (like the succeeding first inversion of IV) functioning fundamentally as an upper neighbor to the structural V; in section (B), departure from and return to a modally transformed IV, and through the dominant on G-flat a clear implication of the unheard Neapolitan of B-flat—both harmonies (the latter enharmonically understood; see ex. 3.11*b*) conventional primary dominant preparations and thus logical harmonic vehicles of retransition; a conspicuous, parallel Neapolitan reference in the first section, in the relation of

A-flat to G; the broadly underlying relation of G-flat to F, a parallel to the uses of Neapolitan association noted above; and plagal embellishment in the closing segments, where the capacity of a tonic to act as the V of its subdominant is exploited as a device of cadential elaboration, as it is in so much tonal music.

Ex. 3.10

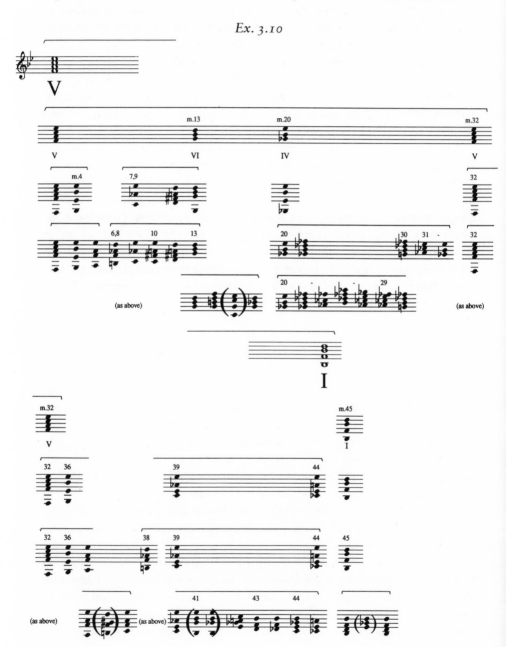

Example 3.10, which obviously has little to do with actual voice leading, suggests that the vocabulary of the Intermezzo can reasonably be regarded as deriving from the elemental V-I, and shows how this may be understood. Although explicit, composed successions are not at issue, there is within each abstracted level a tonal continuity that makes sense and can be heard. Each such level comprises chords extracted from the Intermezzo, exhibiting a stage of harmonic elaboration and amplification in directions of increased chromaticism, essentially linear functions (chromatic chords as neighbors and in passing streams), increasingly ambivalent, ambiguous surface elements, and more distant tonal regions. The harmonic content is thus abstracted and shown in hierarchical degrees of elaboration stemming from the overreaching, functional succession V-I.

Example 3.11 also represents hierarchy, but here the harmonic structure is depicted in linear continuities as ordered in the Intermezzo. A number of octave displacements made in the interest of simplification expose the continuities of voice leading.[6] The encompassing prolongation of V and its ultimate resolution are beamed prominently. Principal tonal regions have been mentioned as the primary B-flat and secondary G. A tonal reference to C-flat is implied, and E-flat and A-flat are tonicized superficially. It is notable that the primary subdominant, E-flat, is approached by its own subdominant, giving another meaning to the pitch class A-flat, as in measures 30–31 and 39–41.

Ex. 3.11a

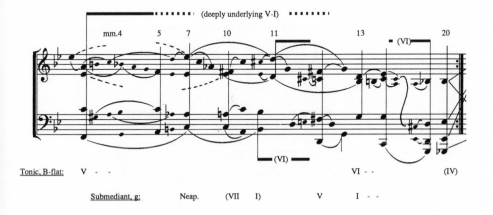

Ex. 3.11a (continued)

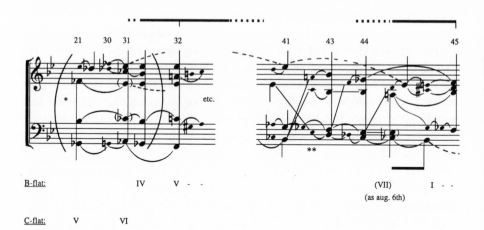

*Only the most basic content of this segment is represented; see foregoing illustrations, especially ex. 3.5.

**To simplify the representation of linear continuities, some notes are shown in octave displacement.

Ex. 3.11b

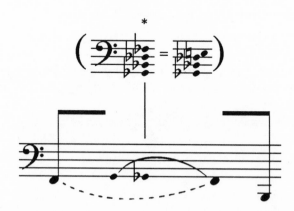

*The enharmonic equivalence is of interest as a principle of tonal continuity, even though Brahms uses the harmony to introduce the B-flat:IV chromatically (by way of its IV), as evident in ex. 3.11a (mm. 21–31), rather than as a primary augmented 6th to reintroduce B-flat:V directly.

As is expressed in ex. 3.11, the fundamental linear relations of F̱–G̱–G-flat–
F̱–Ḇ-flat are of the essence. Example 3.11*b* reveals an interesting relation briefly
noted above: the G̱-flat, prominent in measures 23–24 as the root of V of the
unheard Neapolitan C̱-flat, is at the same time enharmonically equivalent to the
primary German sixth chord, a traditional preparation for the V of B-flat; thus
it is distant in one sense, proximate in another. The augmented sixth is unused in
its conventional terms (see the note to ex. 3.11*b*), and is rather inflected chromatically (G̱-flat to G̱-natural) to yield the IV of IV (on A̱-flat). This is the means
of deriving the retransitional primary subdominant (on E̱-flat). The interior
implication of C̱-flat in its absence is consistent with Brahms's treatment of the
primary tonic in the piece as a whole, and, more locally, analogous to it. The
uses of modal interchange are vital, as in much of Brahms: both as a vehicle of
tonal expansion, and as one means of harmonic variety and chromatic intensity
of linear leaning.

Example 3.11*a* thus shows harmonic structure and inferred, underlying voice
leading by which the structure is articulated; much of the voice leading is by step
relations construed at both near-foreground and deeper levels. Of particular
interest is the disposition of the prevalent, prolonged pitch class E̱-flat, the first
note to be heard, which is manifest in two registers; it is shown moving
ultimately to Ḏ (the fifth scale degree in G minor, the third in B-flat) in both the
form's outer sections. E̱-flat is also of central significance in section (B), which is
portrayed only summarily in ex. 3.11*a* (but more fully in earlier examples), as it
is the pitch class with which the upper-voice melody starts and ends (see ex. 3.5).

Surely, the thoughtful, analytical pianist, aware of and persuaded by some
broad path of demonstrable continuities through a structure, is likely to make
pursuant subtle decisions of articulation and, perhaps, modulations of tempo
calculated to make the continuities clear to the listener. The analyst must argue
that apart from specific decisions of detail to which it may lead, the awareness of
a piece as a compact, documented unity facilitates judgments by which a scale of
events can be conceived: one event may be viewed as preparing its logical
consequence, or as following from the implications of directed tendencies; and
broadly interrelated elements are understood as overreaching. The details of an
interpretation are conditioned by a grasp of broad lines and of whole. This is a
most critical point of relation between analysis and performance, between the
cognizance of large-scale structural functions and continuities (exx. 3.5–7, 3.9,
3.11) and reasoned decisions of interpretation. The awareness of deep structures can guide a performer's conduct through a piece, affording a rational
perspective that can ultimately become intuitive in the interpretive realization.

Because music's framework of underlying, elaborating components can be
viewed and projected in many ways, choices are inescapable. Any thoughtful

performance will expose particular elements and lines of structure and subordinate others. We have seen in Brahms's piece, for example, the suggestion on the
one hand of a dynamic order oriented around a peak of expressive intensity; yet
this melodic apex, which is prominently and deliberately prepared, is at the
same time an upper neighbor to the pitch class B-flat, which is of superior *tonal*
significance. It is inconceivable that a performer not give attention to the
expressively compelling former aspect by remaining faithful to the composer's
directions of dynamic inflection and by interventions indicated above (ex. 3.9).
Still, the B-flat is revealed to the performer as a unifying tonal basis in one sense
"absorbing" the C-flat, making its intrinsic point (in measures 25–26) only if it
is not negated in performance.

With the above general understanding, specific examples of possible interpretive intervention, further to those cited on pp. 53–55 and 57, may be inferred
from the broad analysis of pitch structures in the Intermezzo.

For one thing, the performer must consider an underlying disposition of the
e-flat$_2$ of the piece's beginning—some sense of its meaning in the structure as a
whole, a problem with which ex. 3.11a deals in a particular construct. Or, in a
structure in which tonic delay and evasion are an aesthetic premise, such early,
explicit tonal references as the melodic descent between the first and fifth scale
degrees in the first phrase (ex. 3.5), or the V of measures 5–6 (ex. 3.11a), into
which there is a slight, local crescendo, might be etched prudently, as suggested
for the central melodic b-flat$_1$ of measure 4. Thus interpretation both enhances
tonal indecision (by underscoring the dominant) and mitigates it (by affirming
the reference to B-flat). The basis for such decisions, if they are to be rational
and not merely capricious, is an awareness of important melodic, harmonic,
and tonal structures broadly comprehended.

In the same perspective, such an event as the bass attack at measure 41, a
point of tonal reversal toward final resolution in which the precedent B-natural
has become C-flat, wants some explicit importance in execution, as do the
movement from G-flat to F (into the Intermezzo's first tonic triad!), and the
critical bass descent linking the fourth and first scale degrees at measures 42–
45, recalling that of the upper-voice melody's first phrase. What is indicated is a
special clarity of articulation at these points, one which does nothing to violate
an atmosphere of generally fragile sonorities.

The sense of a broadly unified bass (F, G, G-flat, F to B-flat) suggests attention
to points of linkage in this fundamental continuity—for example, the descent
from G to G-flat at measure 20, especially the second time (ex. 3.12). Comparably, the subdominant of measures 20–21, a vital component in the Intermezzo's
overall harmonic structure, is articulated deliberately even though subdued (as
the object of diminuendo, then piano); the decisively restored tempo, following

a slight hesitation in measures 19–20, is instrumental in this, as is modest
punctuation at the double bar (ex. 3.12).

Ex. 3.12

Where the prolongation of G-flat in the midsection is broken, especially by
the G-natural of measure 30 (which prepares the IV of IV and then points
toward the restored tonic), performance is likely to be un poco deliberato, with
tempo receding from the intensified drive of the preceding bars (ex. 3.13).

Ex. 3.13

Careful harmonic analysis beneath the surface also tells the performer that,
whereas measures 8 and 40 are identical in pitch-class content, the former yields

the subsidiary Neapolitan of G minor, the latter the decisive descent to B-flat, forecasting the corresponding, conclusive descent of measures 44–45 (ex. 3.11). Obviously these are to be treated differently, the latter possibly by articulation un poco tenuto at the second half of measure 40 (within the dynamic level of piano); this would be a valid precedent to Brahms's crescendo and diminuendo scaling of chromatic descent to the tonic at measure 45 (ex. 3.14).

Ex. 3.14a

Ex. 3.14b

[un poco hesitando]

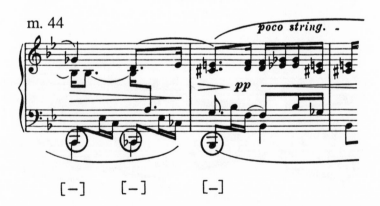

Throughout the final segment Brahms avoids the V that is prominent elsewhere. In the approach to cadence, A-flat again has a critical role: the triad of measure 40 introduces the IV, as it did in measure 31, but now in the unstable six-four position strongly suggestive of I (ex. 3.14*a*). The parallel triad at the second beat of measure 44 (ex. 3.14*b*), now with A̲-natural, acts as a substitute for V (an augmented sixth chord on the primary seventh degree). Again the otherwise prevalent V is avoided, and the subsequent cadential elaborations are altogether plagal. These conclusive cadential articulations require impeccable clarity, particularly that into measure 45, where Brahms implies an unmistakable yet discreet emphasis by the slight renewal of dynamic intensity after diminuendo, and further diminuendo immediately preceding the quickened elaboration by which the tonic of B-flat is sustained.

These practical judgments are examples of many that might be drawn from an analysis of details and broad implications in Brahms's harmonic structure.

Measures 13–20: Formal Process and Interpretation

What have been referred to as closing sections (codetta and coda) merit further comment and investigation because they well illustrate a problem often faced in interpretation: the necessity for judging meaning and function in the formal scenario, especially where circumstances are as ambiguous as they are here.

Are the segments in question areas of contrasting, supplementary thematic exposition (so that the form overall may be read as a restricted application of the sonata principle, including even the direct repeat of a formal exposition)? Or are they areas of conclusive process and cadential elaboration? The answer has an urgent bearing on performance, and the bases on which an assessment is made must be understandable and justifiable.

Measures 13–20, and the parallel tonic repetition and extension at measures 45–52(–55), are thus a problematic example of the issue of place and function in the formal scheme. That they posit a new version of material already presented (ex. 3.3) is not in itself conclusive in assessing these measures as to the discreteness of their thematic implication, because the guise in which the material is stated is decisively contrasted in key, surface rhythmic motion, dynamics, and tempo. (And no reader familiar with Classical precedents will require of a second thematic entity in sonata form distinct contrast of motivic content, so long as tonal opposition is established.)

Furthermore, the material is set off by emphatic cadential arrival on the tonic of resolution, and the succession at measures 44–45 is the Intermezzo's nearest reflection of the conventional V-I in the primary tonic (see above, and ex. 3.11*b*). Each of the closing sections is an almost singular harmonic unity, made up largely of the tonic of resolution (provisional, then final) elaborated by its IV. This technique, as old as tonal music itself, is an extremely common means of establishing finality by giving durational emphasis to the first scale degree within an essentially steadfast cadential resolution. Each cadential segment culminates a broad melodic descent (ex. 3.5), thus embodying linear as well as harmonic arrival. The descent spills into further subsidence through the arpeggiated, prolonged tonic (ex. 3.5). In a context of considerable registral stability, descent is further effected by periodic shifts of fixed pitch-class content to the lower octave (ex. 3.15, representing measures 13–20).

Ex. 3.15

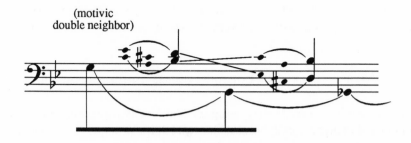

(motivic
double neighbor)

Given the duration of the segment, in the first instance amounting to half that of the preceding material, and the factors of conclusive process cited above, one may judge that the problematic attributes of distinctive content and surface acceleration (the more insistent, doubled sixteenth-notes, and stringendo) are to be understood in performance as relatively casual, superficial motions in place, tentatively attenuating the cadential effect. In their cadential role, measures 13–19 afford almost proportionate balance in relation to measures 1–6 (linear mobility within harmonic consistency) and measures 7–12 (motivic development and relative tonal mobility, with the enharmonic shift of G-sharp to A-flat). Moreover, the cadential process introduces the first explicit succession of a fifth (D-G) in the fundamentally "deceptive" approach to G, which is then prolonged by plagal embellishment, and by superficial chromatic interjections around notes of the secondary tonic triad, in retrospective motivic allusions (exx. 3.3, 3.15). An interesting and additionally pertinent feature of the codetta is an overt deceleration in surface rhythmic values (ex. 3.16), a counteraction to relatively active elements that is decidedly functional in closure. These are the arguments by which the codetta and coda are characterized as being of cadential rather than expository process.

Ex. 3.16

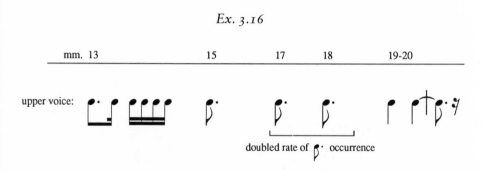

The closing sections illustrate what is a usual feature of cadential process, that of surface progressive tendencies mitigating an essential cadential recession articulated in predominant elements. The sense of cadence is necessarily fortified by extension in the decisively conclusive coda (measures 45–55), while the earlier codetta at its conclusion turns transitionally toward development.

In performance the segments in question should not be inflated beyond the sense of activity in place in a perspective of closure, but rather treated unassumingly and without exaggerated importance, as areas of essential harmonic consummation. Governed by the consideration of essential function, interpretation acknowledges modest shaping events within an appropriate scale. Thus the poco stringendo inflection contributes, with the upper-voice sixteenth-notes, to merely tentative activation. The stringendo, if applied also in measures 15–16 and 17–18 (as is likely), is logically reduced in stages, in accord with a generally recessive tendency and linear descent.[7] Brahms's sostenuto of measures 19–20 has a deliberate, critical role in punctuative recession and ultimately in transition, suggesting that the longer note values be played un pochissimo ritardando (ex. 3.12); this would complement the notated diminuendo and subtly expose the bass's chromatic descent. These interventions are deft but distinct, and they are a necessary basis for the renewed material at measure 21. Those factors in measures 13–20 that the pianist regards as denoting transition toward measure 21 (for example, the elements represented in ex. 3.12) would presumably be accorded particular attention in the repeat of section (A), whereas those contributing to interim closure are more germane to the section's first statement.

The expressive dissonances of the surface are a further sign of activity in place, requiring clear articulation within pianissimo, also on a declining scale, especially in the repeat of section (A). These dissonances might indeed be enhanced gently in the established perspective of closure (ex. 3.17), as might other superficial elaborations playing against the underlying triadic descent: for example, the succession b-flat–b–c_1–a (elaborating g:3), motions around g:5, and parallel factors in the coda.

Ex. 3.17

There are further processive elements to be pondered and, where they are deemed vital to a particular structural continuity or desired expressive effect, conveyed through the fingers. Thus a slightly tenuto treatment of melodic steps in cadential descent within pianissimo may express inferred fragile connections: for example, in the first closing section, that linking the g_1 and f_1 of measures 14 and 16 at an interval of two measures, delicately exposed within an essential rhythmic consistency; or the tonally suggestive pitch-class succession A–B-flat, doubled a third above or sixth below, which undergoes a marked tendency of rhythmic augmentation as two sixteenths, a dotted eighth and sixteenth, and finally two quarters. Again, choices are to be weighed in light of comprehended structure.

To complicate further the scope of potential interpretive detail, the pianist must decide whether to bring out in measures 16–17 the motivic double neighbor (E-flat, C-sharp, D) despite registral transferences, at the same time that B-flat is similarly elaborated diatonically in the upper voice (ex. 3.18). The pianist must also decide how this is to be done, for there are numerous possibilities and a constraining environment of greatly diminished dynamic effect. These are imperative considerations of great difficulty, necessitating reasoned choices that take into account cognitions of structure and content as well as the hazard of confusion in conflicting impulses.

Ex. 3.18

m.16

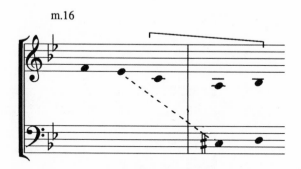

The process and substance of interim closure indicate a conditionally neutral perspective and cautious, modest interventions. These should be consistent with the formal function of tentative arrival extended in unassuming, foreground activity, somewhat aside. Clearly a context of expository thematic digression would imply very different means and ends.

The parallel section following measure 45 is decisive in elaborating the tonic B-flat by plagal actions akin to those of the prior, interim codetta on VI. The final segment by which the material is now extended (measures 52–55) enhances the functions of closure: the prominent recurrence of the broadly significant pitch-class G-flat is a sign of continued plagal elaboration in a last, conclusive gesture. Ideally the importance of this G-flat should be reflected in performance, its final articulation however tempered in the sostenuto, pianissimo conclusion. The extension's brief foreground sweep on IV, at measures 52–54, is to be treated circumspectly in light of the piece's general character and now reduced intensity and consummated recession. Here as before the stringendo of tempo and slight complementary crescendo are a superficial ripple in the prevalent condition of closure.

The coda as a whole embodies tonally decisive lines that offer several interpretive choices. Broad descent through the tonic triad has been noted, but there occurs also a succession of pitch classes B-flat (measure 46)–A-flat (measure 48)–G-flat–F, the last two heard in the inner voice at measures 49–52, then transported in the extension segment to the highest register, ultimately descending to B-flat through a final tonic arpeggiation at measures 54–55. In this depiction of events (ex. 3.19), the transfer of the G-flat's interim resolution precludes punctuation at the tonic of measure 49 as surely as do other tonal and rhythmic factors, and the G-flat is conceived as suspended to an ultimate resolution at measure 54 (ex. 3.19). In these terms, the tonic arrival at measure 49 is regarded as clearly subsidiary, yielding to a continuing cadential extension.

Ex. 3.19

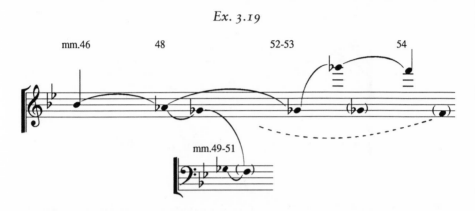

In summary, all surface activity—the descending triadic line, other, complementarily receding lines, and the surface modulations of tempo and dynamics—is circumscribed by a pervasive phased recession toward closure. This makes necessary a performance marked by restraint and a graduated control of tendencies of resolution.

Motivic Occurrences and Textural Interactions

Much can be traced to a fundamental, universal musical idea: that of a leap followed by a reversal by step, evident twice in the initiating melodic segment (ex. 3.20a) and assuming various distinctive forms elsewhere. In its second manifestation the interval components and durational values are reduced; this entity ("y" in ex. 3.20a), marked by a characteristic dotted rhythm and double-neighbor ornament, assumes something of an independent existence in the piece, and indeed wherever the dotted eighth and sixteenth occur the sense of motivic association is aroused.

Ex. 3.20a

Ex. 3.20b

Ex. 3.20c

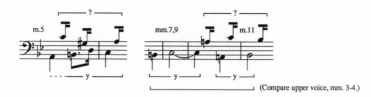

(Compare upper voice, mm. 3-4.)

Ex. 3.20d

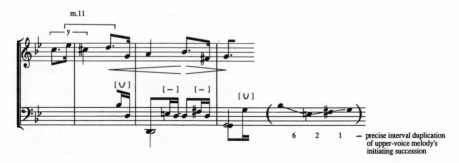

6   2   1   — precise interval duplication
of upper-voice melody's
initiating succession

Ex. 3.20e

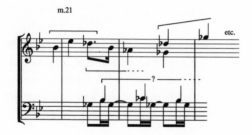

Ex. 3.20f

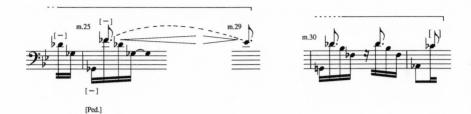

Ex. 3.20g

Ex. 3.20h

This motive y, distinctive, individuated, and omnipresent, requires no particular interventions, although the performer sensitive to its identity and variants will subordinate coincident accompanimental material, especially that of the right-hand thumb, which is a gentle rhythmic propellant through much of the Intermezzo. Further, in the direct repeat of section (A), upper-voice motivic projections are appropriately more relaxed and other, less patent, manifestations brought into relief. Some motivic implications in the voice of the tenor register are discussed below.

Examples 3.20b–h draw attention to certain motivic implications, some of them relatively covert and problematic. The informed interpreter must in each case decide whether deliberate attention is warranted in reference to a particular motivic element.

Again, there is the obvious danger of overburdening the consciousness of the pianist and the listener with motivic projections, allusions, and preoccupations crowding and unnaturally complicating the texture. Motivic occurrences that are abundant and explicit make their point without intervention, whereas those that are most deeply embedded in texture and underlying structure often may not be projected even slightly without distorting imperative continuities. The performer must also decide whether motivic precedents are to be affirmed in some way in their initial occurrences, as opposed to cultivating a motive's gradual emergence through the course of the piece or segment. Any rational interpretive decision to do or not to do requires the probing and thorough study of possibilities; ex. 3.20, though not necessarily exhaustive, is to be read as a series of citations of such possibilities.

The inceptive statements of motive y in measures 3–4 (ex. 3.20b) may be an occasion for circumspectly deliberate articulation, as may the repeated tritonal descent at measure 3, on the exact pitches with which the upper-voice melody sets out. A subtle underscoring of the grouping bracketed with a question mark in ex. 3.20b seems plausible—a condensation of the essential upper-voice content of measures 1–4, and the dissonant preparation of the piece's first B-flat.

Example 3.20c demonstrates that material in other voices may at times be interpreted as motivic, as in the explicit case of the bass at measures 5–6. In this instance certain problematic indications are to be held in balance: the motive is important in and of itself, as a bridge to the cadence, and as a preparation of the second phrase's upper-voice entry, all of which requires that it be distinct yet controlled in a context of cadential diminuendo. The key is a deliberate articulation that is not awkwardly prominent—not an easy balance to achieve, yet one often demanded of performers in light of different, coincident functions of events.

The conceivable motivic implications of the tenor register (ex. 3.20c) are still more problematic: they are potentially intrusive and inappropriately complicating for the texture. Perhaps one such delineation is warranted if it is made with extreme care: that of measures 10–11, following explicit statements in the upper voice. This has a textural value in that it is in contrary motion in relation to the bass, which is motivic as well (ex. 3.20c). The bass at this point is significant too as a reduction of the upper voice of measures 3–4, and its considerable rhythmic augmentation demands a purposeful continuity in performance.

Measures 11–13 raise similar issues (ex. 3.20d). Here the tenor voice yields a motivic derivative that is a precise transposition of the upper voice of measures 1–2; it is also decisive in the tonicization of VI. The concealed melody bears a subtle bringing out on both counts, and given that the concurrent motives in the upper voice are by now self-evident. Brahms's dynamic shading can contribute to the exposure of the tenor motive.

Example 3.20e marks the beginning of the developmental action of the midsection, the only area in which the composer's notation (of the tenor) appears to call for finger pedalling. The tenor's semitonal movement (measures 21–22), an ultimate compression of the characteristic contour, is unmistakably associable with rhythmically identical statements occurring in the upper voice.

The tenor motive's potential, significant role in the forthcoming, climactic progression can be summarized: as a minimal precedent for the upper-voice motive's subsequent intervallic expansion (through intervals 5, 6, 7); as a texturally intensifying, overlapping imitation of the upper voice; as part of a broad tonal reference to an implied C-flat tonic (B-flat–D-flat–F-flat; see ex. 3.20f); and as the basis for an encompassing motivic relation (b-flat–f-flat$_1$–e-flat$_1$; exx. 3.20e, f). The motive is thus to be very soberly considered in performance.

At measure 25 the left-hand thumb takes over the syncopated voice of necessity, and the expansive motivic reference discussed above is thus facilitated; the broadly tritonal content contributes to a dissonant intensity that is a part of this segment's potent drive. In light of these considerations and the notated crescendo, the performer is almost certain to give some articulative weight to the reiterated f-flat$_1$, which must be balanced against the urgencies of the upper voice's ascent. The upper voice is well exposed and registrally removed, so the risk of overcomplicating the texture is minimal.

One factor at the apex of development has been cited as the enrichment of texture at measure 27, the peak of Brahms's crescendo, by an added voice within the octave doubling of the primary melody. This voice is patently motivic (ex. 3.20g): it refers clearly to the basic germinal idea and to its variant occurring at measure 13 and afterward. Of course it has to be heard, even slightly over the upper voice, which is doubled and now receding.

The Intermezzo's later motivic content is much as before. When the material is heard for a third time, relative neutrality and relaxation are called for. A significant departure is that the formerly motivic content of the bass of measures 9–11 is now compromised in favor of a tonal direction which is altered toward conclusion (measures 40–41), and accordingly marked in performance. The coda's motivic references are largely the same as those of the preceding codetta, and include the underlying upper-voice melodic unities that have already been detailed. One possible motivic reference sounds especially persuasive in view of its rhythmic formulation, unique registral exposure, and dynamic inflection as notated by Brahms (ex. 3.20h). Very likely this element is plain enough, given these factors and the vital (though minimal) crescendo by which the element is partly shaped. The motivic contour is also heightened by the modest tempo stringendo by which it is approached—an adjustment to be counteracted by articulating un poco ritardando the final eighth-note of measure 53.

Four Special Problems in Performance of the Intermezzo

This section looks into the particular problems of dynamic inflection within a range between pianissimo and mezzo forte, the stringendo passages, the piece's fundamental tempo, and the final three attacks (measures 54–55).

Even where—as uncommonly—the score is explicit with respect to the placement of dynamic inflections, the performer must decide what is the desirable measure of change, and in what perspective it is to take place. A number of performance directions are given in the Brahms concerning dynamic intensities, and we have a clear idea that the general character is one of subdued articulation. (There is no indication louder than piano, although there is explicit crescendo from piano.)

Content and process in measures 21–27 lead us to conclude that there is a point of maximal dynamic intensity at the approach to measure 27. Once we have decided how far this climactic process is to advance in intensity, we can grasp an overall perspective. If we want the piece to be characterized by an easy lyricism, delicacy, and relative simplicity and directness (Brahms's "grazioso"), and take into account that the score's notated dynamic intensities are prevalently piano and pianissimo, the crescendo into measure 27, although fervent, will take place within a broad perspective of restraint. And other actions of crescendo will also be restricted, always receding through diminuendo to the prevailing condition of piano or pianissimo.

To draw such a conclusion about the critical focal area of development in the piece's midsection is to recognize that there are corresponding intensifying processes inherent in the structural elements themselves—melody, harmonic dissonance, rhythm, and texture. Interpretive intercession in the realm of dynamic intensity, as in that of tempo, largely supplements, complements, goes along with actions built into the structure.[8] The crescendo of measures 41–44, for example, is restrained in the specific context of long-delayed tonal resolution, yet is a factor in clarifying that resolution. Possibilities of surface dynamic nuance other than those the composer indicates are properly considered in connection with cadential and other formal processes to which they contribute. In such a perspective the crescendo-diminuendo inflection of measure 53 would of course be the slightest of all.

The second problem is that of modulating tempo in the passages marked stringendo and poco stringendo and tightly controlling the tempo in these applicable contexts of closure. We may reasonably assume that "poco" or even "pochissimo" applies also to measures 52–53, given the conclusive and decisively recessive process as well as the work's overall character of restrained actions.

It seems difficult to accept that the composer's stringendo applies only to the first two bars of each closing section and not to the thematically and functionally parallel pairs of measures that follow (in a controlling triadic arpeggiation in each case). To put this another way, it would seem awkward and unconvincing if the component units—measures 13–14, 15–16, 17–18, and the corresponding segments of the coda—were treated in a way that set the first unit apart in so decisive an element as tempo, in denial of their explicit concordance of content and function.

The stringendo inflection is thus appropriate also in parallel pairs of measures that follow, but in a diminishing degree comparable with the phased conclusive actions of linear descent and the reduced inflections of crescendo and diminuendo. Therefore, in the codetta to section (A), the modulations of tempo at measures 15–16 and 17–18 are moderated in relation to those of measures 13–14, and finally scarcely noticeable yet a logical outcome of the preceding, corroborating closure. Brahms's indication of sostenuto at measures 19 and 51, further confirming likely nuances of tempo in all three of the two-measure units preceding, restores the prevailing tempo in each instance.

The recessive, circumspect scaling of these interpretive actions is itself an expressive device in agreement with the music's form as assessed in analysis. The actions are of a type and degree often appropriately invoked in performance in the absence of notational directions, and in extension of such directions. In the Intermezzo, the performer has only to imagine the slightest exaggeration of any particular tempo stringendo to appreciate the extent to which the piece's character, and the conditions of cadential arrival, can be violated. The admonition that control must be appropriate to context of course applies especially to the stringendo of measures 52–53. This gesture, played with a modest crescendo, is the gentlest enhancement of anacrustic thrust toward the piece's highest pitch—a sudden but quiescent breaking of registral bonds—and a factor in its final motivic statement.

A third problem is that of general tempo: How is "allegretto" to be understood? As in most such instances, the literal meaning is only somewhat useful: in music the term of course denotes a moderately fast pace, yet one slower than allegro, and if we consider the literal meaning of "allegro" (bright and spirited), we appreciate that the Intermezzo's character should not come across as doleful, as at times it does. But to go further we must ask again what the music's structural elements tell us about reasonably applicable limits of fast and slow. The experienced, sensitive performer's intuitive sense of what tempo "feels" right is by no means irrelevant; it is only inadequate, leaving a margin of uncertainty in which we must invoke analysis as a path to confirmation and resolution.

The relative textural simplicity of the Intermezzo allows a tempo that moves without impairing clarity. But at the same time, the rhythmic content of the surface (constant sixteenth-notes, and the impulsive effect of metrically displaced attacks) itself expresses movement, so that metronomic tempo can well be qualified accordingly. In other words, the rhythmic content, intrinsically and calculatedly unsettling, calls for an easy tempo. There are other elements of structure that dictate caution against too fast a tempo: one is the hazard of trivializing the ubiquitous, motivic dotted rhythm by making the sixteenth-note too short, thus violating the piece's character; and there are times when motivic content and textural density require ample pacing (such as in measures 27–30).

Moreover, as we shall see again in Debussy's song, metrically displaced attacks are balanced by metrically suspended ones that have the effect of holding the tempo and suggest a general context of poise and control; these also dictate an easy tempo, moving but relaxed. All this is to say that relatively impulsive factors of structure demand a context that is balanced and accommodating, not rushed, impetuous, or otherwise exaggerated. The general tempo must also allow for Brahms's stringendo actions—restrained yet modestly restless movements of the surface calculated to fit the piece's easy, grazioso manner and content.

Yet tempo must not be so hesitant as to impair those linear continuities of the middleground that the informed pianist will seek to express, nor so slow as to overdraw an already restricted general pace of harmonic articulation. A too slow tempo also inhibits the richly expansive, built-in effects of progressive acceleration that have been detailed in the analysis of section (B).

One often useful way to zero in on a suitable general tempo is to identify extremes—tempi that are clearly too slow or too fast to allow for communicative exposure of evaluated structural elements to be projected in performance. It might thus be argued that some given metronomic tempo (for example, $\downarrow = 60$) is on all applicable counts too slow, another (for example, $\downarrow = 84$) too fast to accommodate vital content in an appropriate grazioso atmosphere. Within such a range, reasonable interpreters will allow that some latitude is admissible or even imperative, given the varying personal inclinations of musicians and the physical and other circumstances of performance.

The last two bars of the Intermezzo can pose a dilemma for the thoughtful performer. To begin with, they must embody a tendency of restored equilibrium and stability following modulations, however superficial, of tempo and dynamic level in the two measures preceding. These concluding attacks are problematic in part because they are vulnerable to somewhat banal effect (played either too perfunctorily or too pretentiously) and on the other hand because of their critical importance as a stamp of finality: in an ultimate diminution through five octaves, they echo the melodic descent arpeggiating the tonic triad in the coda as a whole.

It seems unthinkable that the above functions are suitably carried out strictly in tempo; rather, their role in ultimate resolution after the very late modulations of pace in measures 52–53, and their melodic content (however meager), suggest an almost imperceptible ritardando nuance, the upper voice carefully and clearly etched, and the penultimate attack rolled moderately quickly, yet not brusquely, in keeping with the Intermezzo's prevailing tempo. The staccato of the two final attacks is observed, but not overdone lest an impression be given of inconsequence.

All these inclinations grow out of an appreciation of content and function. One important aspect of the coda is a singular purity of tonic harmony prevalent from measure 45, albeit with scale degrees other than the first in the upper voice and in contexts of dissonance. The naked, tripled B-flat of measure 55 is of course vital in the final tonal filtering; it requires decisive yet restrained articulation, and in recognition of foreground recessions should probably be in intensity a bit less than the piano of the chord that precedes it. The subtle holding back suggested above lends importance to the final attack by drawing attention to it without overt notice, and strict observance of the preceding rest allows a margin of framing silence in which the critical final sound is best heard.

Chapter Four

SECOND CASE
Berg, No. 3 of Four Pieces for
Clarinet and Piano, Op. 5

With Berg's piece (ex. 4.1), one enters a special world—of sonority, rhythm, texture, and pitch relations—that is very different from those of this book's two other major subjects. Still, many problems of structure and performance are common to all three, notwithstanding their radically different vocabularies; many of the issues posed in chapter 2 arise in all of them, as will certain analytical approaches and directions of solution to common problems.

Some points arising in connection with Berg's piece are particular to chamber music, and it will be important to consider many questions of interaction between the two players in the realization of structural and expressive elements exposed in analysis. More generally, we shall pose the following questions, as in the studies of Brahms and Debussy: What interpretive choices with respect to form, texture, harmony, rhythmic articulation, melodic content, and expressive character may best illuminate critical facets of the piece's structure? And how does the awareness of content, interrelations, and inferred saliences in the structure inform interpretive decisions?

While also true of traditional tonal contexts, it is especially vital in considering the quasi-tonal and other relatively complex pitch and pitch-class relations in the Berg that analysis often reveal diverse plausible views of structural content and consequent interpretive possibilities, and alternative auditory images. The purpose of analysis is again less to plead for one interpretation or another as truth—much less to argue for some antiseptic analysis that solves all problems—than to suggest how interpretive decision can be conditioned variously by divergent analytical constructs, and to demonstrate that insightful interpretation is often a matter of choosing a particular path through a composition, or a network of interrelated paths in some considered unity of the whole. Like all this book's studies, the analysis of Berg's piece projects the insistent principle that, even where structural imperatives are agreed to, choices remain among the possible means of their realization and interpretation in performance.

Of the diverse images of Berg's Op. 5, No. 3, some will be heard as confirming and complementing others, whereas at times one suggested possibility will appear clearly incompatible with another. No performance can try to represent all of these, but the awareness of different reasonable conceptions of structure establishes the necessary basis for choices of interpretation.

Preliminary Notes

One vividly apparent feature of the piece, and of the idiom it represents, is the multitude of relatively precise instructions to the performers in the composer's notation. These include statements of metronomic tempo (invariably these offer an admissible range, or are specified as approximations); relatively exact placements of signs for modulations of tempo; constant, specific directions of dynamic inflection, within a restricted compass of *p* to *pppp*; and unambiguous indications of pedalling in the piano part, including such terms as *ohne Pedal* and *viel Pedal* (without pedal, much pedal). Moreover, hardly a note is without

Ex. 4.1a
Berg, Four Pieces for Clarinet and Piano,
Op. 5 (No. 3)

a specified articulation. The composer gives such directions as the clarinet's *Echoton*, offers general guides to the duration of fermatas, indicates which hand is to be used, and uses directions such as "molto espressivo" (compare "poco espressivo"), *Hände weg* (lift hands), and *so . . . leise als möglich* (as delicately as possible). The composer's indications are best understood as to construed content and process in the structure; they cannot be considered immune to flexibility in performance, and depend on the inferred place of an event in a determined context as well as on the circumstances of performance.

Ex. 4.1b
Berg, Four Pieces for Clarinet and Piano,
Op. 5 (No. 3)

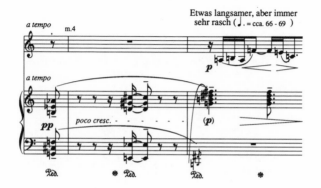

We shall seek in the analysis to reveal likely reasons for these notated directions, and to suggest further specific details of articulation and tempo that are
appropriate in light of analytical findings. Every event in these vulnerable
eighteen measures is vital to a sense of the whole, and there is no reason to
assume, for example, that all staccato articulations are equal, or that others of
any given kind are equal: an analysis is sure to yield some sense of hierarchy
among the notes and larger units. We shall see in at least one persuasive
construct that the stunningly exposed, iterated dyad {C,E} at measure 14 is of
central significance in the structure; the execution *so leise als möglich* must yet
be audible, and impeccably clear—no mean feat for the pianist.

Some inescapable, extremely detailed issues are especially challenging, and
most important to work out in an analytical perspective: for example, the
extent of punctuation between measures 8 and 9 is problematic (see ex. 4.1). Or

Ex. 4.1c
Berg, Four Pieces for Clarinet and Piano,
Op. 5 (No. 3)

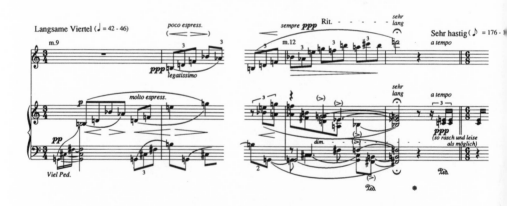

consider the punctuation preceding the anacrusis to measure 14, where the
eighth-rest appears in Berg's notation to be in the preceding tempo (in what
relation to the pronounced ritenuto cadence of measures 12–13?); here the
punctuation must afford a perceptible hiatus before the precipitate "resolution"

that follows, without impairing the piece's progress, and the interpreters must think about a number of functional relations to be considered in analysis, and represented and clarified in performance. These points must be examined with many others, including that of vital rhythmic relations in the piece's formal segmentations.

The analysis which follows is ordered along lines marked by the following topics: (1) the music's formal divisions; (2) items, largely but not only of the piece's foreground, that appear to have "motivic" consequence, thus significant in formal unity and in interrelations between the instrumental parts; (3) matters of inferrable, appreciable "tonality" and of "tonal" fluctuation; (4) further plausible concepts of meanings of the notes, and of relations by which they are processively directed; (5) some particular concepts of broad unity, including that of form; (6) suggestions of underlying gestural, thematic-expressive essences (and a comprehensive unity so conceived); and (7) the special problems of the fermatas, and their roles in punctuating the composition's form and enhancing its intersectional relations.

Ex. 4.1d
Berg, Four Pieces for Clarinet and Piano,
Op. 5 (No. 3)

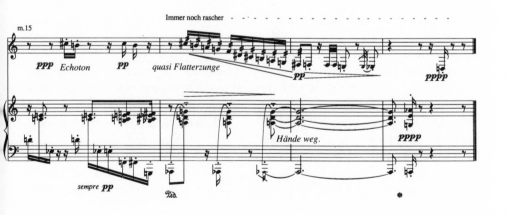

Formal Partitions in Op. 5, No. 3

Berg's articulations of, and rhythmic relations among, the piece's four sections are further treated in a later segment; but it is necessary that these most basic divisions be outlined briefly here, as a preface to further analysis. Unfortunately, copyright restrictions preclude reprinting the entire piece, but much of it—including beginnings and endings of the four main divisions—is given in ex. 4.1, with the clarinet notated in sounding pitches, and all the piece's pitch materials are displayed in this chapter's analytical illustrations. The reader should of course have the complete score for reference.

Section (A) extends through the poco ritardando of measure 3; in it we shall find that hesitant, tentative references to C and D are dispersed in a total chromatic aggregate. These first bars—on balance an area of relative tonal indecision—function in the overall tonal structure as a foil for subsequent, stabler events.

Section (B), from the restored tempo just before measure 4 to the fermata of measure 8, is heard as essentially rooted on G, a C:"V" against the clarinet's C:"V"-"I". It is therefore an area of opposed harmonic elements and implications far less equivocal than those of the preceding section. At its cadence, tonal analysis will suggest a conceivable implication of D pertinent to later events.

Section (C), also patently G-rooted, extends from measure 9 to the restoration of tempo just before measure 14. Analysis will suggest that this section (a slowly arpeggiated C:"V") and the first attacks of the following one are tonally the piece's least ambiguous phase, except for the cadential harmony of measure 13, which gradually emerges in measure 12 and is a point of multiple implication. In section (C) the two instrumental parts, in contrast with their opposed dispositions in section (B), are unified in harmonic substance while imitatively interactive in a texture that compensates for harmonic inactivity and slow tempo.

In the concluding section (D), analysis will reveal an unequivocal reference to C yielding finally to D. The former is exposed in a sudden harmonic and textural simplification that yields to circumstances of chromatic accrual. These lead in turn to a "modulation," comprising quasi-conventional elements, toward D and the dyad {D,F-sharp} that prevailed in Op. 5, No. 2. (Op. 5, No. 4, confirms C.)

Motivic Elements and Textural Interactions

"Motivic" chords and other recurrent pitch-class associations

In Brahms's Intermezzo, a vital unity was traced in one or more central motivic ideas of distinctive intervallic content, contour, and rhythm; in the example by Berg, where pervasive unities will be seen to derive from a number of elements, there is no central, permeating motive of comparable distinctive content and identity. But no analysis can fail to identify terms of other kinds that are "motivic" owing to their associable recurrences. These are particular, distinct groupings of notes and intervals (that is, pitch-class groupings, linearly and vertically disposed, occurring in transpositions and other variants). Some such motivic associations of importance in the piece and Op. 5 generally are given in ex. 4.2. Although any of these can be considered in analysis as an abstracted transposable collection, and explored on these terms with respect to all conceivable permutations, the intention in ex. 4.2 is to emphasize concrete, definitive, inversionally related interval structures as denoted by arabic numerals at the right, rather than citing as motivic every conceivable pitch-class grouping of abstractable corresponding elements, however delineated in the composition and however accessible in experience.[1]

Ex. 4.2a

5 6
6 , 5

Ex. 4.2b

5 8
8 , 5

Ex. 4.2c

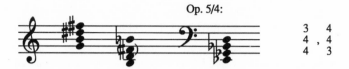

Op. 5/4:

The structure given as ex. 4.2*a* is especially notable in Op. 5, No. 1, where, for example, it is prominent in measure 4 and in measures 8–12, the piece's conclusion. In Op. 5, No. 3, the following instances can be cited: measure 4 (piano, right hand); measure 9 and following measures (both instrumental parts); measure 13 (a complex structure posing a number of implications of function and relation—but note the directly superposed notes of the piano's left-hand part, and the piano's lowest four pitches, a symmetrical array in which the motivic chord occurs twice); and measure 18 (piano—A, E-flat, A-flat).

The grouping shown in ex. 4.2*b* is evident in measure 18 (piano, right hand), as at the beginning of measure 3 (piano and clarinet), measures 6–8 (piano), and measure 9 (piano). Or see Op. 5, No. 1, measures 1 and 9, as well as Op. 5, No. 2, measure 2. In No. 3, it is striking that the pitch classes G, E-flat, and A-flat occur in the same vertical ordering at each of the piece's two primary cadences: measure 8 (by which the form is decisively bisected) and measure 18. (Both include as well the pitch class A, which has a particular significance; the pitch classes D-flat/C-sharp and E, sounded at measure 8 and prominently in the approach to the piece's final cadence, further interrelate the two events. The grouping given as ex. 4.2*c* occurs most distinctly in the third piece of Op. 5, and is durationally prominent at measures 5–7.[2] (See also Op. 5, No. 1, measures 4, 6, and 7–8.)

Although analysis will lead any thoughtful performer to deliberate questions of interpretive approaches to these materials, it seems unlikely that exx. 4.2*a* and 4.2*c* (both of which are recurring terms in Berg's vocabulary) warrant any particular notice in performance. These elements are prominent in Op. 5, No. 3: the former especially as the lower notes of measures 9–11, the latter in measures 5–7, where its mere recurrence makes a strong point.

Another matter is ex. 4.2*b*, where intervallic correspondences constitute a vital overreaching relation of the two primary cadences, a factor of significance potentially important for performance. The pitches g_1, d-sharp/e-flat$_2$, and a-flat$_{2, 3, 4}$ are repeated in measures 6–8 and in that sense self-evident; yet it is critical that Berg places articulative stress on the recurrences of A-flat (within exceedingly subdued dynamic levels), and especially that the chord of measures 16–17 (including A-flat) be caught by the piano's pedal. Moreover, the related chord of the piano at the piece's end, although transparently exposed and lacking competing factors, requires care in resisting any tendency of merely perfunctory articulation: this is one reason for the direction *Hände weg*, and the immediately preceding release of the pedal. Both cadences have vital roles in formal, tonal, rhythmic, and other broad configurations, requiring precise, controlled execution.

The augmented triad

An inferrable, pervasive augmented triad, explicit in Berg's piece in three of the triad's four possible transpositions, can be heard as a further motivic factor.[3] It has been observed that Op. 5, No. 2, concludes on the augmented triad {B-flat, D,F-sharp}, a neighbor of that which opens Op. 5, No. 3, symmetrically enclosing (in a pitch-class sense) the latter's constituent dyad {C,E}, which is a fundamental element.

The augmented triad containing the pitch classes C-sharp, F, and A is not an integral entity in the piece, but a striking pattern can be traced involving the other three augmented triads, quite apart from the significance of the sonority itself as a factor of motivic unity. This is seen graphically in ex. 4.3 (not a pitch-specific representation), which depicts a succession of which all components are not merely present in the composition but demonstrably exposed. In the illustration, parentheses denote less explicit occurrences and triadic members that are nonconcurrent, as is A-flat in relation to C and E at the piece's conclusion.

Ex. 4.3

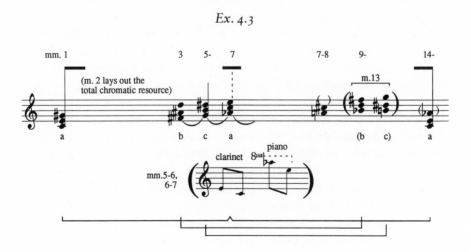

The most explicit components in the inferred continuity are those of measures 1, 3, 5, and the following measures, 6–7. Especially prominent in the composition is the element designated "a"—obviously a factor of overreaching unity in the content of pitch as well as that of pitch class; even at the end, a stark iteration of the dyad {C,E} is complemented by a subsequent iteration of A-flat in the bass of measures 16–18. Of the augmented triads, that labeled "c" is, as a pedal in measures 5–7, also especially prominent. These structures are also related in connections other than those of motivic unity and continuity.

The piece's first three notes, vulnerable and easily lost to the ear, demand a clarity and security of impression not easy to bring off at the requisite tempo and dynamic level; Berg's legato is a pertinent resource in this regard. And what of further interpretive needs and possibilities assuming and following from the continuity traced in ex. 4.3? The piano's third chord in measure 3 has cadential exposure, and agogic emphasis in that it reverberates (figuratively) through the subsequent rests: an awareness of the relation of this chord to that of measure 5 can motivate an appropriate sense of connection in which the intervening two chords are a subordinate anacrusis. (Indeed, the augmented triad of measure 3 will be viewed as a quasi-dominant to that of measure 5, quite apart from the stream of continuity suggested in ex. 4.3.) And the augmented-triad component recurring in and after measure 5 requires nothing except meticulous articulation, notably set by Berg to occur exactly where the clarinet line does not move.

In the extreme foreground, the composer's poco ritardando and crescendo of the piano part in measure 6 (with the notated modest stress on A-flat) serve to project the critical juxtaposition of two augmented triads. At this point one might question Berg's notation: it would seem better to articulate two distinct voices with both hands rather than with the right hand alone, and this would facilitate projection of the motivic descent F-sharp–F–E. The interior chromatic ascent in the piano's left-hand part at measure 7 is integral in the model represented as ex. 4.3 and vitally counteracts the clarinet's chromatic descent. Here Berg's ritardando and precise pedal changes help to achieve clarity in a context of extremely fragile sonorities.

In measures 9–13 precedence over other factors is taken by such explicit elements as the motivic chord in the piano's low register and especially by an overriding, quasi-tonal unity of function in preparation of the return of the dyad {C,E} at measure 14. But the implicit, linking augmented triads are nonetheless appreciable, in an elaborate pitch-class complex at measure 13. Indeed, in one of several inferences to be drawn from this complex, the two triads make up six of its seven pitch classes immediately before recurrence of the focal pair {C,E}, and they may be viewed as a functional harmonic unity in the approach to that central element.

Finally, no deliberate strokes other than of meticulous (and problematic) clarity are indicated at the naked exposure of {C,E} at measure 14—which is at once a provisional "resolution" and a springboard for final actions of chromatic dispersal. Moreover, the A-flat of measures 16–18 is the piece's lowest pitch, and it is sustained by the pedal; a phased diminution in durational values of its rearticulation complements the diminuendo and demands a steadfast fidelity of rhythmic execution.

Motives as contour-intervallic melodic formulations

Motive in the usual melodic-rhythmic sense is far more equivocal here than in traditional formal procedures: encompassing, fundamental unities are rather of such quasi-motivic factors as have been described, and other pitch-class relations yet to be traced.

There are however two melodic patterns in the Berg that should be viewed as motives in the more traditional sense. The first of these is illustrated in ex. 4.4: a direct, registrally unified, linear chromatic succession of three attacks (that is, two semitonal steps: 1–1). It would of course be foolish to ascribe to just any chromatic succession such motivic significance, one criterion of which must be distinctiveness. Rather, I draw attention to those formulations of which a point is made in the compositional textures and groupings. Thus, although the piano's left-hand part at measures 1–3 describes a straightforward descending chromatic scale, the attacks are grouped rhythmically, yielding the impression of a motive exposed in a definite, distinctive form. The motive is emphatic also in measures 6–8, where in both instrumental parts its rhythmic content is again short-short-long, even to the extent of equivalent durations of the motive's first two attacks, F-sharp–F, in the clarinet. Example 4.4 traces this idea throughout the piece.

Ex. 4.4a

(precedents)

Ex. 4.4b

Ex. 4.4c

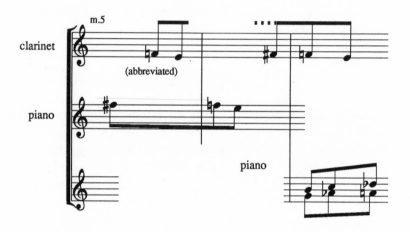

Ex. 4.4d

Ex. 4.4e

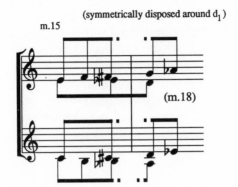

(symmetrically disposed around d_1)

m.15

(m.18)

Ex. 4.4f

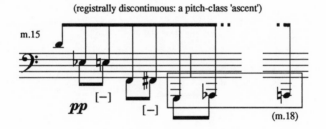

(registrally discontinuous: a pitch-class 'ascent')

m.15

pp   [−]   [−]   (m.18)

Ex. 4.4g

m.17

The motive's original rhythmic aspect, insistent in measures 1–2 and reflected in augmentation in measures 6–8, is later abandoned. But its property of readily apprehensible linear-melodic formulation is pervasive, as shown in ex. 4.4. The chromatic element is moreover in striking contrast to a second basic melodic configuration (ex. 4.5), with which it is merged in the registral scattering of chromatic succession at measure 15 (piano, left hand; ex. 4.4f) and measures 4–6 (piano, upper voice). Two factors worth noting are the clarinet's repetition and completion at measures 17–18 (ex. 4.4g) of the chromatic descent initiated in measures 6–8 (ex. 4.4c), with an overlapping pitch-class succession in the lower register, and the mirroring of that descent (using the *pitches* of the clarinet's precedent) in the piano's upper voice at measure 15 (ex. 4.4e).

The contrasting motivic element, which must be characterized somewhat more generally, is traced in ex. 4.5: a melodic unit comprising a leap followed by a step in reversed direction (that is, an appoggiatura).[4] Although its definitive character is thus essentially one of contour and intervallic relation, the leap is normally up, the step down; probably the sense of resolving the leap, which is often dissonant, is stronger when the second motion is descending.

Ex. 4.5a

Ex. 4.5b

Ex. 4.5c

Ex. 4.5d

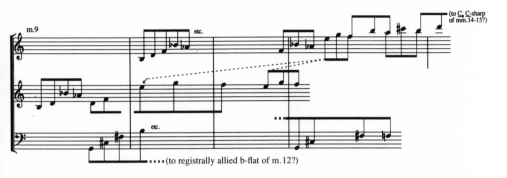

Ex. 4.5e

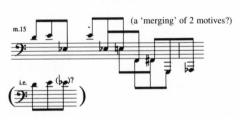

The second attack—the object of the leap—is often though not always accented; this complements its active quality. As ex. 4.5 shows, the reversed, associable pattern of step followed by leap is also in evidence. The illustration brings out the special importance of the motive in measures 9–13, where the specific chromatic-rhythmic idea is discarded, and the appoggiatura amplified as a series of leaps before the opposing step. This idea too has its initial exposition in the opening bars, in the clarinet.

The performer will see that both motives are prominent at the outset, the chromatic three-attack unit aggressively so despite a restricted dynamic intensity. The clarinet's appoggiatura motive into measure 2 is a vital precedent, its notated, controlled stress on the e-flat₂ critical. Similarly functional in motivic delineation is the piano's crescendo at the broad anacrusis to measure 5, from the final attack of measure 3; this expansion of the motive is represented as ex. 4.5b. The appoggiatura motive's definitive content in the clarinet of measures 5–7 (ex. 4.5c) is fortified by critical foreground crescendo inflections and slightly slower tempo. Comparable inflections of the surface shape the motive in measures 9–12.

The present discussion of melodic motivic content must include reference to areas of critical textural interaction to be brought out. Significantly, these are at stages of comparative harmonic inertia: the imitations on the chromatic motive exchanged between piano and clarinet at measures 6–8, in pitch-class duplications; and like interactions involving the appoggiatura motive, in *pitch* duplications, at measures 9–10 (now in a context of absolute harmonic immobility). The latter of these instances of textural activation must not overlook the freer motivic relation between clarinet and piano in measures 10–11. Slight stresses at the appoggiatura peak are particularly functional in this environment of harmonic inaction and slowest tempo, as is Berg's concentration on the relatively active appoggiatura idea as opposed to the more recessive chromatic motive, which has just undergone expansive descent in its most drawn-out presentation (clarinet, measures 6–8).

Such occurrences require the performer's awareness of their positions, and an understanding of the reasons for correlative performance directions in the score: for example, the elaboration of each note of the clarinet's augmentation at measures 6–8, by articulative stress followed by flutter, all taking place in a register left to the clarinet. Berg exposes essential ideas by such controlled factors as registral contrast (as between the instruments at measures 6–8) and, strikingly, by textural openings, as when the piano fortuitously vacates the clarinet's register at the moment of the latter's vital entry at measure 10.

A noteworthy challenge of realization is the requisite delineation of upper-voice motions of the piano at measure 6—the chromatic descent that the clarinet will imitate expansively, where melodic-motivic content and other vital factors suggest that the texturally concentrated material be negotiated by two hands, as pointed out above. Also problematic is the interior chromatic movement in the piano's left-hand part at measure 7, in the area of most subdued dynamic level, where each ascent has melodic, harmonic, and motivic significance; this must be articulated lucidly yet with extreme delicacy.

A further interpretive difficulty in delineating motivic content can be seen in the last four bars, where the piano and clarinet interact in culminating statements of the chromatic motive (ex. 4.4e–g). Here the performers' sense of interrelation in their different approaches is imperative, as the clarinet's final chromatic descent answers the piano's motivic ascent a measure and a half earlier.

Inferrable Tonal Functions and Relations

Especially in an idiom that depends relatively little on the normative syntactic terms of a traditional tonal system, there are likely to be different ways of hearing relations and continuities. This is not to deny that there may be absolutes in which circumstances of form and structure are unmistakably singular and elemental; but where structure is interestingly complex, divergent possibilities of a piece's narrative—choices to be made on demonstrable grounds—may be offered by the divergent constructs according to which a piece's elements can reasonably be interpreted by the performer and by the alert, experienced listener.

The following approaches to the Berg suggest means of interpretation analogous to those of conventional tonality, although obviously different from them. There often are in the piece different, plausible ways of inferring tonal relations, at times because the music is ambivalent (a condition which can itself be functional in relation to points of comparatively clear tonal focus), or because more than one construct can be reasonably deduced from experience, and from evidence in the notes.[5]

Although this is not the place for a comprehensive commentary on tonality, it is appropriate to state certain assumptions underlying the analysis:

1. The music is heard against the background of its tradition (and ours), and harmonic and melodic formulations that are significantly analogous to tonal conventions of the eighteenth and nineteenth centuries are likely to be experienced as being of parallel implication.

2. Distinct and prominent contextual manifestations of natural, elemental consonances (in this case the major third) may in the absence of decisively negating opposed elements be grasped as being appreciably structural and implying resolution.

3. Such conventional harmonic forms as dominants, which are understood as tonicizing (that is, as directly or indirectly supporting and tending to confirm tonic status), often have analogues in less restrictive musical systems, where they may function comparably. These analogous, tonicizing harmonic structures (characterized by semitonal leaning toward resolutive consequents, and at times by a root relation of the perfect fifth as well) often have functional significance in quasi-tonal contexts.

4. There are three kinds of confirmative or corroborative contextual associations that tonicize resolutive pitch-class structures: reflexive (the referential quasi-tonic element has been recently heard), concurrent (the referential element is heard at the same time or within some defined, narrow time frame), and anticipative (the referential element is heard subsequently). In a reflexive relation, a referential element, once established, may retain its focal implication well beyond its actual audible presence—a problem of perceptual retention impossible to specify for all circumstances.

5. Active chromatic aggregates may effect a sense of relative tonal neutrality and dispersal, in which chromatic elements are neither apprecia-

bly subsidiary to focal points of orientation nor referential in relation to them, and in which the chromatic resource is not demonstrably evident as the expansion of a diatonic basis.

6. The whole-tone collection similarly conveys a sense of tonal neutrality until the intrusion of semitonal factors effects a basis for, or furthers, tonicization (see also ex. 4.10 and the accompanying text).

Although I emphasize inferred tonal implications in Op. 5, No. 3, it should be noted that tonal references to C̲, D̲, and G̲ can be adduced in Op. 5 as a whole. Indeed, in the work's overall scheme, the G̲ of No. 1 and the C̲ of No. 4, appreciable especially in the final cadences of these outer pieces, are broadly functional.

Also readily apparent is the predominant D̲, and the dyad {D̲,F-sharp}, of Op. 5, No. 2, a quasi-tonal basis veiled at the piece's conclusion by the addition of B̲-flat, in a cadential augmented triad associated with that which opens No. 3. The final pitch classes of No. 2 and the first three of No. 3 thus constitute one of two whole-tone hexachords; this is one of the piece's important resources, linearized in longer notes of the piano's upper voice at measures 2–3.

To analyze tonality in the Berg piece is not merely to identify and document quasi-tonic pitch classes, but also to view an articulated structure in which relatively explicit rootedness (in measure 14, for example) is opposed to more unstable, dependently ambiguous conditions (as at measures 1–4). We can thus see and hear vital polarities in the structure: between references to C̲ on the one hand and D̲ on the other; between quasi-dominant and quasi-tonic functions; and between tendencies of clarity and ambiguity, stability and mobility. Factors of stability are of course extremely ephemeral in a context of such sweeping, extreme brevity, and of richly diverse content and expression that are vividly evident in, for example, tempo changes alone.

C̲-references

Section (A) is essentially an area of tonal ambiguity and dispersal. Its exceedingly brisk tempo is a factor in this, for the impression it gives is so fleeting that potential tonal implications are unlikely to cohere even after the piece has been heard repeatedly and become familiar to the listener.

One can in theory make a case for a G̲-reference in the first seven notes of the clarinet part (ex. 4.6a), which constitute the complete diatonic scale of G minor. These notes can thus be shown to relate to forthcoming G̲-pedals in the piece's interior, and to Op. 5, No. 1. Moreover, the piano's right-hand part in measure 1 moves around, from, and to g_1, the pitch of the pedal at measures 5–8, at the same time as the clarinet's allied diatonic set is unfolded.

Ex. 4.6a

Ex. 4.6b

└ Note complementary triad concluding Op. 5/2.

Ex. 4.6c

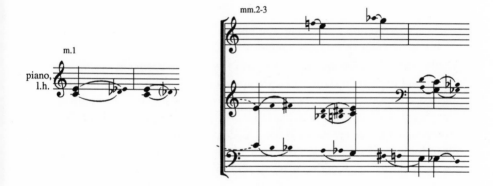

piano, l.h.

piano

Ex. 4.6d

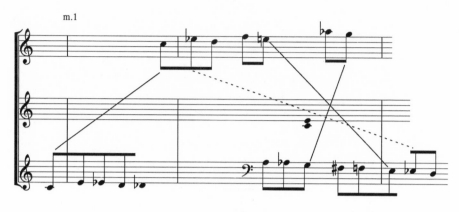

Ex. 4.6e

The first seven notes of the clarinet phrase are the loudest in the instrument's immediate context (*ppp!*) and temporally the most concentrated. The notes are plainly heard because of their judicious rhythmic placement, ascent into an unimpeded register, and timbral distinctiveness. Any deliberate attention to the phrase's component elements by whatever overt means would of course be a distraction. Still, a local tonal implication of G, subsidiary to an essential immediate context of tonal ambiguity, is demonstrable. And the crucial, subsequent diminuendo in both instruments, leading up to the cadence in measure 3, can be regarded as functional in associating measure 1 and the G-pedal of section (B).

An aspect of the predominant tonal ambiguity of the first bars is their susceptibility to diverse tonal inferences, one of these detailed above. Example 4.6*b* views the piano of measure 1 as an elaborated C-triad with chromatic neighbors, and as prolonging into measure 2 the important dyad {C,E}.[6]

Example 4.6*c* reveals an inferred C-element the components of which are compositionally exposed. Especially striking is that part of ex. 4.6*c* which represents measures 2–3: the focal pitches of the piano's right-hand part leading to a recurrence of the C-triad in measure 3. We are to return to these measures in relation to events later in the piece. Example 4.6*d* depicts interactions between the two instrumental parts with respect to variously exposed C-factors. And ex.

4.6*e* points up the chromatic descent into measure 3, significantly falling just short of c, and plausibly including the registrally allied c-sharp/d-flat of the chord following the descent. The pitch class $\underline{C}$, here considered the focus of orientation in these bars and the initiating basis for the descent and its almost achieved outcome, may thus be deemed expected. It is also notable that $\underline{C}$ is avoided altogether in the chords that follow.

These events, which occur in a very fleeting context, are thus tentative signs of $\underline{C}$-reference in a prevalent condition of tonal ambivalence shared to a significant degree by the piece's outer sections. The first notes are critical as a motivic reference to Op. 5, No. 2, and to later events in No. 3; while the e_1 is emphasized by duration, performance must guard against loss of the c_1, and thus of the initiatory element $\{\underline{C},\underline{E}\}$. Further, if the pianist is aware of the importance of this dyad at measure 2, on the same pitches, this can help to enforce the sense that measure 2's first piano attack is, with measure 1, an in-place basis for the rapid chromatic and whole-tone descents and dispersal that immediately ensue. The return of c_1 in the piano's left-hand part in measure 2 is vital also as culminating the immediately preceding chromatic descent from e_1 and reinitiating chromatic descent toward d (and c-sharp) in measure 3 (ex. 4.6*e*); thus care has to be taken to preclude its easy concealment. Indeed, in a sensitive performance it is likely to prevail gently over the simultaneous, staccato c-sharp$_1$.

Implied here is a view of measure 1 as requiring a sense of comparative stability of tempo, however fleeting, with an "imagined" slight acceleration in measure 2, a feeling that complements its harmonic context of precipitate tonal dispersal and enhances the sense of tentative cadence, poco ritenuto, in measure 3, where the concluding augmented triad can be construed as a preparatory associate of that of measure 5. As suggested, the diminuendo of both instruments in measure 2 is vital to the perception of relation between measures 1 and 2 as characterized here.

One point of conceivable tonal references cited here and later (to $\underline{C}$, $\underline{D}$, and $\underline{G}$) is to underscore a primary condition of multidirectionality. However provocative the conventional relations of these three pitch classes, the structural context of tonal suggestiveness calls for a parallel realization of comparative neutrality, for everything to be projected with impeccable purity and transparency, utterly without piano pedal or gratuitous articulative prominences, and for the notated dynamic levels to be scaled (and rests observed) precisely. The rest in the piano in measure 2, exposing the restored $\{\underline{C},\underline{E}\}$, is essential. Linear and vertical occurrences of triadic groupings, some of the immediate foreground and others under the surface, are self-evident as relative consonances; that of measure 2 is supported by the interactions of the clarinet (ex. 4.6*d*).

For all the detail laid out in ex. 4.6, and in subsequent further explorations of tonality in measures 1–3, what must finally be urged in performance is an awareness of introductory preparation, and of structural content serving the functions of bridging (the second and third pieces of Op. 5). No marked interpretive interventions are implied beyond absolute fidelity to composed durations, articulations, and differences of dynamic intensity explicated and corroborated by analysis.

Although other implications are to be seen in sections (B) and (C), in these regions of the piece's interior references to C̲ are most persuasive. Examples 4.7a and b deal with such references in the chords at the upbeat to measure 4 and within the measure.

Ex. 4.7a

Ex. 4.7b

Ex. 4.7c

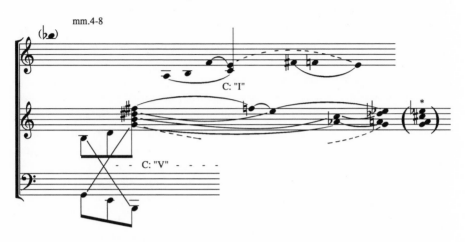

*See ex. 4.14 and related text.

The chords can be interpreted with respect to a number of tonal analogues by which the forthcoming $\underline{G}$-pedal and the tonicization of $\underline{C}$ are prepared:

1. The augmented triad of the preceding cadence, last heard at the end of Op. 5's second piece and complementing that of the first three notes of the third, is an inferred chromatic lower neighbor—a complex of leading tones—of that to be sustained in measures 5–6 (ex. 4.7a).

2. The upper-voice notes ($\underline{A}$-flat/$\underline{G}$-sharp–$\underline{F}$-sharp) are the encircling chromatic neighbors (and an "augmented sixth") in relation to the approaching $\underline{G}$-pedal (ex. 4.7b).

3. The middle-register succession e-flat_1–d_1 (ex. 4.7b) can be conceived as expecting the delayed $\underline{C}$—specifically the focal c_1 of the clarinet in measure 5.

4. In its own register, the augmented triad of measure 3 moves directly to the structure {$\underline{C}$-sharp/$\underline{D}$-flat,$\underline{F}$,$\underline{B}$}, an "augmented sixth" directly related to $\underline{C}$ (ex. 4.7a).

5. The entire chord at the end of measure 3 can be conceived as a "V" of $\underline{C}$, the traditional prototype of which it vividly resembles.

6. The chords leading into measure 5 omit the pitch class $\underline{C}$, thus enhancing its strong affirmation in measure 5.

7. The related voices of the bass and right-hand thumb, intervallically equivalent and involving registral exchanges of $\underline{G}$ and $\underline{B}$, arpeggiate a further manifestation of C:"V" in a direct approach to that of measure 5 (ex. 4.7b).

These factors, illustrated in exx. 4.7*a* and *b,* with the indicated tempo poco ritenuto just preceding the decisive return to tempo at the first of the chords, the notated legato connection fortified by the piano's pedal, and the poco crescendo, support the sense of preparatory anacrustic function. This can be conveyed by directing the chords so that they move toward measure 5, and by observing precisely the off-beat placement of the second chord.

These chords are among the piece's most challenging events, and embody further elements of process to be brought out later. In their diversity, the many inferrable, functioning elements pose again the issue of interpretive choice. Although some tonal factors can be assessed as simply there to be heard, others are capable of circumspect projection. On the other hand, an example of potentially overburdened interpretive intent and contradiction can be seen in the incompatibility of the lower-voice arpeggiations noted as item 7 above with the descent from e-flat$_1$, which is probably subsidiary (ex. 4.7*b*).[7]

Example 4.7*c* depicts the entire section (B), incorporating references to $\underline{C}$ and one of the piece's two explicit references to the dyad $\{\underline{C},\underline{E}\}$. It centers on the relation to the clarinet's melodic segment in measure 5, echoed in measure 6, of a protracted "V" (implied in the piano's chords, and explicit in the $\underline{G}$-pedal).[8] Berg's active, subtle context ornaments and expressively complicates this tonal reference, but it is evident that the clarinet melody entering at measure 5, and through the two subsequent reiterations of c_1, in itself clearly suggests $\underline{C}$.

Measure 5, although piano, is the loudest point so far. The slightly restrained tempo (*etwas langsamer*) is vital to the significance of this phase as a preliminary focus of the piece's tonal structure, as are an insistent legato in the clarinet and strict observance of the strategic dynamic inflection in measure 5, its crescendo intensifying the dissonance of two implied voices converging toward c_1 and e_1 (ex. 4.7*c*). The diminuendo expresses tentative arrival, and complements the descent of f_1 to e_1. An immediate context of active dissonance is created by the opposition of $\underline{F}$ to the piano's $\underline{F}$-sharp, and the modest supremacy of the $\underline{F}$ over the $\underline{F}$-sharp is heightened by the clarinet's crescendo.[9] All in all, the significance of measure 5 is inescapable in any $\underline{C}$-oriented construct for the piece, and the clarinet melody of measure 5 demands an expansive realization fitting the context, however provisional, of interim arrival and relative focus in the tonal structure.

The piano's articulations are by contrast unassuming: significantly, the exactly placed reiterations of the quasi-dominant chord are at points where the clarinet line does not move. Motivic entries and exchanges in measures 6–8 were discussed earlier, and other implications of events in measures 6–8 come up later.

Section (C) sustains the G̲-pedal in a harmonic context that is yet more explicit as a dominant analogue in measures 9–11. This yields to a complex chord (still arguably like a V) evolving at measure 12 and emphasized by fermata at measure 13. In one sense this section prepares the starkly exposed "tonic" {C̲,E̲}, which follows. This essential harmonic role is complemented and intensified by both tempo and the fermata's long duration. Among the properties of the protracted chord of measures 9–11 is its motivic status in a harmonic structure comprising intervals 5 and 6 (ex. 4.8a).

Ex. 4.8a

Ex. 4.8b

The c-sharp ultimately to B, m. 13 (see text).

**Note direct juxtapositions of C̲-sharp, D̲ and F̲-sharp, F̲, m. 9, third beat.*

***As to the relation {C̲-sharp, B̲}, compare clarinet at end of m. 12, clarinet at mm. 15–16, and Op. 5, No. 4.*

Ex. 4.8c

Ex. 4.8d

*Trichord comprising at m. 13 clarinet's $\underline{D}$ with lower voice of each piano segment; compare the harmonic succession linking $\overline{Op}$. 5, Nos. 2, 3.

Ex. 4.8e

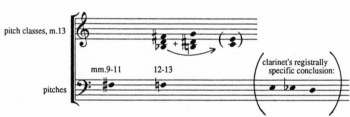

Ex. 4.8f

(associated with $\{\underline{C},\underline{E}\}$ dyad as at piece's beginning)

(compare:)

Ex. 4.8g

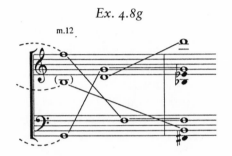

The second part of ex. 4.8*b* shows, in the piano's second voice from the top, a chromatic descent from c-sharp$_2$ to g$_1$ entering at the upbeat to measure 11, in a specific-pitch relation recalling the piano part of measure 1 and referring too to the clarinet of measures 15–16, as well as reflecting more locally the piano's lowest pitches of this same section. The pitch classes C-sharp and G function decisively as D-references at the end of the piece; in section (C) they may suggest that implication but are incorporated into and subordinate to a prevailing C:"V" (ex. 4.8 *b*). The C-orientation in these measures is paradoxically fortified by the absence of C, except for its passing occurrence in the chromatic descent, and its lack altogether in measures 12–13 (which also withhold E, except for one auxiliary occurrence early in measure 12 in the clarinet).[10]

In part because of the union of harmonic structure of the two instrumental parts, as contrasted with those of section (B), the material refers most strongly to C; it does so in a spatially amplified, protracted "dominant" of strongly dissonant form (extended to the ninth, A-flat), as illustrated in ex. 4.8*b*. The G-pedal, distributed registrally around that of its pitch in section (B), is compounded in the piano's g$_2$ and bass G (restoring the low register of the anacrusis into measure 5). The reiterated B and D over and under G, and the "diminished-seventh" structure in the clarinet, are powerful dominant analogues in which the clarinet's B-flat is understood as a motivic appoggiatura (ex. 4.5*d*). The neighbors and double neighbors inferred in ex. 4.8*b* are persuasively summarized in the clarinet's ascent at measure 12.

To draw conclusions for performance is largely to verify the composer's abundant directions. For example, the relation of auxiliary notes to essential harmonic notes in both instruments is fortified by crescendo and diminuendo actions in the foreground and the poco ritardando approach to measure 11; both these inflections corroborate the sense of appoggiatura contours and dissonant content. A consistent realization of the piece's slowest tempo (and *langsame Viertel*), and a fitting legatissimo (aided by the piano's *viel Pedal*), are essential in this area of the piece's maximal harmonic stability, harmonic fusion of the two instrumental parts, and quasi-tonal functionality. Textural activity is most important in this environment, and manifest in imitative exchanges: the clarinet, *ppp*, sounds "under" the piano, yet in an open middle-register space where its distinctive timbre is unencumbered in a composite, active texture. Faithful execution of the surface rhythms of two against three also contributes subtle ripples of activity in a context common in tonal music: the relative immobility of harmonic protraction—a fixed field of pitch-class and pitch content—against active elements of dissonance and vital textural motions. (The harmonic condition of measures 9–11 as relatively fixed, and against which surface undulations take place, is independent of any particular interpretations of tonal possibilities.)

These examples of interpretive imperatives follow from, and are corroborated by, the analysis of inferred structural content and process. In measure 12 the composer's articulative stresses, especially important in the context of the diminuendo by which they are circumscribed, convey in the piano a phased harmonic change toward the approaching cadential chord. The ritardando unfolding of this process both clarifies the change and prepares the long, forthcoming fermata. The softer clarinet part, which continues the harmonic protraction of the preceding bars (ex. 4.8b), is subsidiary to that of the piano, which fluctuates harmonically; this is especially problematic in light of the clarinet's ascent into a register of more penetrating timbre. Throughout the section the keenest balance is required between essential and auxiliary factors, and between the instrumental parts. And in the area of fixed harmonic content, elements once established are as a matter of principle tempered in their rearticulations.

A further detail: the pair {C-sharp,B} in the piano's low register at measure 12, which we relate to the same pitch classes in the clarinet at measures 15–16, and which is important in Op. 5, No. 4, bears discreet attention (particularly the C-sharp, for the B is stressed and sustained into measure 13). The pair not only plays a motivic role but is also a chromatic pitch-class encirclement of the C of measure 14.

The provocative verticality of seven pitch classes at measure 13, which comes about gradually in measure 12, is subject to a number of inferences that can bear differently on performance. In the present context one notes in particular the inferrable tonal implication with respect to C̲, and the pair {C̲,E̲}, two of the five pitch classes withheld in measure 13. Example 4.8c shows the complex to be made up of the continued G̲-pedal and two major triads interpretable as tending toward the C̲ to come, and the harmony to be thus related to that of measure 5. Example 4.8d points up the B̲-flat augmented triad comprising the clarinet's D̲ and the lower voice of each piano trichord; the augmented triad is thus delineated in actual registral positions. In this sense, measures 13–14 recall the succession linking Op. 5, No. 2, and No. 3.

Example 4.8e shows the complex as embracing two augmented triads, inclined toward C̲, that are inferred in ex. 4.3 as functional in a fundamental overall structure. Here the F̲ (specifically the pitch f) is viewed as part of a long-range, registrally unified chromatic descent consummated with the piece's final attack (this construct is also illustrated in ex. 4.15a). And ex. 4.8f interprets the complex as being made up of the G̲-pedal plus tendency notes oriented to the pair {C̲,E̲}, recalling associations established very tentatively at the beginning, and more decisively at measure 5.

Finally, ex. 4.8g exposes in analysis the conventional C:"V" factors (measure 12 begins with an explicit dominant ninth), and registral transfers of these. Here too the composed texture is supportive in the direct juxtapositions of G̲ with D̲, and comprises the tonally critical tritone {B̲,F̲}.[11] Example 4.8 thus details a number of reasonably inferrable implications of these notes, and of their registral and textural setting in relation to surrounding events.

In light of its multiple implications, the performers could well decide that measure 13 is to be played in the best attainable balance—as neutrally as possible. Indeed, as a "V" complex preparing the dyad {C̲,E̲}, the harmony can be heard essentially as sustaining the implication of the preceding, slowly paced events in a "reverberation" transformed in texture, with E̲-flat the only added note, and the tonally critical tritone {B̲,F̲} underscored in the clarinet of measure 12. The inescapable question of how to perform measures 12–13 engages the analysis undertaken here even if the interpretive decision is to project all elements clearly, allowing Berg's stressed articulations as the harmonic redistribution takes place in measure 12.

The notated stresses of the piano at measure 12 (tempered in the prevailing dynamic intensity and diminuendo) mark the transfer of the G̲-pedal to an upper voice, and the movement of the bass to F̲-sharp coincidentally with B̲ a fourth above, the B̲ tending toward C̲ and not to be neglected. The motion from F̲-sharp to F̲ is also most important in relation to the E̲ of measure 14, and more distantly in relation to the descent toward the final cadence (ex. 4.8e). A decision to favor the F over the simultaneous, stressed B-flat thus seems arguable on the basis of immediate and overreaching references.

Berg's tempo ritardando and fermata are imperative if the cadence is to be expressed unambiguously in all its inherent implications, not the least of which is purely formal. It is uncertain whether the indication *viel Pedal* applies to measure 12, where a clear delineation of the harmonic shift appears to require that pedal be restricted. Perhaps the pedal should be changed precisely at the second beat, where harmonic motion begins, and conceivably with each articulation afterward, with the utmost care taken to sustain with the fingers the notes that are tied into measure 13.

In ex. 4.9, the measures following the fermata are heard as locally realizing the C:"V" implication of measures 9–13, yet as abruptly redirected toward the pitch class D of the clarinet's ultimate arrival.

Ex. 4.9

mm.14-16

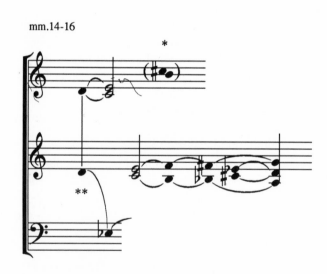

Compare C-elaborations of Op. 5, No. 4.
**Initiating the D-A pitch-class "ascent"; see ex. 4.16b.*

Somewhat paradoxical in its intricate language is the presence in Op. 5, No. 3, of a fixed pedal note through half its measures, and far more than half the time it takes for the piece to be performed. The G that has been unyielding since measure 5, almost entirely in the lowest-sounding voice, is compellingly displaced by the piano's sonority rooted in $\underline{C}$ at measure 14, although temporarily so, and the motivic and tonally referential dyad is plainly exposed in its accustomed register.

Example 4.9 represents the $\underline{C}$:"I," and its symmetrical auxiliary d_1, as the basis for the almost immediate chromatic "modulation," toward $\underline{D}$; in this respect this section can be likened to section (B). Section (D) thus embodies locally the piece's tonal structure at large: there are bipolar references to $\underline{C}$ and $\underline{D}$ (the section thus reflects the immediately surrounding pieces of Op. 5), and fluctuations between conditions of relative focus and mobility.[12]

The piano's pedalled, iterated thirds that follow the cadence at measure 13—difficult, fast, *ppp*, and *leise*—are articulated with a certain insistence, as a transient resolution of the preceding trenchant dissonance and temporal hiatus. The neighbor d_1 entering at the end of the bar (staccato, and now without pedal) wants equivalent articulation, in recognition of its initiating role in the subsequent modulatory process.

The clarinet's dyad $\{\underline{C}\text{-sharp},\underline{B}\}$ at measure 15 (ex. 4.9) at once elaborates the established $\underline{C}$ (as in the fourth and final piece of Op. 5), and sets in motion a descent toward $\underline{D}$ that is whole-tone, then chromatic (ex. 4.16). In this ambivalent relation to the preceding $\underline{C}$-reference and the forthcoming cadence on $\underline{D}$, the staged dynamic progression (*ppp*, then *pp*, at measure 15) functions decidedly as a factor of emergence complementing tonal process. The slightness of the change, in an extremely subdued general dynamic condition, makes its realization as difficult as it is crucial, especially in the requisite tempo.

$\underline{D}$-references

Berg's structure, embodying functions analogous to those of traditional tonality, evidences bipolar references to $\underline{C}$ and $\underline{D}$. $\underline{D}$ is obviously the ultimate goal of directed successions in Op. 5, No. 3 (as is $\underline{C}$ of No. 4), whereas here it is subordinate to implications of $\underline{C}$ through most of the piece. Thus one way to characterize the tonal structure is as a progression from $\underline{C}$- to $\underline{D}$-orientation. In this framework, what $\underline{D}$-references can be inferred, however tentative? And what might they suggest in performance?

Whole-tone formulations are much in evidence, particularly at the outset and conclusion of the piece. In measures 15–16, the clarinet projects distinctly the whole-tone collection containing $\underline{C}$-sharp/$\underline{D}$-flat. Example 4.10 reflects in a special way a principle stated earlier: the whole-tone collection is tonally neutral but potentially functional in tonicizing an element of the other whole-tone set (for example, through semitonal consequents of such structures as the French sixth).

Ex. 4.10

In measures 2–3 of Op. 5, No. 3, the whole-tone collection comprising the two augmented triads linking this piece with the preceding is linearized in the eighth-notes of the piano's upper voice, starting with F-sharp and descending to A-flat (and conceivably including a return to the pitch class F-sharp at measure 5, as hypothesized in ex. 4.11). Because this resource is well exposed, and in view of the prominent G of the forthcoming pedal and of the bass immediately preceding measure 4, it can be heard as a quasi-tonal preparation for G, as suggested earlier with respect to the upper voice of the chords (A-flat–F-sharp) leading into section (B).

Ex. 4.11

On the other hand, these preliminary measures are the piece's most diverse in pitch materials and ambiguous in potential implication, and the illustrated whole-tone succession is only one inferrable principle of association. In fact, the other whole-tone set, that of ex. 4.10, is represented (less explicitly) in the piano of measure 1, and the tritone G, C-sharp/D-flat, repeated in measure 1, potentially implies C as well as D (ex. 4.12). Admittedly it is questionable whether either reference is contextually persuasive; yet the ambivalence of this harmonic resource is interesting with respect to a predicated bipolar tonal basis in the piece as a whole, to C-references detailed earlier, and to the D of Op. 5, No. 2, even in this initiating context of essential tonal dispersal and ambiguity.

Ex. 4.12

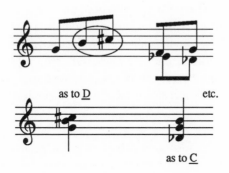

Moreover, the pitch-class pair {B,C-sharp}, circled in ex. 4.12, becomes in effect a diminished third in its role of elaborating the C later in Op. 5, No. 3, as well as in the next, last piece of Op. 5. When this dyad is emphasized by the clarinet in measures 15–16 it refers first to the harmony rooted on C (measure 14), then to the D of the final cadence (ex. 4.16). Like tempo, this condition of tonal ambivalence is a factor of convincing relationship between the piece's outer sections.

Example 4.13 displays a further conceivable reference to D in measures 1–3, supported in the upper voice's metric accent on D at the first beat of measure 3, but dispersed in the continued whole-tone descent. This formulation, enforced by the piano bass's chromatic descent to a cadential D, is in any event a vivid anticipation of the piece's final outcome, specifically of the clarinet part of measures 16–18.

Ex. 4.13

Compare clarinet, mm. 16–18.

Elements shown in exx. 4.12 and 4.13 are suggestive of D, although section (A) is largely neutral in tonal implication; these elements reflect and anticipate more cogent tonicizations in a tonal structure which subsequently comes into focus.

An awareness of the special functions of the pitch-class pair {C-sharp,B} and the tritone {C-sharp/D-flat,G} with respect to both D and C suggests to the pianist some useful guidelines. These include the imperative of transparent clarity of the passage's tonally suggestive longer notes and its stressed articulations of the outer voices, and the importance of a general atmosphere of tentativeness to which the very swift tempo contributes, as do later the diminuendo and poco ritardando cadential actions through the suspenseful rests of measure 3.

In measures 5–8, a modulation may be inferred: from a strong reference to C in the clarinet's explicit, diatonic statement in measures 5–6 against the piano's supportive G-pedal, to the motivic, chromatic shifts in measures 7–8. Example 4.14 isolates the gradually evolved pitch-class complex surviving at measure 8, including the preceding and following G-pedal. Clearly, D is contextually manifest at the cadence of section (B), a phase in the broadly traced emergence of a referential D that reflects the comparatively veiled implication of the beginning and anticipates the decisive final outcome.

Ex. 4.14

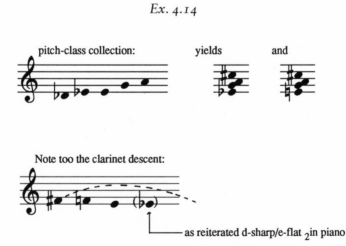

Precise execution of the notated piano pedalling is needed to project the modulation and motivic statement in the chromatic shifts of section (B), and the slowing of tempo, diminishing dynamic intensity, and ultimate fermata are

functional at this principal interior cadence, in a pointed implication uncon-
firmed until (and overreaching to) the piece's end. Complementing these tendencies of approach to the cadence are Berg's textural and rhythmic simplifications
culminating in the clarinet's residual echo-tone, and a pronounced but not
disruptive punctuation at the double bar, followed by a decisive resumption at
measure 9 (radically contrasting in most of its elements, but retaining the
insistent G). In its extreme fragility—its restraint of eventfulness, unfulfilled
expectancy, and hesitancy—the cadence is one of the piece's especially intense
moments, and is likely to be the subject of much thoughtful rehearsal. Not the
least of its requirements is a precisely coordinated release of the piano pedal and
clarinet e_1 at the end of measure 8.

That no section of the piece is without a degree of bipolarity in tonal implication is borne out also in study of measures 9–13, even though this passage is
justifiably construed as the least equivocal in its implication of C. Consider in
illustration of this prevalent condition of tonal ambivalence ex. 4.15a. The
f-sharp from there is a chromatic descent in measure 12, one of the stressed
events of harmonic change at that point, has been fixed in that register since
measure 9 as part of an ostinato complex, in one sense recalling chromatic
descents from the pitch class F-sharp in both instrumental parts at measures 6–
8. In this light, it may be heard as again inclining toward a D inferred in the
harmony of measure 8 (ex. 4.14), where the descent has been aborted, and now
as specifically inclining toward the pitch d in the register of the clarinet's
ultimate articulation at measure 18. (The motivic chromatic descent thus takes
place in three registers: that of f-sharp$_2$, piano, measure 6; f-sharp$_1$, clarinet,
measures 6–7; and that of the lower octave.)

Ex. 4.15ab

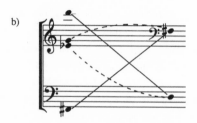

b)

This is one of the cited bases of justification for the stressed articulations of measure 12: the F̱ thus derived is important in an immediate tendency toward the goal of {C̱,E̱} achieved at measure 14, as well as in a plausible, deeper linear direction toward the ultimate cadence.

Example 4.15b portrays yet another sign of subsidiary reference to Ḏ in and approaching the intrinsically active, multifaceted verticality at measure 13: the pair {Ḏ,F-sharp} of the outer voices, coinciding with an exposed, auxiliary dyad {E-flat,G̱}. The dyad itself is conceivably a subsidiary tonal object by virtue of a registrally allied "V six-five" at the center of the preceding, protracted complex based on the "V" of C; see ex. 4.15a. One might point also to the preceding, exposed tritonal elements {G̱,C̱-sharp} implying Ḏ and thus related to the outer voices of measure 13: this tritone is explicit in the chromatic descent initiated at the upbeat to measure 11, and in the two lowest iterated voices of the piano, measures 9–12.

The richly suggestive pitch-class content of measure 13 offers various interpretive possibilities of place in an overall tonal construct. If one conceives of the chord's primary role as a "V" setting up the C̱ to follow, might one favor in articulation the tritone {Ḇ,F̱}? Or might a subtle edge be accorded the E̱-flat element in expressing an essential inclination toward Ḏ? Can both implications be respected by favoring the two upper voices of each of the two piano trichords (the clarinet's d₃ is irrepressible), thus conveying the sense of a fundamental ambivalence? Dubious among these possibilities would be a tendency of *suppressing* factors of immediate relation (to C̱) in favor of those more overreaching (toward Ḏ). Again one may opt finally for a balanced, impartial execution in which all the notes, and all implications, are clearly represented and potentially apprehensible.

In performing this prominent cadence (one mark of which is the clarinet's highest pitch overall), it is important to be aware of factors of purely textural dissonance (that is, complexity) that are tentatively resolved in the exceedingly simple formulation that follows. Also impinging on interpretive choices is the motivic significance of the components of measure 13: the four pitch classes of the piano's chord of measure 5 as well as its transposed inversion (in measure 13's upper four voices); and its lowest trichord (ex. 4.2a) as a recurring sonority preceded in measure 12 by a transposed inversion (piano, left hand). It is apparent that any interpretive decision to favor a particular structural constituent rests on a considered analytical image of harmonic and melodic lines to be traced, items to be brought discreetly into relief, and integral features vulnerable to neglect by default.

In the piece's final bars, the anticipated arrival on C is regarded as giving way to fluctuation, in which an elaborating d_1 (end of measure 14) is the basis for symmetrical chromatic progression to a structure built in fourths, which is centered on D and refers to it (measure 16; see ex. 4.9). Example 4.16a illustrates the functional tritone {C-sharp,G} of the whole-tone segment of the final clarinet descent, followed by a consequent segment linearizing {F-sharp,D} chromatically in resolution. It can be seen that the tonally critical minor seventh (A, G), penultimate goal of the piano's harmonic process into measure 16 (ex. 4.9), survives in the final chord's two lowest voices (ex. 4.16c), immediately preceding the clarinet's concluding, isolated d. Over that final note, prepared by such forms of D:"V" as the clarinet's tritonal whole-tone span and the piano chords of measures 16–17 and measure 18, it is possible to infer a D-triad implied by preceding semitonal neighbors, as suggested in ex. 4.16c.

Ex. 4.16a

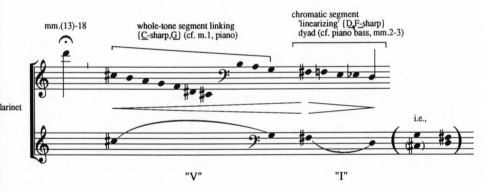

Ex. 4.16b

Ex. 4.16c

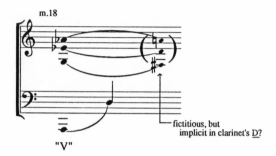

m.18

fictitious, but
implicit in clarinet's D?

"V"

Other striking features of the final tonicization of D can be pointed out. One, portrayed in ex. 4.16b, might be termed a "pitch-class ascent" in the piano's bass, a complete chromatic filling of the interval between the pitch classes D and A, scattered registrally and trenchantly allied to the clarinet's subsequent chromatic filling, in descent, of the third from F-sharp to D. Another highly functional aspect of the cadence is textural: apart from tonal implications, the piano's expansion from the bare content of measure 14 to a fuller, more dissonant, spatially distributed penultimate sonority lends a stunning perspective for the clarinet's final utterance, which in its severe, sudden textural reduction is all the more telling.

A further important factor is the way in which the melodic content of section (D) fulfills a tendency heard in section (B), where both piano and clarinet articulate the motivic, tonally implicative chromatic descent F-sharp–F–E. This element is recalled in the opposing ascent of the piano's upper voice in measure 15, involving the same pitches as the clarinet's in measures 6–8, and finally answered by the clarinet's decisive chromatic descent, also from F-sharp but now recessively in the lowest of the three octaves exploited in this absorbing interrelation overreaching much of the piece. Finally, all the elements described and represented in ex. 4.16 reflect the clarinet's prominent d_3 of measure 13, the d_1 neighbor of the interim "tonic" dyad {C,E} at measures 14–15, and references to D throughout, including those of measures 1–3, which notwithstanding the context of relative tonal dispersal resemble the formulations of the clarinet's final two measures (compare exx. 4.16a and 4.13).

The imperative of perfect clarity is especially challenging in the piano part, the technical severities of which are exacerbated by Berg's instructions *so rasch . . . als möglich,* then *immer noch rascher*! Yet the abrupt, fast tempo is crucial to the requisite sense of resolution, and is related to that of section (A).

A number of details of execution are essential in delineating central elements of content inferred in analysis. The pitch-class "ascent" from D to A in the piano's bass requires that the left hand articulate incisively each registrally unified chromatic step (e-flat–e, and so on), possibly with very circumspect stress on the second degree of each such step—a difficult but effective interpretive stroke if carried out with sensitive control. Once the piano has attained at measure 16 the D:"V" (object of the wedged progression), engagement of the pedal sustains the harmony in a context of recession of which the most obvious feature is diminuendo, and in counteraction to which is the progressive rhythmic diminution of its recurring A-flat upbeat, an element of rhythmic mobility requiring meticulous timing.

The clarinet's dyad {B,C-sharp} has ambivalent tonal meanings, and motivic significance with respect to Op. 5, No. 4. Berg's phased crescendo (clarinet, measures 15–16) helps spring this initially tentative element into the final descent toward D of which it becomes an integral part. In the descent, the exact pacing of Berg's crescendo and diminuendo, as notated, helps delineate the juncture between whole-tone ("V") and chromatic ("I") segments.

A further, compelling rhythmic subtlety is the off-beat attack of the final note, something readily appreciated when one imagines the potential banality of an on-beat cadential impulse—for example, displacing the piano's final chord to the third eighth and the clarinet's attack to the fourth. Both these events, extremely short, are set at the lowest dynamic level (*pppp*), yet if the piece is to end and not merely cease they must be articulated urgently and incisively. The players are likely to feel an exacting intensity, and the direction *Hände weg*, which prepares the piano's final attack, facilitates a clear, precise, sharp staccato. As indicated in the score, the pedal is lifted just before the attack.

Finally, it is essential that there be a margin of silence in which the decisively resolutive, difficult, and precarious events concluding Op. 5, No. 3, can be assimilated. This is well understood when one considers the deleterious effect of doing the opposite: entering the following piece too soon, or violating the intense hiatus which is the true terminal event of Op. 5, No. 3, prematurely abandoning the posture assumed during the final bars, turning pages, or making other distracting movements.

A further look at multifaceted tonal factors in section (A)

Section (A) establishes a prefatory perspective of tonal dispersal: a preliminary environment of relative tonal ambiguity and uncertain tonal implication. The configurations adduced in the analysis of section (A) point variously, in a rapidly unfolding succession of triadic, whole-tone, diatonic, and chromatic groupings, the sum of which is arguably a virtual tonal neutrality.

The piece's two interior sections on the other hand are relatively clear in tonal implication, in a structure that can in one sense be defined as a line of contrasts between comparatively decisive tonal references interacting with the more nebulous tonal conditions of other segments.

There are still further demonstrable lines of content and derivative structures in the manifold context of measures 1–3. The criteria by which these structures may be assessed are: articulative stresses, longer notes, motivic groupings, delineations by rests, and registral associations.

Ex. 4.17a

Ex. 4.17b

The lower staff of ex. 4.17a shows the chromatic line of the piano's left-hand part partitioned into inferrable motivic groupings. The up-stemmed notes are those of motivic inceptions, the down-stemmed ones those of durational or stressed accents, which expose the line's arpeggiations of two of the three diminished seventh chords with respect to the specific criteria.[13] The up-stemmed series would have as its next constituent C, which is deliberately withheld. The down-stemmed series, enhanced by the clarinet's concluding e_2–g_2–b-flat$_2$ over the piano's e, would in traditional terms have D as one of its four potential pitch classes of reference; with the insistent accents by which it is arpeggiated, it is the more emphatic of the two linearizations, and the line comes to a stop on D in measure 3.

Example 4.17b deals with the piano's right-hand line, the variant doublings of which constitute an interesting textural process to be explored later. The central tritone {C-sharp,G} of measure 1 is of course an element in the most strongly projected of the two left-hand arpeggiations, while the piano's middle-voice accents linearize the other (the up-stemmed notes in ex. 4.17*b*).

A paradigm of inherently ambiguous structures is thus exposed here, complicated by concurrent, opposed, implicative lines. These lines are unfolded at great speed in circumstances of essential tonal hiatus that await later focus and are a basis for it. To an extent, the analysis in ex. 4.17 reinforces inferences of tonal allusion that likely enhance, reflexively and anticipatively, more potent references before and after. But the essential point of the network of mingled implications in section (A) is one of dispersal, substantiated in the analysis of all constituent structures with respect to intrinsic factors of grouping and emphasis, including those of ex. 4.17.

This may further underscore the need for impeccably balanced execution faithful to every notated detail of articulation, to the very fast tempo, and to indicated modulations of tempo and dynamic level. The absence of the piano's pedal until section (B) is a necessary aid to incisive clarity. In such a perspective, elements represented as tonal referents, for example the accented C-triad of measure 2 and its surrounding associations portrayed in ex. 4.6*c*, may well emerge self-evidently by virtue of their inherent properties of exposure; but to throw anything into relief in measures 1–3 risks denying an essential preliminary perspective for events to come. On the other hand, the performer's choice, guided by the thorough analysis of possible interpretations and their implications, may be to etch circumspectly one or more of the inherent formulations that anticipate clearer tonal references during the later course of the piece.

With the necessity of meticulously representing many details of integral elements and continuities that constitute a point of departure for later events, the hushed, taut first section of Berg's piece is likely the most difficult in an extremely arduous whole. Exhaustive analysis is the necessary basis for choices to be made.

Berg's Notes: Supplementary Considerations

Two practices that affect the workings of Op. 5, No. 3, are the apparently purposeful exclusion of pitch-class resources in particular segments of the piece, and the use of certain intervallic relations that appear to be deliberately processive. Both are important to performance, especially because they relate to processes of dynamic intensity, rhythm, and other elements in tendencies of complementary or counteractive effect, and because they tend to confirm other, particular structural implications of the notes.

Section (A)

Against the piano's comprehensive chromatic resource, the clarinet phrase unfolds ten pitch classes, lacking B̲ and C̲-sharp (ex. 4.18). B̲ has a fundamental role in the section following, as a primary leading-tone (in both instrumental parts), and C̲-sharp has a parallel function, principally in the structure's ultimate tonal course. And the clarinet part in section (D), which lacks C̲ and B̲-flat, features B̲ and C̲-sharp prominently, an aspect of fulfillment in the section's overreaching relation to the first.

Ex. 4.18

lacking B̲, C̲-sharp (integral
in clarinet at mm.15-16)

The analysis of pitch-class content in section (A) tells the clarinetist something about approaches to later developments. For example, the C̲-sharp initially withheld makes no appearance in the clarinet part until its prominent occurrence (directly related to D̲) in measure 12, where the slowing tempo can be used in a subtly deliberate articulation of the clarinet's c-sharp$_3$ and b$_2$ at the end of the bar. Furthermore, fidelity to the diminuendo at this point can have the effect of subordinating the B̲ and thus discreetly enhancing the functional relation of C̲-sharp to D̲ (the d$_3$ of measure 13 is the clarinet's longest and highest note). Assuming that the piano's left hand speaks clearly, the clarinet's C̲-sharp and B̲ may be heard to imitate the same pitch classes three octaves below; and the two notes are reiterated in the pedal complex of section (C), and articulated simultaneously in measure 11.

Example 4.19 deals with a further structural aspect of the notes in section (A): controlled intervallic expansion and contraction in processive, directed actions. It can be seen that this applies to measure 2 at the slightly under-surface level of the motive, and that the textural process strikingly complements the rhythmic and intervallic expansion at the absolute foreground (that is, in the anapestic motive; see ex. 4.19*b*). Intervallic contraction at the cadence in measure 3 (ex. 4.19*b*) can be felt as an element of intensity through the rests (ritardando) that follow.

Ex. 4.19ab

a)   piano, mm.2-3

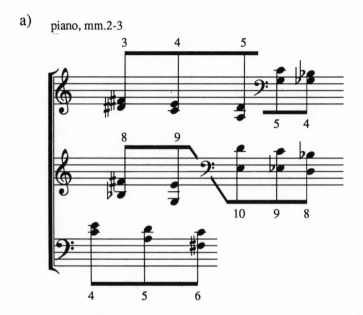

(a consequence of concurrent
chromatic and whole-tone
successions)

b)   compare, at   and, at m.3:
        microlevel:

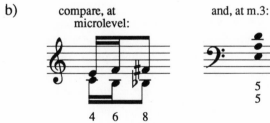   

Although these observations hardly suggest any particular, overt interventions in performance, the awareness of such elements of process can confirm the performer's sense of encompassing shape in the sweep of the first phrase, and further corroborate the functions of articulative stresses, where the controlled intervallic changes are evident. The shape delineated by lines of intervallic expansion, then contraction, function actively with the concurrent processes of diminuendo and ritardando, and with rhythmic recession toward the cadence. Specifically, one might conjecture that the process of intervallic contraction (in the coordinate relation of smaller intervals and greater density, presumably a factor of dissonance) counteracts that of recessive slowing and thus constitutes a subtle psychological element of penetration across the cadential punctuation. In other words, the textural condition can be felt as one factor in an active cadence, supportive of a linear relation between the augmented triads of measures 3 and 5.

Section (B)

Scrutiny of the pitch-class content of measures 5–8 also reveals evidence affirming links of continuity; here B-flat and D are excluded (ex. 4.20).

Ex. 4.20

(cf. exx. 4.3, 4.28)

The B-flat is last heard in the clarinet and piano at the cadence in measure 3, and although D is heard in the second of the anacrustic chords entering section (B) it is withheld altogether in measures 5–8; both pitch classes are restored prominently in measure 9. Example 4.20 (compare exx. 4.3 and 4.28) depicts a stream of continuity illuminating one basis for the calculated avoidance of the dyad {B-flat,D} in measures 5–8. In this perspective, the harmonic succession in the piano at measures 6–8 (ex. 4.7c) expects the dyad in a chromatic succession which goes through the pronounced cadential break at measure 8.

At measure 9, the B-flat consequent occurs in a register consistent with that of the preceding succession, and the D occurs below and ultimately above. It is surely deliberate that the B-flat, which is registrally consistent, is placed at the apex of surface crescendo inflections (piano, measure 9; clarinet, measures 10–12), and is the melodic peak of legato, foreground motivic statements. And the understanding of its linear relation to contrapuntal movements and pitch-class context in the preceding measures underscores and clarifies the precise placement of dynamic inflection around the b-flat$_1$ (not altogether clear in the notation), as does its position in the appoggiatura motive.

Like the preceding section, section (B) reveals a factor of controlled intervallic distribution in the anacrustic chords and central phrase's essential harmonic material (ex. 4.21*a*); this also is a noticeable, shaping aspect of texture.

Ex. 4.21a

mm.3-5,8 (chords as constituted)

9 - 10 - 11   - 8   4 - 5 - 6   4 - 3 - 2

Ex. 4.21b

Concurrent modulations of dynamic intensity and tempo can be understood as parallel processes, and again a textural concentration of density at the cadence counteracts the recessive actions of ritardando, rhythmic deceleration (ex. 4.26), and diminuendo, exerting a kinetic influence through the cadential fermata and punctuation.[14] Bilinear structure in the clarinet of measures 5–8 (ex. 4.21*b*) embodies more modestly a related principle of textural contraction. The cognizance of such obviously deliberate elements can enforce the interpretive tendencies of shaping gestures, even of physical approach, while confirming the contributive functions of notated details of execution.

Example 4.22 shows some additional, intriguing details of the chords of measures 3–5, in which intervallic opening (ex. 4.21*a*) can be heard as complementing registral expansion (see note 14). Both these tendencies are plausible, appreciable aspects of anacrustic preparation. The following elements of structure in the chords are of particular interest:

1. They articulate nine pitch classes, excluding the B̲-flat just heard in
both instrumental parts, the A̲ of the approaching clarinet entry, and the
tonally critical C̲ about to emerge in its first cogent tonicization.

2. They embody several distinct elements of process: (*a*) From the cadence in measure 3, space opens dramatically. (*b*) Pitch-class volume progresses, then recedes—from three voices (in the preceding cadential chord)
to six, five, and four. (*c*) With regard to degrees of harmonic change, the
first anacrustic chord in relation to the preceding triad embraces six new
pitch classes, the next chord two (three are carried from the first chord, for
minimal harmonic change), and in the chord of measure 5 three of four
pitch classes are new in relation to the immediate precedent, reflecting
enhanced change. (*d*) The chord of the foregoing cadence and that of
measure 5, which are motivically related in interval structure, lack tritones.
In the line of succession into measure 5, the tritones are in the first chord
the two tonally prevalent ones, {C̲-sharp,G̲} and {B̲,F̲}, then one in the
second chord, then none, the absence of a tritone in the harmony of
measure 5 conceivably enhancing the important forthcoming tritonal statement and resolution in the clarinet (ex. 4.21*b*). (e) In textural density, or
quantity (as the number of simultaneous pitches), progression and recession correspond almost exactly to the element of pitch-class content, because there are few doublings: thus there are three components at measure
3, then six, five, again six, and four as the space closes again. These
relations are summarized in ex. 4.22.

Ex. 4.22

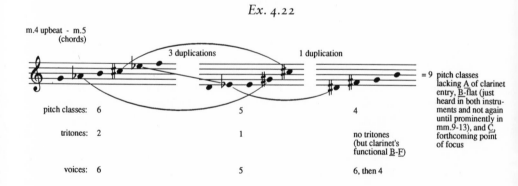

m.4 upbeat - m.5
(chords)

pitch classes:	6	5	4	= 9 pitch classes lacking A̲ of clarinet entry, B̲-flat (just heard in both instruments and not again until prominently in mm.9-13), and C̲, forthcoming point of focus
tritones:	2	1	no tritones (but clarinet's functional B̲-F̲)	
voices:	6	5	6, then 4	

However little is known of such matters, one feels that the crescendo and
decisive resumption of tempo complement such presumably intensifying processes as pronounced harmonic change and recontraction of texture into measure 5, whereas a textural reduction from six to five to four would be sensed as
counteracting the intensification and thus a factor in preparing the (slightly)

slower tempo and radically slowed harmonic pacing of section (B). Music must commonly project such functionally complementary and counteractive lines of action as those represented in ex. 4.22.

Here again analysis suggests specific justifications for interpretive details. For example, the registral space deliberately established at measure 5 is maintained by the piano pedal exactly to the middle of the bar, a vital consideration in the process traced; and the piano's diminuendo in measure 5, in addition to throwing into relief the critical clarinet phrase, appears to be functional as the space recedes and elements of activity in the piano part are suspended. The off-beat attack in measure 4 complements the progressive tendencies of quantitative growth and crescendo. Playing measure 5 as an outcome of the large anacrustic gesture is appropriate to its steadied tempo and pronounced harmonic change, its textural concentration, and its inclusion of the dyad {G,B}, which is important immediately and over the long range. In the chords leading into section (B), such functional elements as crescendo and decisively resumed tempo, which are channels of activity and directed thrust, are ideally controlled according to the performer's sense of the place and role of these elements in an expressive scheme.

Section (C)

As may be expected in light of its importance at measure 14, C is withheld in measures 9–13, except for one fleeting occurrence in measure 11, while the G and C-sharp of the preceding cadence are maintained in the lowest register as a factor of continuity and conceivably of ultimate tonal functionality. The nine pitch classes of measures 9–11 exclude, in addition to C, the tritone {A,E-flat} of measure 8 in favor of the reiterated D-reference {C-sharp,G} (see ex. 4.23).

Ex. 4.23

These first notes of measure 9 will be caught by the piano pedal, reflecting the tonally significant preceding cadence: they should not be lost in the upsweep of grace notes. A deliberate punctuative silence between measures 8 and 9 contributes to the clarity of the initiating, reflexive harmonic content.

The examination of direct intervallic succession in melodic and harmonic motions within section (C) is of particular interest,[15] and significant in a processive relation to section (A), which has consistent, direct successions of relatively small intervals. The intervals articulated between contiguous attacks in measures 9–11 are shown in ex. 4.24.

Ex. 4.24ab

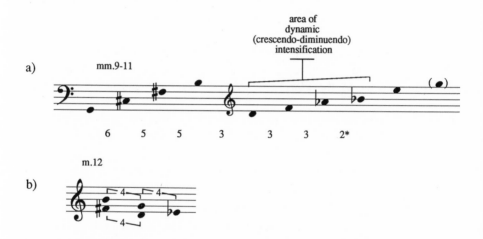

*Note: (1) the diminishing interval series constitutes a perspective for semitonal successions in m. 12, initiated at m. 11; (2) there is no direct occurrence of interval 4 until m. 12—a factor of preparation for m. 14.

Within this area of the piece's most pervasive harmonic stasis, the unfolding through gradually diminishing interval sizes is a persuasive aspect of shaping: it may be described as a textural crescendo, assuming that smaller intervals in higher registers denote progressive intensification. Especially striking is the absence until measure 12 of interval 4 (see ex. 4.24b), in general a motivic and tonal element. This circumstance supports the notion of the interval as focal and ultimately resolutive. Just as Berg's withholding of a particular pitch class can enhance the sense of achieved goal when the pitch class is finally introduced, so an implication of fulfillment and resolution is conveyed by the naked exposure of interval 4 as a quasi-tonic dyad at measure 14, anticipated in direct occurrences only in the relatively complex textures of measures 12–13.

The sensitive performer may judiciously underscore inherent musical processes that analysis has illuminated—for example, by applying such interventions as circumspect crescendo or acceleration, often so slight as to be virtually imperceptible, yet experienced as part of the total construct. In the matter of such intervallic shapings as those detailed above, there is little if anything to do overtly; indeed, interpretive consciousness of an act of intervention may well cause exaggeration beyond the cautiously supportive, all but unnoticed nuance that stops short of drawing attention to mannerism over substance. The vital role of the clarinet in unfolding the culminating, small-interval stage of progression comes through, however pianissimo, by virtue of timbre, assured registral exposure, and notated dynamic inflections, for which we now see further justification. Similarly, the clarinet's proliferation of occurrences of interval 2 in measure 12 occurs in a context of slowing tempo and ascent into a penetrating register.

There is perhaps another clue to the importance of the chromatic entry in the piano into measure 11: beyond its role as a linearly filled mirror of the low, ostinato harmonic element {G̲, C̲-sharp} that is its precedent, it is an ultimate culmination of the tendency of intervallic contraction traced here. This texturally new entry may warrant modestly greater attention than the outer-voice components which are by now well established. Berg's foreground inflection of crescendo and diminuendo can be construed as applicable specifically to the chromatic descent, which occurs nonetheless within a governing context of harmony rooted on G̲. Further, the structure profiled by graduated interval changes also justifies the stressed chromatic steps of measure 12.

Further Elements of Broad Structural Continuity

Overreaching tonal elements have been treated in detail; and a path through Op. 5, No. 3, that traces occurrences of the augmented triad (and its component interval 4) is shown in exx. 4.3 and 4.20, and is further examined in ex. 4.28. The following pages deal with a particular attribute of form, especially its rhythmic delineations, and with the piece's essential melodic-thematic substance.

Rhythmic articulations of form

One dimension of structure in the Berg is of course that of form, not significantly in the traditional, recapitulative sense, but as a partitioning of the piece's narrative into contrasted yet interdependent phrases overtly punctuated by cadences and resumptions. Of the three punctuative cadences, that separating sections (A) and (B) is the least marked, which is obvious from Berg's placement of double bars and fermatas.

One of the form's strongest delineators—perhaps the most perceptible—is that of tempo, an aspect of rhythm. This includes not only metronomic tempo, the role of which is readily appreciable, but the modulations of tempo in such instances as the gradual slowing toward each of the two fermatas. In fact, all three preliminary cadences are characterized by retarded tempo, which makes the rush of the piece's final cadence all the more compelling.

It can be assumed that tempi are within the metronomic ranges specified, taking into account varying acoustical conditions and the capacities of the instruments to speak clearly. The general effect to be felt and conveyed in realization can be described as analogous to an extended, gradual diminuendo (that is, antecedent slowing) followed by an abrupt crescendo (that is, accelerated affirmative consequent) within the rhythmic element of tempo. With this overall construct, analysis illuminates a number of details of modulation of tempo, and suggests caveats of interpretation respecting these.

The cadence at measure 3 is effected in substantial part by a moderate holding of tempo, poco ritardando. Obviously it is much too early for the piece to stop, and the slowing, in the context of a very swift tempo, is phased to extend through the rests. The upbeat to measure 4, in a restored tempo deciso, reflects a modest change of content and character, pointing to measure 5. A functional, controlled rate of attack in the area linking sections (A) and (B) is important. Here the increasing temporal intervals between attacks are a composed hesitancy contributing to the sense of phrase downbeat at measure 5 (see ex. 4.25), and thus of the preceding anacrusis counterbalancing the crescendo and restored tempo in measure 4; they require impeccable rhythmic precision in performance.

Ex. 4.25

Section (B) is only slightly slower (*immer sehr rasch*); the textural and harmonic simplifications in this section themselves complement the experience of a slower tempo.

The tempo poco ritardando at measures 7–8 is, like that of measure 3, tempered in the context of fundamental swiftness, but here it is applied over a greater distance, in which the pace will recede to an increased extent. With the fermata it can be conceived as exactly preparing the following, slowest section, in a phased adjustment complementing the diminuendo, the piano's textural reduction, and the augmentation of motive in the clarinet—all these factors limiting the ritardando. Moreover, the slowing is again in considerable part composed: it is shown in ex. 4.26 in terms of a declining rate of attack and increasing intervals of interruption in the rate, further qualifying the degree of actual change in tempo. (The surface poco ritardando in the piano part at measure 6 cannot in this context be deemed a true slowing, but rather an articulation un poco deliberato to facilitate motivic statement in the moving voice.)

Ex. 4.26

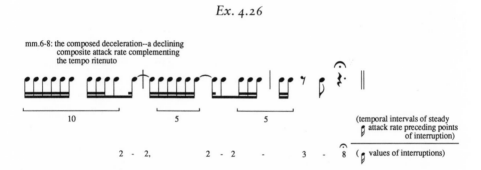

The slow tempo of measures 9–13 is a vital element in the piece's inner core, an area of arrival in broad recession of the overall tempo structure, and in this sense fittingly conceived in performance as a plateau of action. In analysis this is found to be an area of relative stability, though at the same time one of counteractive dissonance, imitation, active surface rhythms, and foreground dynamic inflections. The metronomic value of the quarter note is more than twice as long as that at the piece's beginning, and the felt pulses—the dotted quarter in 6/8 and the quarter in 3/4—are in the relation 5:3.[16]

The ritardando of measure 12 can be governed by the clarinet's increasingly deliberate triplets, affording time for the chromatic articulations in the piano (where harmonic change takes place in stages); but the sense of the broad quarter, as a fundamental pulse never sacrificed to the triplet eighth, and of already restricted tempo and harmonic rhythm, must limit the slowing.

The tempo of the final section is somewhat less rushed than that of the first: the original eighth-pulse, at MM 216, can be compared with the eighth at about 180 in section (D). But of course the tempo measured by rate of attack is more active in measure 14, and the actual metronomic tempo is accelerated in the last three bars. Berg's *als möglich* is to the point: the tempo is driven just to the threshold of audibility of discrete attacks, an imperative complicated by the piano's pedal.[17]

Thus there is overall an apprehensible macrorhythm of tempo relations among the formal divisions, slowing, then quickening. The linking stages are always conceived and conveyed with an interpretive sense of past and future conditions, and the underlying tempo and its inflections are moderated by an understanding of intrinsic, composed process (that is, within harmonic, tex-tural, and other elements).

Further elements of encompassing unity

Of the piece's many pitch-class and other interrelations, some overreach the entire piece, or major portions of it. Among these are cited tonal references, motivic recurrences, tempo as a comprehensive rhythmic process, the recur-rence of the element $\{c_1,e_1\}$ from measures 1–2 in the same register at measures 5–6 and 14 (see also ex. 4.28), the clarinet descent of measures 6–8, regarded as fulfilled in 17–18, and the inferred stream of augmented triads in chromatic succession.

Example 4.27 affords a further view of the bisecting and final cadences, and the factors of harmonic content closely relating them. As is evident in the illustration, the two cadences are very nearly parallel in pitch-class content, except for the final cadence's lack (or resolution?) of the C-sharp/D-flat of the bisecting cadence—a notable sign of interrelation and fulfillment.

Ex. 4.27

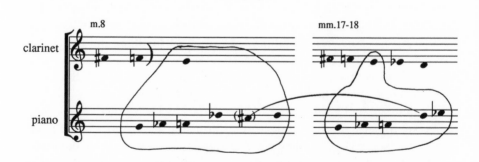

Example 4.28 represents (largely in specific pitches) the cohering, registrally fixed recurrences of the dyad $\{C,E\}$, and a chromatic stream of thirds linking these. This is a more consistent derivative of the hypothesized, corresponding succession of augmented triads given as ex. 4.3.

Ex. 4.28

*Note precise registral identity of three occurrences: mm. 1, 5–6, 14.
**Most explicit elements.

Example 4.29 shows an underlying voice leading that can reasonably be inferred; it is given initially as a simplified pitch-class representation in which the resulting consistency of register clarifies the construed connections. The derived structure is made up largely of chords of primary motivic and tonal function, linked in overreaching associations of common tone, diatonic and chromatic step, and arpeggiation.

Ex. 4.29

(The notes are given mainly as pitch classes in a registrally consistent simplification, except in the lower sketch. The natural sign is used only to cancel a directly preceding sharp or flat.)

*The tritone {B,F} refers back to m. 5, clarinet (ex. 4.7c).

To draw from deeply inferred continuities conclusions about details of performance is problematic especially with respect to the complexities of ex. 4.29. On the other hand, some overreaching elements, for example that of the tonal-motivic dyad {C,E} so vividly exposed at measures 5–6 and 14, are readily apprehensible so long as performance does nothing by misconstruction or default to obscure them. The following are three examples of considerations of structural continuity with implications for performance:

1. At measure 8, the piano pedal, diminuendo in the clarinet, fermata, and following silence enhance the sense of abeyance and hence of resolution in the tonally consequent events to come.

2. The determination in analysis that nearly all components of the structure shown as ex. 4.28 have inherent exposure in cadential function, duration, repetition, or some combination of these, suggests that they require as a rule no deliberate enforcement. However, a justifiable intervention might be for the pianist to cling slightly to the final chord of the cadence in measure 3, in the interest of its having effect through the subsequent, interrupting silence.[18]

3. The interpreter concerned with such a portrayal of structure as that of ex. 4.29 might for example attribute particular importance to the upper voice of measures 4–5 (and the intervallically equivalent, chromatically associated fourth-chord at the middle of measure 12, anticipating its appearance in measures 16–18).

All the cited elements are there as resources among choices of interpretation. Some are likely by virtue of their inherent exposure to be inescapable in any clear realization of the music; others may bear attention in interventions that do not distort or obscure other imperatives, even at the cost of elements deemed less vital.

These possibilities point up again the hazards of an overburdened consciousness in performance, and of the error of projecting contradictory images. But they point up no less the urgency of analysis that takes interpretation—as a complex of chosen elements—beyond the uninformed impulse.

A Thematic Essence in Op. 5, No. 3

The sweep of Berg's structure can be examined in yet another dimension: one that is derived at midlevel in a digest of primary content, and which paraphrases in summaries of thematic and expressive materials of each section the essential message of the piece. This difficult and problematic procedure—an individual, interpretive reading and hearing—is in a way re-creative, even though all its

Ex. 4.30a

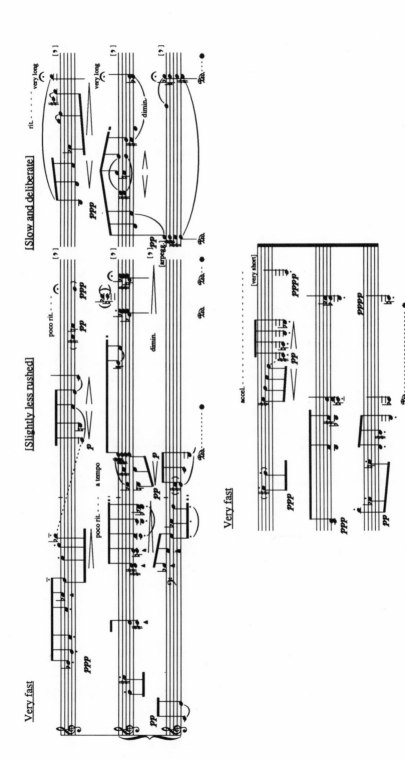

137

working secrets are taken directly from Berg; it is one musician's generalized reflection of the true piece, an attempt to grasp its essential entities of theme and pitch structure, and identify by exclusion certain elements that elaborate the midlevel essence.

Every good analysis is a rendition, a learned investigation ultimately more or less subjective, and the present representation is especially so. More than many it requires getting inside the composition experienced as a thematic and expressive statement.[19]

The illustration incorporates material directions of the piece's essential content interpreted without formulaic preconceptions. Substantive melodic and harmonic interrelations of sections can be heard, as can the function of section (C) as an area of fusion of the two instrumental parts. As a synopsis of principal, distinctive contours and gestures, the reconstruction encapsulates midlevel underlying motions and distinctive elaborating detail, the latter excluding direct retracings of the piece's surface in measures 9–12.

Example 4.30a is thus a type of distillation that can be effected for many pieces, analogous to a loose, broad-brush graphic sketch. As it is read or played, the piece's most basic tempo relations and dynamic inflections are generalized, and the sketch can elucidate a gist of distinctive content, which suggests to the performer the component units and entities of directed process essential to the composition.

Perhaps ex. 4.30a can also be read as a figurative speeding up of the piece's substance, or as an improvisation (again, analogous to the strokes of a broad brush). An exercise of this kind affords the performer a perspective—a living image of fundamental information to be articulated—and represents a mode of encompassing conceptualization by which to resist any tendency of over-absorption in ultimate details of the surface.

A compelling unity in the clarinet part is visible in ex. 4.30b, where the pitch-class representation of a particular continuity is seen to embrace a large part of the composition. Interestingly, the residual trichord {A-flat,C-sharp,F-sharp} occurs prominently in measures 9–12 and 15–18 (piano and clarinet in both instances), and in the upper voice of the chords leading into section (B)—a further indication of importance in this voice.

Ex. 4.30b

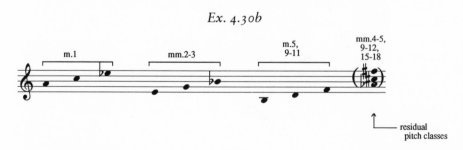

residual
pitch classes

Some interpretive guidelines and questions may be said to follow from the analysis that is the basis for ex. 4.30:

1. Is it possible for the clarinetist to convey a connection between the b-flat$_2$ of measure 3 and the consequent a of measure 5? This is a difficult but critical issue: such a connection can often come across, and even the physical factor of holding the instrument ready through the intervening time can fortify the impression of the events of measure 5 as an outcome of the preceding phrase. (Again, imagine contrary distractions impairing the connection.)

2. The piano's descending diminished triad (bearing accents in measures 2–3, left hand), one element in the prefatory environment of general tonal dispersal, is vividly apparent in ex. 4.30*a* as mirroring the clarinet's important, concurrent ascent through the same triad.

3. The question of interpretive choice in the anacrustic chords initiating section (B) arises again, as do those of essential actions of motivic statement, tentative tonal arrival, and subsequent modulation in measures 5–8—these are vital elements that appear magnified and thus illuminated in the synopsis.

4. The conception of measures 9–13 as a focal area to and from which the broad structure is directed induces an appropriately expansive approach to Berg's *langsame Viertel:* relaxed, yet active in dissonance and textural interchange, treated with a sense of consequence, core, and turning point, slow and deliberate.

5. The thematic synopsis substantiates the role of measures 15–18 as an abrupt, swift resolution. Except for a suggestive implication in measure 8, the exposed C-sharp has its first occurrence in the essential overall line of action; this is another criterion of its significance in the final section and further justification for Berg's crescendo approach to the c-sharp$_2$ of measure 16.

6. The tight interdependence of clarinet and piano in the final section is persuasively exposed in the condensation: it is a different manner of interdependence from that of measures 9–12, where the two instruments are harmonically allied. In section (D) the piece's fulfillment is a matter of reconciliation between the piano's provisional C and the immediate fluctuation toward D, in which the clarinet leads. In the resolution, the most urgent phase of interdependence unites the piano's "V" (measures 16–18, the final two chords in ex. 4.30*a*) and the clarinet's "I" (measures 17–18, summarized in the illustration and in ex. 4.16*a*). An implication of this is that the piano's final attack is assuredly not an end, but yields rather to the clarinet's conclusive consequent. Again it is instructive to imagine what physical behavior this observation implies: the pianist must maintain pos-

ture and attitude not only through the clarinet's decisive arrival, but through its reverberations in the ensuing silence.

7. Example 4.30*b* suggests that the clarinet's two diminished triads of measures 1–3 are precedents to the sequential entry of the third of these— B̲,D̲,F̲—tentatively at measure 5, decisively at measures 9–13. Although the triads are compositionally explicit and emphatic, care must be taken to preserve their integrity in the initial whirl of complex activity, and the third triad, ultimately prevalent and far-reaching, must be regarded (on suggested tonal bases) as an aim of progression and a central element. (In this view, and in light of its inferred reference to C̲, the clarinet's b of measure 5 bears attention: it is in intensity at least the equal of the preceding note.)

This list of performance issues and necessities could go on. In any event the performers' consideration of these and like matters is enhanced by a comprehensive hearing of the piece's essential streams of formal and tonal articulation in a broad, interpreted grasp of its thematic essence.

The Particular Problems of the Fermatas

The question of the fermata is: How long, and in what rhythmic relation to local and broad contexts? Of course no answer respecting a given case is likely to apply to all circumstances of performance. Berg's punctuations at measures 8 and 13 have many functions with respect to structure: they articulate form in an encompassing rhythmic process, they are points of active dissonance, they have crucial harmonic implications of tonal direction, and they hold key positions within certain broad continuities. Insights into the structural conditions of these decisive cadences should suggest approaches to the interpretation of the fermatas.

Although the fermata enhances the effect of formal punctuation and of tonal as well as intrinsic dissonance, the elongated cadential event is always susceptible to exaggeration, and the piece's progress to impairment. Because a fermata is a constituent of rhythmic structure with a direct bearing on tempo, some sense of its interpretation can be derived from its relation to tempo: as a rule, the faster the tempo, the shorter the fermata. The fermata of measure 8 is less pronounced than that of measure 13 not only on this ground, but because the latter culminates the piece's area of central convergence and prepares the rapid close. This is borne out by Berg's notated clues (*ziemlich lange, sehr lang*).

Most crucial is the place of each fermata in the overall structural configuration of deceleration through measure 13. Measure 8 is an interim but critical stage preparing the slowest tempo, and measure 13 culminates the process. The interpreter who is aware of comprehensive rhythmic process will understand one imperative contextual significance of the fermatas.

A necessary factor in the approach to the fermata of measure 8, the fermata itself, and the subsequent punctuation is a processive, syntactic relation between sections (B) and (C). The fermata long enough to convey a sense of interim arrival, yet precluding exaggerated interruption, is best conceived as a moderately pronounced extension of the poco ritardando tendency initiated at measure 7, followed by a decisive break, the clarinet's release coinciding exactly with that of the piano pedal. The realization shown in ex. 4.31 reflects this value, and affords a fitting sense of indefinite suspension as well as the necessary absence of regularity integral to the idea of fermata. In this interpretation, the measured (yet in the ritardando context unmeasured) cadential event falls naturally into place as a step in the underlying scheme of gradual slowing, which continues into section (C). The silence may be construed as equal to the quarter-note pulse of the forthcoming section (about 42), and is thus itself a factor in the transitional rhythmic process.

Ex. 4.31

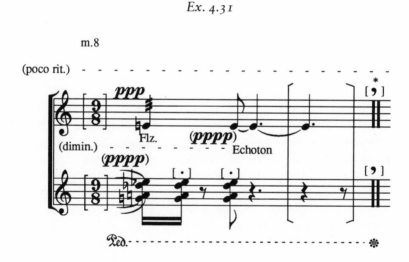

m.8

*A punctuation roughly equivalent to the quarter note of section (C).

The technique of mentally repeating through the fermata of measure 13 the rhythms of measure 12 in a continuing ritardando inclination yields a duration appropriate to the requirements of the fermata's position in process, and affords suitable emphasis conforming to the place of measure 13 as a fundamental point to and through which identified actions are directed. The realization proposed in ex. 4.32 reflects these considerations, advancing also the notion of an added, slowed pulse within the fermata's duration. The fermata and punctuation thus embody the values of processive consistency, irregularity of duration, and suspended dissonance (of meter as well as tonal implication), without the exaggeration by which continuity would be violated.

Ex. 4.32

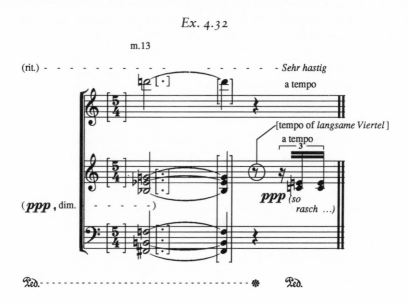

The requisite attributes of asymmetry and unpredictability are served by maintaining the slow, and slowing, tempo through the eighth-rest following the fermata, as much as by giving the fermata a duration not in accord with established mensural units. The longer eighth-rest seems indispensable to the sense of dissonant hiatus, as is confirmed by the unsettling effect of too short a break following the fermata; this would be a clear error of interpretation also hindering exposure of the forthcoming entry of {C,E}.

Of course no two performances would be identical, lest an established regularity dull the performer's own sense of hiatus and impair the fermata's meaning. Such constructions as are shown in exx. 4.31 and 4.32 are matters of preliminary conceptualization and rehearsal that can condition a suitable rendering having ultimately an ostensibly unmeasured effect. In both cases, the feeling of a continued ritardando tendency through the fermata contributes to the effect.

The quality of the experienced fermata must be one of ideal balance in relation to context, especially rhythmic context, and at the same time of suspended activity through a considered temporal interval that is set with the appearance of spontaneity and never mechanically. Ideally, the requisite intensification during the interval is vitiated neither in regularity, nor in a break so long as to effect disruption or contradict character (in the Berg, one of restless vigor held tensely in abeyance at measures 9–13). The interval of indefinite hiatus is informed and conditioned by careful prefatory thought about meaning and place, yet conveying the impression of performance caught in an uncertain moment of suspended time.

Chapter Five

THIRD CASE
Debussy, "C'est l'extase langoureuse" (Verlaine), No. 1 of Ariettes oubliées

The Song's Tonal Idiom

Claude Debussy's setting of Verlaine's "C'est l'extase langoureuse" is a resplendent specimen: the affecting, cogent musical portrayal of a poem rich in directed structural elements and poignant images. The song is representative of a sumptuous tonal idiom which, while profoundly influential in much twentieth-century music, is something of a fragile, transitory byway in any broad historical perspective.

These preliminary pages offer some general thoughts concerning that idiom, and regarding certain basic techniques of harmonic and contrapuntal usage which are fundamental to Debussy's and related styles. Debussy's musical language is clearly one of tonal functionality, often appreciable in a forthright, basic structure underlying a richly elaborative surface of neighboring and passing sonorities. In Debussy, such elaborating elements are tightly woven into the structure in compact contrapuntal lines ultimately traceable to the fundamental, functioning harmonic basis, often consisting of V and I.

Distinctions and relations among linear and tonal elements

Harmonic and melodic elements in tonal contexts are usefully considered with regard to two principal classifications of significance and capacity, linear and tonal. Considering a tonal structure as a leveled system (from a fundamental, often prototypical and formulaic content, through midlevels of increasingly detailed elaborations, to the composed surface), the tonal function of a harmony is its position and role in such a structure, ultimately in relation to I, or tentatively in relation to a secondary harmony. Its proximity to I, or to a secondary, interim goal can be gauged according to such an array as the descending cycle of fifths, or by another, given standard. Tonal functionality (of the surface, of a midlevel, or deeply fundamental) is implicit or explicit in such terms as V, secondary dominant, pre-dominant, tonal resolution, deceptive resolution, tonic substitute, fifth-related, and the like.

Linear function is, on the other hand, assessed according to the position and role of an event in a specific continuity of line, heard in the context of a particular level—that is, in a relation between directly contiguous components, or underlying and overreaching the surface in some degree. Linear function is implied in such terms as neighboring, auxiliary, elaborative, passing, and paren-thetical, which are commonly represented in graphic analyses by the symbols "N" (neighbor) and "P" (passing), by slurs marking near or distant linear associations of subsidiary elements to more basic ones, and by comparable devices.

All harmonies have linear function, even those of some ultimate background, in their direct or overreaching implication in constituted lines. Most harmonies have at some level of implication both linear and tonal function; the latter is of variable significance, as is evident for example in comparison of the passing V six-four (between I and its first inversion) with the allied cadential V, or the first inversion of IV linking two Vs with the IV introducing V in the authentic cadence.

It is a factor of style that in late idioms tonal (or roman-numeral) func-tionality is at times obscured or relatively eclipsed, so that particular harmonic events, in this sense detached from the tonal basis, have essentially or even purely linear significance.[1] Such components in the structure are often charac-terized as nonfunctional (that is, tonally nonfunctional), a not quite apt term that however connotes an absence or remoteness of tonal identity and implica-tion, with linear function primary, often in rich space-filling and time-filling processes.[2] Whatever the extent of severance from a tonal basis, linear func-tionality implies tightly interwoven connections of voice leading and counter-point.

Contexts that embody elements of primarily or purely linear function reflect a spectrum of possibilities: tonal functionality can be understood as tenuous, remote, negligible, or utterly inapplicable. In these conditions the underlying tonal basis, even at midlevels, is often of compensatingly direct or even primi-tively simple harmonic content.

Tentative examples

The excerpt sketched as ex. 5.1 occurs early in Debussy's song (which is in E), and has evident tonal implication: an auxiliary passing chord links V and I, its "dominant" structure analogous to the dominant ninth that initiates the succession and indeed opens the song. (A quick look at exx. 5.4*a*, *b* reveals that the V prevails through measures 1–8, the I through measures 9–14.)

Ex. 5.1

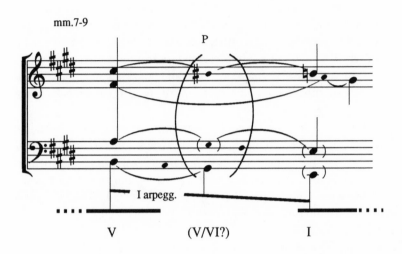

In this case, the auxiliary chord participates in a bass arpeggiation of the tonic triad, as illustrated; its sense of tonal detachment is mitigated by voice leading and by the functional implication of G-sharp as a dominant of E:VI, the latter critical especially in the second stanza, and a common associate of the tonic in the terms of traditional tonality. Still, the contextual role of the G-sharp chord is significantly one of linear connection and elaboration.

Example 5.2 exhibits the characteristic derivation of an auxiliary chord by voice-leading adjacencies yielding a structure, the prevalent major ninth sonority,[3] of negligible tonal relevance; it recurs at measure 14. Here the chromatic neighboring chord elaborates E:I, this time as a vehicle of linear progression toward V.

Ex. 5.2

mm.11-14

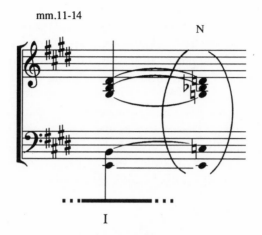

An important distinction may be drawn between the subordinate harmonies of exx. 5.1 and 5.2—the latter represents a more severe tonal severance, and is thus more particularly and singularly of linear significance. In other words, as a dominant the first chord suggests C-sharp, diatonic to E major and an appreciable tonal factor in the song's subsequent developments;[4] the second refers to F, of which neither condition applies.

As a further preliminary illustration, ex. 5.3 shows an excerpt from the song's tonally digressive interior, demonstrating as did ex. 5.1 the extent to which the organization of the bass line may condition details of harmonic content.

Ex. 5.3

mm.26-37

pitch-class
succession:

In ex. 5.3, which is a pitch-class summary, the stemmed D is depicted as an interim goal of progression, occurring tentatively at measures 29 and 31, then decisively at measure 34. Its larger role is clear as a passing element in the motion toward B (and E:V), and later analysis will reveal the D, in its most overreaching implication, as a registrally conforming lower neighbor of initiating and concluding cadential occurrences of the tonic pitch class E.

The D̲, derived by a partly chromatic pitch-class "descent," is tonicized by its dominant (measures 28 and 30; ex. 5.19), and it alternates at the cadence with D:IV, in a plagal elaboration (measures 32–34). It thus has significant tonal function as a cadentially exposed secondary tonic of quasi-modal relation to the primary E̲, in addition to its vital linear functions. Beyond its prominence as the goal of harmonic development in the second stanza, the local and farther-reaching linear functions are distinct, inescapable factors in the structural meaning of the D̲.

The above examples afford tentative views of tonal and linear functions of harmonic components. They document degrees of potential predominance of one functional capacity or the other, and the tendencies of chords to assume essentially linear significance in idiomatic contexts of detachment from explicit roman-numeral identities and relevant tonal foundations.

The Poem

The text of Verlaine's poem is of course of crucial importance to interpretation, and its form and organization have an intimate relation to the form and structure of Debussy's setting. Interestingly, not all the poems in Verlaine's set "Ariettes oubliées" are included in Debussy's collection, and not all the songs in the collection are based on poems from the set.[5] The poem is given below, together with a translation in which elements of rhyme and meter are sacrificed in the interest of literal rendering.[6] With "C'est l'extase langoureuse," Verlaine included two evocative lines from Charles-Simon Favart (1710–92): *Le vent dans la plaine/Suspend son haleine* (The wind on the plain/Holds its breath).

> C'est l' extase langoureuse,
> C'est la fatigue amoureuse,
> C'est tous les frissons des bois
> Parmi l'étreinte des brises,
> C'est, vers les ramures grises,
> Le chœur des petites voix.
>
> O le frêle et frais murmure!
> Cela gazouille et susurre,
> Cela ressemble au cri doux
> Que l'herbe agitée expire . . .
> Tu dirais, sous l'eau qui vire,
> Le roulis sourd des cailloux.

Cette âme qui se lamente
En cette plainte‾dormante,
C'est la nôtre, n'est-ce pas?
La mienne, dis, et la tienne,
Dont s'exhale l'humble antienne
Par ce tiède soir, tout bas?

It is the ecstasy of languor,
It is the exhaustion of love,
It is all the tremors of the forest
In the embrace of breezes,
It is, in the grey boughs,
The chorus of tiny voices.

O the delicate and fresh murmur!
It twitters and rustles,
It resembles the tender cry
Which the excited grasses breathe ...
One might say, the muffled rolling of pebbles,
Beneath the turning water.

This spirit that laments
In this sleepy plaint,
It is ours, is it not?
Mine, and *thine*,
Whence flows the humble anthem
So softly through this warm evening?

Elements of Poetic Structure

Meter

Verlaine's meter is of two or at times three stresses to a line.[7] The most patent regularity—rhythmic, not metric, in that it is independent of accentual patterns—is in the number of syllables per line: it is consistently seven as the poem is spoken, and in the musical setting follows the pattern 8-8-7, 8-8-7 for each six-line stanza (sestet), a regularity observed faithfully by Debussy.[8]

This rhythmic element can be seen to correspond exactly to the rhyme scheme. A vital implication of the purely syllabic rhythm (and of the rhyme scheme) is a tendency to divide the stanzas into halves (tercets), the shorter, seven-syllable line functioning cadentially at the close of each stanza. (The tercets are not self-contained in sense and syntax, and in that respect, except possibly in stanza 3, are open structures.)

In considering musical realization, foreground patterns of accent can be read variously, depending on whether the line's first metric unit is iambic (*Ce-la*), anapestic (*Tu di-rais*), or longer (*C'est la fa-tigue*). Except for the fifth line, where a comma follows the first word, there are no units beginning with an accent, although a trochaic tetrameter is problematically suggested in Debussy's treatment of certain lines (3 and 6 of the first stanza, 4 of the second).

A structure of two primary accents to the line (*C'est l'ex-tase lan-gou-reuse*) underlies a more superficial organization involving subordinate accents (*C'est l'ex-tase lan-gou-reuse*). And although the former, deeper structure is considerably uniform throughout the poem, the latter articulates a fluctuating meter susceptible to varying inflections according to poetic sense and imagery. Indeed, degrees of musical accent (durational, registral, and other) are shaped in Debussy's setting with regard to an irresistibly scaled progression of poetic content, and to the subtle but deliberate highlighting of focal words and images in an expressive contour.

Rhyme

The regularity of linear rhythmic recurrence in the musical setting (8-8-7, and so on) corresponds to that of rhyme (A-A-B, C-C-B) in the factor of departure at each third line and in the implication of symmetrical divisions of the stanzas into syntactically incomplete units of three lines. Debussy's setting makes a point of the poetic rhyme only to a limited extent—notably in that of the first two lines and phrases (*-reuse*), and deliberately moves through mid-stanza junctures as sense requires. Yet the elements of syllabic rhythm and rhyme are manifest properties of rhythmic unity, and the former especially are appreciable in the song as in the poem.

Threes

The poetic structure is marked by a number of ternate, or tripling, elements: three stanzas (and thus three primary formal segments in the music); three rhyming pairs in each; the division of each sestet into two tercets marked by rhyme and syllabic rhythm; the occasional three stresses per line (a trimeter); and the use of three principal images (described below). Debussy's 3/8 meter, usually reinforced by the actual musical accent, appears relevant, as is the poem's susceptibility to this musical organization. The song's pervasive relation of threes constitutes one of many vital aspects of unity.

A poetic contour delineated by three imaginal phases

No doubt the most critical element of poetic structure, and a vital determinant in Debussy's setting, is a progressive line of development with respect to three focal images and referential states, one for each stanza. These focal images reflect progressive intensification toward the inward, personal references of stanza 3. In very general terms, the progression is from a basic tableau of scene and feeling, through portentous connotations of variously interpreted sounds to which the speaker refers, to ultimate allusion to the lovers' selves—a reference in a way recalling the beginning of the poem and the song, but marking a climactic phase of content and imagery far beyond the relatively cool, lethargic state reflected in the opening lines. More specifically, stanza 1 evokes appearances and ambience: the subjects' dreamy awakening; the rapture, languor, and exhaustion of the act of love and its aftermath; the scene of trembling trees and the chirping of voices by which the final line turns toward the next sestet. Stanza 2 develops the sound-image (*des petites voix*): a murmur, a twitter, a cry, and finally a calmed reference to the muted roll of pebbles under water. The poignant reference to a "cry, as breathed by agitated grasses" is central, the evocation of (*le*) *cri* having unmistakably subjective implication. In the third stanza, the foregoing images climactically and inevitably become personal ones: our voices, our dreamy lament, our humble anthem. The final line looks back to the initial scene of tepid evening and faded twilight, out of which the structure has gradually emerged and developed: from subjective but indefinite, through objective and metaphoric, to subjective and personal.

Another way to regard the poetic structure and its musical setting is to trace its emergence through nine specific allusions by which the central sound-image is variously interpreted, for once scene and sentiment have been evoked, it is in these allusions that the line of expressive contour, and of progressive intensification, is most clearly felt:

> le chœur des petites voix
> le frêle et frais murmure
> gazouille, susurre
> (le) cri doux que l'herbe . . . expire
> le roulis sourd des cailloux
> cette âme qui se lamente
> cette plainte dormante
> la nôtre(!)
> l'humble antienne

Debussy's music constitutes a wondrously elegant, concordant rendering of Verlaine's text and a commentary on it. The medium of expression, far from

having melodramatic fervor, is one of fluidity, multifold and multilayered implication, tremulous but restrained feeling, and suggestive understatement.

The Music's Formal Divisions and Delineators

Three main divisions in the song correspond to the poem's three stanzas.
Principal, delineating cadences occur at measures 18 and 34 (exx. 5.4b, 5.4d). A
subsidiary cadence splitting stanza 1 occurs at measure 9 (ex. 5.4a), setting off
the first two, preliminary phrases, which are in both text and music introductory, from the shifted directions of musical and poetic content at measure 11.
The first two phrases (a period) are introductory in that they establish the
structure's tonal basis (in E:V-I); eight of the ten bars project an inert dominant
ninth, in an attitude of quiescence appropriate to the poetic awakening, and
preceding reference to the modestly active surrounding scene. This material,
which restricts tonal content, is of course also in tempo (the structure's slowest
except for the last few bars) an introductory basis for developments to come.
(See exx. 5.4a, b; some performance indications are added in square brackets.)

Ex. 5.4a
Debussy, C'est l'extase langoureuse,
No. 1 of "Ariettes oubliées"

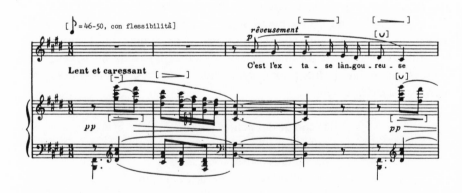

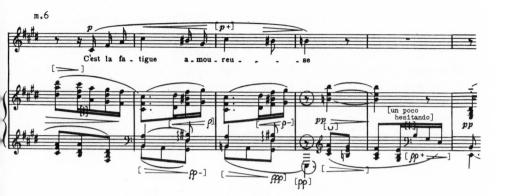

From *Ariettes oubliées, copyright 1913, Société des Editions Jobert. Used by permission of the publisher. Sole representative, U.S.A., Theodore Presser Company.*

Ex. *5.4b*

From *Ariettes oubliées, copyright 1913, Société des Editions Jobert. Used by permission of the publisher. Sole representative U.S.A., Theodore Presser Company.*

Stanza 2 is also divided (exx. 5.4c, d), not cadentially but in a marked change of attitude and musical content from measure 28; that content includes relatively stable reference to the secondary tonic D̲. There is also an unindicated change of tempo here. The text setting following measures 11 and 29 is relatively declamatory (quasi-recitando) in contrast with more lyric approaches preceding each of these points of subsidiary interior division.

Ex. 5.4c

From Ariettes oubliées, *copyright 1913, Société des Editions Jobert. Used by permission of the publisher. Sole representative, U.S.A., Theodore Presser Company.*

Ex. 5.4d

From Ariettes oubliées, *copyright 1913, Société des Editions Jobert. Used by permission of the publisher. Sole representative, U.S.A., Theodore Presser Company.*

By contrast, stanza 3 (exx. 5.4e, f, g) is a pervasive continuity, and in this sense a dynamic and "agogic" consequent. Viewed in this way, the form as a whole is a progression comprising increasingly expansive continuities.

Ex. 5.4e

From Ariettes oubliées, *copyright 1913, Société des Editions Jobert. Used by permission of the publisher. Sole representative, U.S.A., Theodore Presser Company.*

*Compare the rhythmic notation in m. 45, where an editorial clarification is introduced in brackets (ex. 5.4f).

Ex. 5.4f

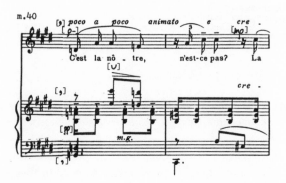

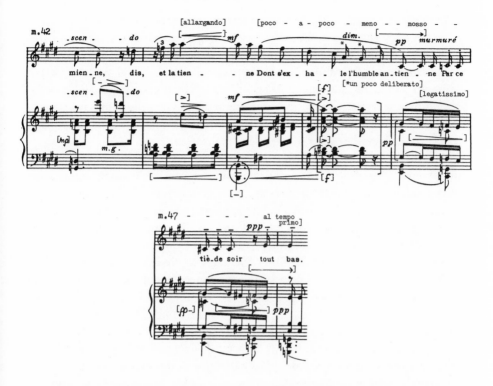

From Ariettes oubliées, *copyright 1913, Société des Editions Jobert. Used by permission of the publisher. Sole representative, U.S.A., Theodore Presser Company.*

Ex. 5.4g

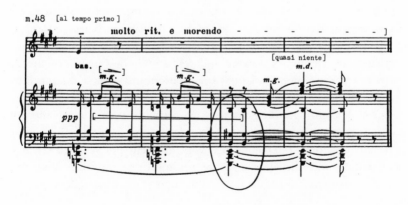

From Ariettes oubliées, *copyright 1913, Société des Editions Jobert. Used by permission of the publisher. Sole representative, U.S.A., Theodore Presser Company.*

Each stanza begins with the voice relatively unencumbered by directly competing motivic material in the piano: see the song's opening, and measures 20–21 and 37. Related to this and further delineating the form are the voice's exits at measures 9, 18, 28, and 34, marking major divisions as well as those within stanzas 1 and 2, and stanza endings marked both by the voice melody's descent into its lowest register and by the most literal piano-voice doublings (unisons at measures 17–18 and 46–48, octaves at measures 32–33). These are important aspects of cadential process in the poetic realization.

Although tripartite, the form is obviously not recapitulative in the conventional sense, even though some critical distinctions (notably tonal) that characterize stanza 2 are clear from analysis, as are certain parallels between 1 and 3. There is a significant durational correspondence among the stanzas: measures 1–18, (18–)19–34(–35), and (35–)36–52. To be sure, a number of tempo changes affect real-time durational relations. For example, the final ritardando cadence extends the agogic relation of stanza 3 to the two antecedents. A near balance of division that is comparable pertains to interior punctuations in stanzas 1 and 2: measures 1–9, then 9–18 (V-I, I-V); and measures (18–)19–27, then 28–34(–35). Indeed tempo has in itself a compelling progressive effect overall, and the three stanzas embody three principal advances in tempo: un poco mosso, animato, and, it will be argued, un poco più animato. The increased compact unity of stanza 3 is an attribute in this general perspective, as are the changes midway through stanzas 1 and 2 at measures 11 and 28, especially in tempo: più mosso in the first case, meno in the second, the latter in reaction to the preceding animato.[9] Stanzas 1 and 2 thus manifest a vital tempo relation: slow—faster, faster—slower.

These broad considerations of tempo suggest one general perspective by which the interpretive consciousness is informed. Another can be understood with respect to the critical sense of cadence and resumption pertaining to formal divisions. Interpretive factors germane to these decisive junctures are tentatively suggested in exx. 5.4b, c and 5.4d, e. Other elements of formal delineation in performance are Debussy's slowing and deliberately declamatory enunciation at measure 17, a point of cadential preparation and of first reference to the central poetic image; the restored tempo at measure 18 (that of measure 11, not of measure 1); slightly marked dynamic intensity (yet piano) at the entry of the motive in measure 18, and the motive's presentation as modestly more active than its introductory statements in a very different poetic context; and the gentle but deliberate thrust at measure 20, appropriate both to text (frêle et frais) and to the launching of the musical structure's main tonal developments in stanza 2.

Examples 5.4d, e display the other major formal division, that separating stanzas 2 and 3. Notable here is a slight slowing in measure 33, fitting to both text and cadential arrival (on <u>D</u>, significantly in a very low register). The thrust at measure 34, an aspect of which is urgent, pressing articulation in the piano's right-hand part within the pedal's cohesive effect, prepares renewed development while obviating exaggerated punctuation. And the imperative sense of poetic and musical directions to come is served by underscoring the propulsive dissonance at measure 36 by the preceding diminuendo, by Debussy's sforzato attack at measure 36 (circumscribed within a generally restricted scale of dynamic possibilities), by mild articulative stress on the motivic entry at the second beat of measure 36, and by the indicated, cautious further advance in tempo at the same bar.

Although the formal design of Debussy's song is not recapitulative in the usual sense, some interrelations of melodic and harmonic content are worth noting. For one thing, it is apparent even at this preliminary stage of analysis that stanza 2 is the scene of marked tonal fluctuation, whereas stanzas 1 and 3 substantially correspond in tonal content, broadly E:V-I-V in the first, and V-I in the third. The outer segments thus project the most fundamental, overreaching succession dominant to tonic, manifesting a compelling frame for the singular tonal events of the second stanza.

A few especially pertinent, interlinking motivic factors should also be noted in connection with broad formal design. Thus, the seminal thematic idea that opens stanzas 1 and 2 (the piano, measures 1–4 and 18–20), and that predominates in both voice and piano through the introductory bars, 1–11, is expansively recapitulated in stanza 3 (voice, measures 43–46). And exx. 5.5 and 5.6 demonstrate a relation of somewhat generalized pitch contour between major segments of the voice melody of stanzas 1 and 3 (ex. 5.5), and stanzas 2 and 3 (ex. 5.6), reflecting in this sense the role of the third stanza in summarizing and commenting on prior thematic substance.

Ex. 5.5

voice,
mm.11-17

mm.37-40

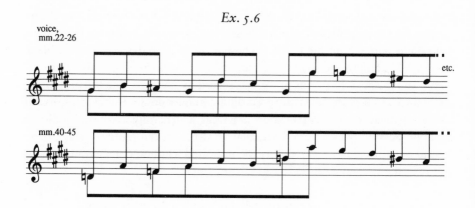

Ex. 5.6

voice,
mm.22-26

etc.

mm.40-45

Motivic Components: Generative and Derivative

As in the studies of Brahms and Berg, I am in a general sense regarding as
motivic any minimal, distinctive component that functions in unifying recurrence, commonly in varying appearances, and is vital to a piece's particular
identity. In exploring Debussy's song, it may be helpful to summarize some of
the very general senses in which motives and motivic factors may be regarded:

1. As a characteristic grouping of notes constituting a recurring term—a
complex of pitch classes demonstrably associated and its transpositions, in
other words a distinctive array of intervals presented as a simultaneity or in
linear succession (for example, the citations from the Berg piece, ex. 4.2).
Excluded may be commonplaces that are so ubiquitous as to lack distinctiveness in a given idiom. Motivic status is often ascribed to a melodic-
intervallic particularity of which a special point is made in a given context,
however, such as the descending third cited in Beethoven's Fourth Symphony (ex. 2.5).

2. As an identifiable melodic contour marked by directional changes and
distributions of leaps and steps, or of larger and smaller intervals (exx. 5.5
and 5.6, or the appoggiatura configuration in the pieces by Brahms and
Berg).

3. As a motive in the most usual sense: a specific, distinctive melodic-
rhythmic entity, a basis for variance in recurrence, and for development
(the piano's opening descending gesture in the Debussy—ex. 5.10).

A motivic grouping recurring usually as a distinctive chord

What is in traditional styles termed the "dominant" major ninth chord—a
favored, distinctive sonority in impressionism—is in the ears during much of

the Debussy, variously transposed, functioning both in elaborations of the surface and in articulation of the song's tonal basis.

The chord (as a simultaneity) is manifest in varying positions and distributions, and ordered melodically as well; we can view it in one sense as a grouping of pitch classes, given in ex. 5.7a in the interval sequence 2-2-2-3(-3). When we consider its potential intervallic content (which includes all the intervals between any one of the five components and any other), we find interval 2 to be the most prevalent, and the semitone to be uniquely inapplicable. Example 5.7b points to an occurrence among contiguous notes of the voice melody over the second part of stanza 1.

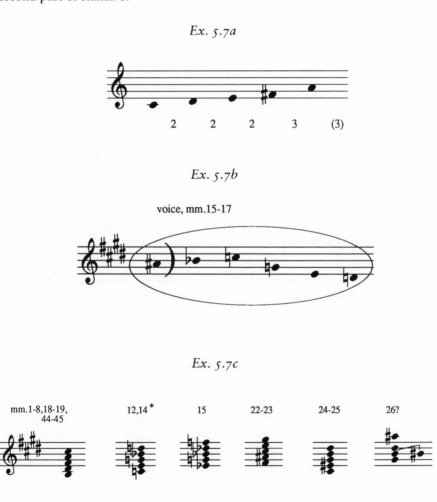

Ex. 5.7a

Ex. 5.7b

voice, mm.15-17

Ex. 5.7c

mm.1-8,18-19, 44-45   12,14*   15   22-23   24-25   26?

*Compare ex. 5.7b.

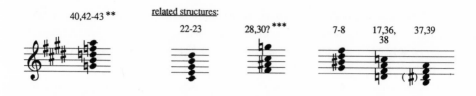

***The G of m. 42 pertains also to m. 43.*
****Or: a diminished seventh chord on A̱-sharp, with the F̱-sharp—as an anticipation, then suspension, of the focal D-triad—"representing" E̱.*

Example 5.7c documents the collection's prevalence as a chord, listing as well certain closely related sonorities that in an important sense extend its influence.

The above potently illustrates the capacity of such an intervallic complex to dominate the harmonic materials of a structure, and thus as one of many elements to lend it a pervasive unity. For almost half the song's real-time duration the sonority is heard, its effect enhanced by closely related chords (ex. 5.7c). As the structure of a number of auxiliary chords as well as the primary E:V, the major ninth thus affords a predominant harmonic flavor, and in its distinctiveness is arguably motivic especially in the flanking outer stanzas.

One aspect of expository content in the introductory period (measures 1–10) is its virtually uninterrupted dominant ninth, the protraction of which as a functional tonal basis occurs in the song's slowest tempo, performed *rêveuse-ment,* almost hesitantly and listlessly (*langoureusement*). The almost constant major ninth chord of the opening segment, marked by a sense of drift in its postponement of resolution (and in its relatively loose tonal implication compared with the minor ninth and related diminished seventh), overreaches to the briefer, yet intensely climactic, occurrence at measures 44–45. But for these critical framing occurrences, the prevalence of the sonority may suggest compensatory attention in performance to contrasting harmonic structures, especially in stanza 2, and its understatement in interior occurrences: in an essentially surface role (for example, at measure 15) at times dimmed by inversion (measures 12 and 14), and in less explicit manifestations (measure 26) or rhythmically subordinated ones (measures 22–23). Although they are appreciable factors in unity, the subsidiary occurrences in the structure's interior are to an extent caught in the sweep of developing tempo and tonal fluctuation, and often have a clearly auxiliary harmonic role.

Other, less prevalent motivic chords

There are other, less prevalent chordal sonorities that have quasi-motivic status. These are the major seventh chord (measures 11 and 13 as E:I, and intermittently in measures 29–33 as D:IV and I, before this locally referential harmony becomes a triad at measures 34–35), as well as what we may refer to as the major triad as six-five, here more precisely I as six-five (at such formal junctures as measures 20 and 46–47). These structures, both employed significantly as active surrogate tonics, are to be interpreted as ongoing in their dissonant implication: they are factors of propulsion at measures 11 and 13, and of merely tentative arrival at measure 20 (the prominent C-sharp of which is isolated a measure later as the vehicle of tonal departure) and measure 46 (where the voice doubles the compromising C-sharp, and where the characteristic six-five structure is maintained into the passing chords of measures 48–49).

Example 5.8 suggests that in their clear tonal relation to E:V and its major ninth these sonorities can be construed in terms of the suspension of dissonant factors: see measures 9–11, 18–20, 28–29, 31–32, 45–46, and 47–48, and ex. 5.40.

Ex. 5.8

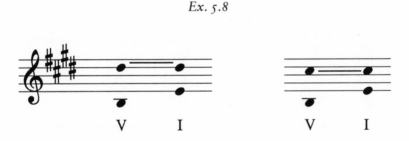

A fundamental motivating thematic idea as object of reference*

The motive stated by the piano in measures 1–4 is the structure's fullest and most explicit such entity, and a vital germinating idea. Apart from its particular melodic-rhythmic formulation, it can be considered in generalization as a basic, motivating gestalt pervading the entire composition. One can see encapsulated in it something of the structure's essential substance—contour, dissonance and metric character of appoggiatura, central component qualities of harmonic sonority, and especially primary tonal content. The abstraction given as ex. 5.9, which initially spans measures 1–10, thus represents in significant ways the structure at large.

- Ex. 5.9

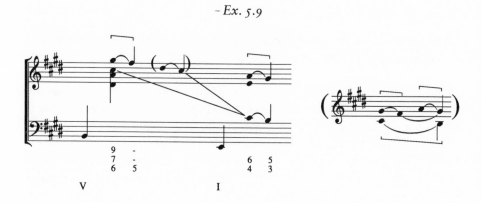

It is possible to feel in the abstraction at least two essential necessities of interpretation applicable to it as motive (measures 1–4, etc.), and to larger areas conditioned by its content (measures 1–10 and 44–52). These are expansive action followed by a recession in dynamic intensity, and a characteristic, surface molding of the two-note appoggiatura factor itself, with slightly pressing articulation of the dissonance followed by a modestly scaled diminuendo into the consequent note (Debussy's *caressant*). The latter is an interpretive gesture [_____] that is recurrently pertinent, though varied in degree according to changing intensities of context.

The primary, initiating, generative motive itself

The most explicit melodic-rhythmic manifestation of the abstracted basic idea, the statement with which the song begins (ex. 5.10), embraces the appoggiatura component as well as other subunits that have in some degree independent existence as derivatives; these are tentatively identified in ex. 5.10*a*.

Ex. 5.10a

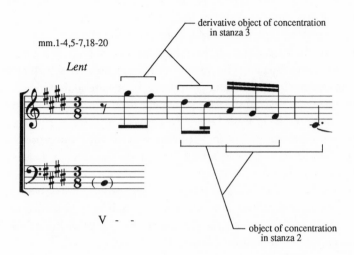

Ex. 5.10b

Ex. 5.10c

The integral motive is absent from measures 11–17 and 20–43, thus articulating a widening interval (that is, rhythm) of distribution appropriate to its saturation of the introductory ten bars. Yet its recurrences are unmistakably literal, having a strategic punctuative role in linking stanzas 1 and 2 (recalling early musical and poetic states before the digressive actions of stanza 2), and in grandly enhancing the climactic goal of stanza 3, a point to which elements are broadly and compellingly directed. Interestingly, the literal motive is confined to the piano except at this culminative statement. And except for the interim tonic at measures 9–10, it appears largely in active dominant harmony; or, more precisely, its appearances are in V (measure 1–7), in I (measures 9–10; ex. 5.10b), then twice in V-I (measures 18–20, 44–46; ex. 5.10c). This is in itself a palpably functional ordering.

When at a later stage we go further into the broad expressive contours of poem and music, and of their interrelations, we shall be in a position to consider fitting, correlative changes in variant interpretive approaches to this central motive, especially in moderate adjustments of tempo.

The two-note derivative fragment

The most basic derivative of the initiating, primary motive is the two-note descent bracketed in exx. 5.9 and 5.10a, most often a step, and usually in the guise of appoggiatura entering on the second beat (dissonance and resolution, the former metrically stronger).

The derivative motive's occurrences, following its precedent as a component of the thematic element stated at the song's outset, are largely literal, especially in its predominance in stanza 3. But there are items that can be regarded as variants (see ex. 5.11), as indeed may the final three sixteenth-notes of the larger motive, imitated by the voice in measure 4. On the other hand, one might argue that such properties as dissonance content, pitch accent, and metric placement are necessary to its identity. At what point does an entity so ubiquitous as a descending step lose distinctiveness and lack true motivic significance?

Ex. 5.11

*Compare last three sixteenth-notes, upper voice, m. 2, distinguishable in leap-step-step-leap succession heard also in m. 6, immediately preceding the bass "imitation" of m. 7. (See also exx. 5.13 and 5.14.)

In all the motive's appearances, its distinctiveness clearly is as much a product of interpretive molding (a cautiously intense, coaxing attack and a diminuendo into the resolution note, as noted in exx. 5.4a, b, e) as of the inherent properties noted above. Debussy indicates this shading even in the hypothetical variant in measures 22–23. Interesting possibilities of dynamic shading arise in measures 7–8 (ex. 5.4a), where sensitive and discreet interpretive interventions can contribute to the appropriate sense of gradual emergence implicit in the poem. For example, the singer's underlying descent from c-sharp$_2$ to b$_1$ (ex. 5.20a) can be construed and dynamically shaped as a midlevel motivic occurrence spanning the two bass descents in measures 7 and 8.

Example 5.4a incorporates the factor of diminuendo within diminuendo as the primary motive's course continues through measure 6. The three-note descending bass of measure 7 is sloped correspondingly, and again in measure 8 but slightly further, to *ppp*, thus scaled according to prevailing recession in the phrase and in the tonal structure.[10] Against this tendency, the ascending foreground progression of the piano's upper voice (measure 7) is interpreted in slight crescendo (again, less in measure 8), supporting the voice's notated crescendo (*amoureuse*) in a counteractive diversity of dynamic implication that is itself functional in the poetic atmosphere of incipient emergence.

All these examples of potential interpretive intervention demonstrate that an awareness of motivic constituents is a vital basis for judicious controls in performance, according to contributive functions in changing contexts. Interpretive stress complementing dissonance, pitch accent, and off-beat attack is especially pertinent to the motive's function in accelerative drive in stanza 3, the basis for which is laid with the motive's announcement in measure 36. Its entries here can almost be impatiently jumped as the progression, in which the propulsive motive's insistent recurrence is so notably functional, advances after measure 40. This motivic component implies expressive urgency in the markedly dissonant contexts of stanza 3.

The motivic, three-component appoggiatura contour

The appoggiatura contour (typically upward leap, downward step) is also derived from the initiating, primary motive, and related to the descending-step fragment recurrent in the song, yet distinct from it.[11]

The usual role of the second note as an accented dissonance is characteristic, but the melodic contour can itself be viewed as definitive; it is clearly associable with true appoggiatura even when the second note is consonant, as in the voice melody of measures 24–25, or when the object of the leap is metrically weak, as in the voice at measure 22. The leap may itself be regarded as of dissonant implication, whatever its harmonic context, in the expectation of consequent directional change.

The motive's capacity as a vehicle of intensification, and its characteristic dynamic shaping in performance, are represented in ex. 5.4*c*, from stanza 2. Example 5.12 portrays in a sketch of the excerpt's melodic outline certain elements of progression that carry poetic content from a relatively passive condition (*le frêle et frais murmure*) to the subsequent, tentatively climactic reference (*ressemble au cri doux*). These are intervallic expansion, registral ascent (against the piano's descent), and telling changes in the metric position of the second (normally dissonant) note, which finally takes a metric accent as the object of the widest leap, as noted in the illustration. A corresponding overall dynamic intensification is suggested in ex. 5.4*c*.

Ex. 5.12

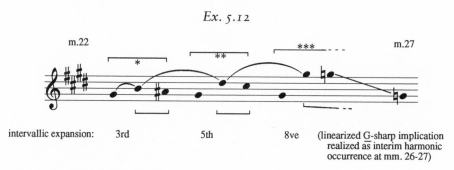

Among factors of progression:
*Chord note, off *weak beat.*
**Dissonance, on *weak beat.*
***Chord note, metric accent, *object of largest leap.*

A *further motivic derivative*

Example 5.13 illustrates a further motivic component running through Debussy's structure, and also derived from the primary statement in measures 1–4. (See also note 10 and related text.)

Ex. 5.13a

Ex. 5.13b

mm.3-4

... l'ex - ta - se   lan - gou -   reuse

Compare bass of mm. 7–8 and 48–50, as well as top voice of mm. 22–23, as augmentations.

Ex. 5.13c

m.6

C'est   la   fa - tigue ...

Ex. 5.13de

d)   e)

mm.7-8   mm.22-23

Ex. 5.13fg

f)

mm.24ff. (ultimate intervallic contraction)

g)

mm.28-29 etc.

Ex. 5.13h

m.32 etc., 46-47

As is often the case, the discrete identity of this derivative is problematic in its transformations, for example where the diatonic basis of its chromatic variant at measures 24–25 (exx. 5.13f, g) can be read as the descending-step motive with on-beat rather than characteristic off-beat placement. This of course documents kinship and common origin. Yet it seems useful to review the sixteenth-note derivative as a special term of which the development, concentrated in stanza 2 and recalled finally at measures 46–47, will be viewed as allied to that of poetic imagery.

As is evident in ex. 5.13, the progress of the motive is thus toward ultimate intervallic compression in the chromatic variant, recurring after its emergence at measure 24. (The process of intervallic compression can be heard vividly when one compares the descending sixth of measures 2–3 [a_1 to c-sharp$_1$] with the fifth marked by the piano's ascent in measures 7–8, and with the cited chromatic transformation.) The alliance of the chromatic variant to the poetic *cri doux* is explicit in measures 24–26, and we shall in fact refer to it as the *"cri* motive." In the song's interior, this chromatic motive becomes critically prevalent to the extent that such chromatic successions as the extension into measure 27 and the piano of measures 44–45 are significantly associable.

The motive is traceable from measures 2–3, neglected in the second part of stanza 1 but then occurring in almost every bar of stanza 2 after measure 22, often in piano and voice, and often with concurrently opposed directions of motion.

What inescapable or speculative observations can we make with respect to performance? For one thing, awareness is again imperative as a basis for deciding to bring a given statement into relief or leave it alone, as irrepressibly evident, or to be heard in passivity on grounds of context, as well as for deciding the degree of any intervention. In this fundamental regard, special importance attaches to a motive's original occurrences: in the present case they suggest the pianist's cautious, delineating punctuation in measure 2 and like contexts (see exx. 5.14, and 5.4*a*).

There is also the critical matter of interpretive awareness in a motive's relatively covert manifestations, such as that of the piano's middle voice at measure 22, the clear delineation of which requires a deliberate technical control not easily achieved.

Where a motive is restated immediately (in the same pitches, transposed, or shifted registrally), as is often the case in Debussy, serious interpretive issues arise: the need to avoid redundancy may suggest a modest withdrawal in dynamic intensity the second time, or the performer's awareness of contextual process, as when the motive recurs within an intensifying stream of action, may well demand otherwise. In this sense, the evolution toward the acute chromatic variant in stanza 2 is a matter of which the enlightened performer can scarcely be ignorant. Indeed the same variant becomes a vehicle of resignation by way of registral drops—tentatively at measures 28 and 30, then at 32 and 33, and ultimately at measures 46 and 47. Its extension into measures 26–27 is moreover a device of musical and poetic redirection, and of musical dissolution and modulation in a number of elements to be considered later.

Some further points about performance are made in connection with ex. 5.14.

Ex. 5.14

rhythmic grouping?:

Apart from functional intervallic transformations detailed in ex. 5.13, the motive appears also in rhythmic variation as an aspect of its vital existence in the piece's course, and as a further issue of interpretive study and opportunity. Thus, the sixteenth-note portion is at times apparently construed as the metrically weak second of two impulses in a trochaic whole (see for example Debussy's slurring at measures 7, 8; 22–25; 32, 33; and 46, 47). According to this conception the motive is heard as receding, suggesting diminuendo at least in descending forms, although we have seen that the ascents of measures 7 and 8 (see ex. 5.4*a*) can imply controlled crescendo inflections opposing inherent metric structure. Immediate recurrence of the trochaic form, where the sixteenth-note portion is a reactive consequent, also suggests slight punctuation between the two statements (for example, at measures 7–8).

At other points, the sixteenth-note segment is heard as anticipative—the first part of a weak-strong, two-impulse whole that points toward the accented (longer) note in an iambic unit; see for example Debussy's slurring at measures 2–3, or measures 28–29 and 30–31.[12] In these instances, the metric functions and relative positions of component impulses dictate enforced connection between the sixteenth-notes and the consequent accent as a rule within a prevailing diminuendo.

Elsewhere, important choices remain of interpretive shape and connection. At measures 10–11, for example, continuity over a formal division seems to require that the sixteenth-notes be directed toward measure 11, the notation notwithstanding. The same treatment may well apply for other reasons in the piano part at measures 33–34, where variety could well be a criterion and governing value dictating an enforced continuity between the cadence-forming measures 33 and 34, in contrast with the punctuation between measures 32 and 33, and despite the notation.

The above considerations are subtle factors to be explored at the fringes of analysis of a single element, that of the ultimate details of motivic unity and development. At times implications overlap: thus, for example, the piano's longer impulse of measure 7 is both the goal of the sixteenth-note anticipative group of measure 6 and the initiator of the trochaic motivic variant that occupies measure 7. On all counts, the performer must have a developed sense of immediate context and broad implication as a basis for decisions of articulation.

Unifying accompanimental figuration

Although clearly lacking a distinctive identity of melodic shape and intervallic content, and thus not a motive in the strict sense, the recurring accompanimental figure consisting of the ♪ ♪ ♪. ♪⟩ foreground articulation is yet a factor of material consistency. Once introduced at measure 11 (where it is an aspect of tempo un poco mosso), the figure is used in 27 of 42 measures, or for nearly two-thirds of the song's duration.

As for the functions of this rhythm, the second attack (the eighth-note following the sixteenth) both anticipates and extinguishes the measure's second beat, and the next attack (a dotted eighth, or an eighth followed by a sixteenth) is both premature and delayed in relation to the regular pulsation.

The pattern thus, in all its guises a corroborating unifier, contributes in one sense to an effect of propulsion, of moving ahead of established pulsation. In another sense, it can have the effect of delayed articulation in relation to established pulsation. The figuration is restrictive in that it is most feasible in slower tempi.

Any particular expressive tendency in this ambivalent rhythmic backdrop depends of course on context, as must the performer's approach to it: on dynamic intensity, metronomic tempo, in-process modulations of tempo, conditions of other elements (tonal and textural), and especially on the governing demands of text. Clearly poetic imagery is decisive in the voice's few commensurate syncopations in measures 15 and 41–42, and that of measure 20 is an unmistakable factor of thrust toward the vitalizing motions of stanza 2.

As a general principle of performance, the figure's prevalence dictates discretion, even understatement: the accompanimental material is by and large felt more than heard. Yet it is susceptible to subtle inflection, as when the pianist slightly leans into its advance in a way that supports developing tempo.

In its precedent appearance at measure 11 (see ex. 5.4b), after the lassitude of the introductory phrases, the rhythm is a factor in establishing new directions of poetic content, and certainly in a controlled yet palpably moved tempo. Debussy's notated articulations (slightly pressing, separated attacks) further these same ends, and on the other hand are clearly useful, like the piano's syncopations, in arresting established motion at the forthcoming cadence (measures 17–18), which is formally, tonally, and texturally important.

Limited occurrences at measures 24–25, where the figure is aborted, support and stimulate the voice's intensity of activity at a critical moment (ex. 5.4c); that of measure 27 is functional in halting developed activity; and those of measures 28 and 30 seem calculated to compromise a governing process of recession in a judicious balance. (Measures 26–27 are to be discussed as embodying a receding process in all but the tonal element; here again rhythm contributes to recessive effect.) All these subsidiary occurrences of the accompanimental figuration require perfect clarity without insistence, and are served by Debussy's detached articulations (exx. 5.4c, d).

The restored rhythm affords at measures 34–35 a factor of continuity through cadence (exx. 5.4d, e), as well as a vital stimulant into the climactic stanza 3 and virtually throughout it. And the occurrences at measures 48–49 are quiescent reminiscences, necessarily retardative in effect while serving the imperatives of unity and confirmation: these statements, succeeded by a functional augmentation in the piano's middle register at measures 50–52, represent a mere ripple of residual activity, yielding to a gradual subsidence in all elements.

Harmonic Basis: Continuities of Line and Tonality

The structure's ultimate basis in E: V-I has been evident in, for example, the interrelations of introductory and subsequent literal statements of the primary motive, which cast a controlling influence over the whole. Example 5.15 reviews the harmony of measures 1–10, then looks ahead to the relation of these measures to all that follow. The illustration thus represents a broad unity utterly unequivocal in its basic tonal functionality. The notes to ex. 5.15 draw attention to certain significant details, one of them an ostensible relation between early implications of C-sharp and important midlevel references to C-sharp in stanza 2.

A point of theory embodied in ex. 5.15 and in those that follow is the derivation of harmonic elements at foreground and at deeper levels with regard both to voice-leading proximities and adjacencies (often chromatic) and to governing principles of formulation in the bass (for example, that of the E-triad outlined in the essential bass of measures 1–10). These are decisive points of compositional technique.

Stanzas 1 and 3

There is a point in comparing the outer stanzas directly, as is already somewhat apparent: although disparate indeed in the elaborative musical surface, form, and shaping poetic content, they are nevertheless parallel in a shared tonal basis

Ex. 5.15

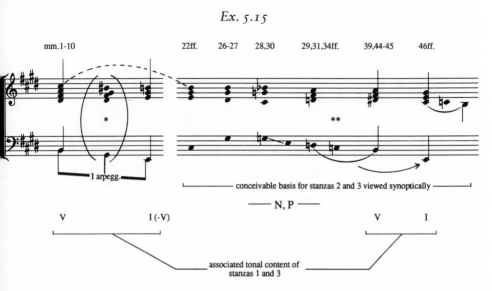

*Compare the voice's prominent references to C-sharp in subsequent stanzas. Specificities of elaborative harmonic content are here and elsewhere traceable in part to governing formulations of the bass, as discussed in the text.

**The auxiliary "four-two" on D introduces E:V at the entry to stanza 3; compare the cadence to the first stanza, mm. 17–18.

consisting of clearly functional elements. These elements are compositionally enriched by linear resources of compelling surface continuities of voice leading, partly explored in preliminary analysis.

Example 5.16 provides two representations of the elaborated, fundamental I-V of measures 11–18. As in all illustrations in this series, the harmonies are shown in registral simplifications by which voice-leading implications are made visible, and the notes of piano and voice are combined.

A generally relevant factor is evident in the bass of measures 11–18 (ex. 5.16a): its disposition in a governing, symmetrical intervallic sequence, here 1-3-1 in doubling parallel fifths. The interior components, E-flat and C, form a pivotal link between the tonic and dominant degrees.

The segment's structure is also regarded as transpiring in two harmonic stages, each internally formed of primary and subsidiary elements that are step-related and largely chromatic (ex. 5.16b). In this sense, the I is elaborated by chromatic lower neighbors, the V by diatonic and chromatic upper neighbors. The neighbor relation is explicit in the bass and evident in voice-leading condensations in the sketch.

The next illustration (ex. 5.17a) digests the whole of the tonally reflective stanza 3, a detail of which is the preparation of its initiating V (measure 37) by

Ex. 5.16a

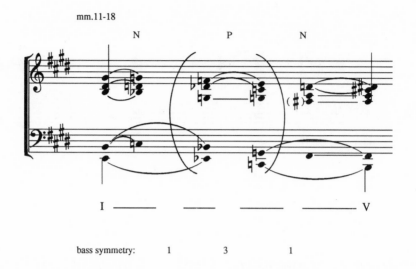

Ex. 5.16b

the dissonant neighbor that had the same function at measure 17—a D-rooted four-two. (The auxiliary harmony, rooted on D, can also be regarded as looking ahead, as a dominant, to the tonally deviant linear harmony based on G in measures 40 and 42.) Again the harmonic structure is conditioned in significant part by symmetries of intervallic sequence in the bass: an expansive succession 4-6, 6-4 over the larger span, then in local elaboration 4-5-4. The latter interval 4 and the superposed harmonies (measures 46–47) are reminiscent of the elaboration E-C (I, and its neighbor) at measures 11–12.

Ex. 5.17a

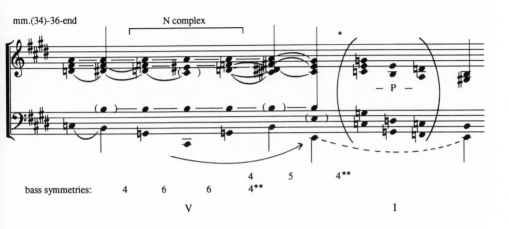

*Compare I elaboration at mm. 11–14.
**Note elaborations of the fifth and first scale degrees, both involving interval 4 (a major third) below.

Measures 37–45 can be seen to embody a deeply returning harmonic motion, a prolongation of V through a complex of symmetrically disposed neighbors extracted and illustrated in ex. 5.17b. Clearly, a further determinant is that of depicted pitch-class unities, or common tones; these, with the tritonal bass motion at the heart of the symmetrical succession, go far toward accounting for the particular components of harmonic elaboration.

Ex. 5.17b

In the broad returning motion V-V, the initiating occurrence is relatively tentative (measures 37, 39); the second (measures 44–45), which is decisive, is underscored by a number of elements of focal intensity, and a point of central orientation in the poem (*la tienne*). The area between the two articulations, comparatively detached tonally and having a mobility that strongly supports a predominant progressive tendency, may be heard to recall the important references to D̲ of stanza 2 in the relation {G̲,C̲-sharp}.

Stanza 2

The essential tonal direction traversed in measures 20–34 is from E̲ to D̲. The latter pitch class is noted in two senses: as a secondary tonic in the second part of stanza 2 (measures 28–34), and in a deep linear relation as the lower neighbor to the primary tonic.[13] (The register of the first E̲ as tonic arrival, measure 9, corresponds to that of the cadential D̲ at measure 34—a register otherwise unoccupied.)

Example 5.18a, a pitch-class representation of the lowest voice, portrays initially sequential fifth-relations underlying the tonal fluctuation in stanza 2. These, bracketed in the sketch, comprise factors diatonically related to E̲; moreover, the harmonies on B̲, F̲-sharp, and C̲-sharp, all dominant forms, are respectively V, V once removed, and V twice removed—signs of a conventionally tonal basis (measures 18, 22–23, and 24–25) underscored in the roman numeral analysis given (where E:VI-V of V-III can also be heard as B:II-V-VI). Example 5.18a encapsulates the concluding fifth-relation of plagal approach to D̲ (measures 32–34) with the corresponding bass succession at the first tonicization of D̲ (measures 28–31).

Ex. 5.18a

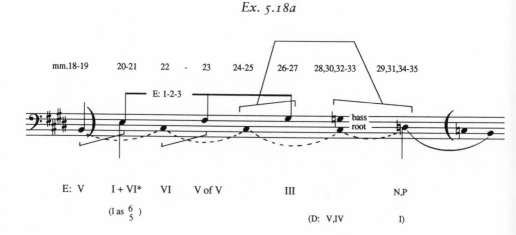

*VI is separated from I as a point of tonal departure at m. 21. As for the harmonic structure at m. 20, compare the song's final cadence, and the tonic's interim appearance at mm. 46–47.

The above clearly indicates the vital role of stanza 2 as the site of relative tonal mobility, an aspect of which is the ambiguity of striking chromatic events in measures 27–28 (provisionally resolved at measure 29 and in the comparatively stable content of measures 29–34). These considerations arise again later in the perspective of inclusive processes involving a number of elements cofunctioning in stanza 2 in direct relation to the text.

Examples 5.18b, c explore further pitch-class interrelations complementary or alternative to those represented in ex. 5.18a. Example 5.18b focuses on the overreaching succession C-sharp–D against the implication of chromatic-diatonic descent from G-sharp (measure 26) to the cadence. And in another reference to tonal factors capable of interpretive projection, ex. 5.18c reveals a discernible set of symmetrical intervallic relations (compare exx. 5.16, 5.17), drawing attention also to two triadic linearizations (E:VI, D:IV) the tritonal root relation of which is itself oriented toward D, and an adumbration of the prominent, auxiliary relations {C-sharp,G} in stanza 3 (ex. 5.17b; measures 40–42).

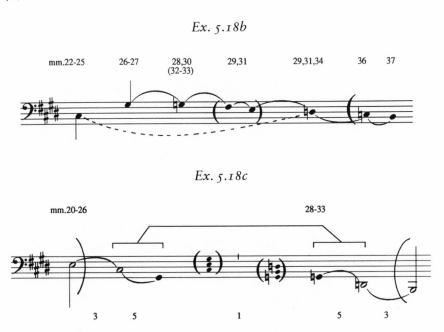

Ex. 5.18b

Ex. 5.18c

This intense chromatic phase is detailed as ex. 5.19 (compare ex. 5.3), again largely a pitch-class representation. Its most telling constituent is the slip from G-sharp to G, an altogether singular chromatic inflection highlighted by the voice's sudden descent by interval 3 after a series of semitonal steps, and especially by the surprising relation of the voice's concluding G to the preceding, registrally equivalent G̲-sharp of the piano, the decisive inflection thus occurring across a timbral separation.

Ex. 5.19

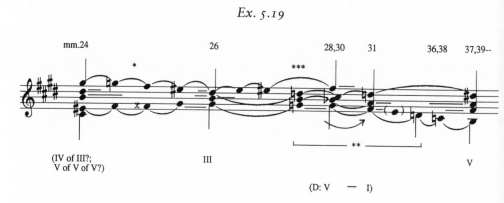

mm.24   26   28,30   31   36,38   37,39--

(IV of III?;   III   V
V of V of V?)

(D: V — I)

*Note the exchange G̲-sharp–E̲-sharp.
**Area of principal chromatic linear functions and maximal tonal fluctuation, cadentially exposed, toward "modal" lower neighbor of I.
***See also ex. 5.31 regarding coincident D̲-sharp, D̲-natural.

Stanza 2 is thus a region of marked, eventful tonal divergence, and of inferrable, demonstrable, cogent relations to the outer segments, which confirm E̲.

The Voice Melody in the Tonal Structure

Voice notes are included in the foregoing sketches; but the supplementary examples that follow illuminate critical factors of tonal and linear structure in the voice melody itself, to a degree independently perceived, as well as certain aspects of tonal relation between the two instruments.

The voice's pitch classes complement those of the harmony, and especially in the quasi-recitando segments following measures 11, 29, and 40 can often be construed as clearly deriving from the harmony. There is of course nothing surprising in this: it is simply to recall the obvious point that harmonic structure is in tonal practice a point of departure for all pitch-class materials, shaped into motivic unities and interesting, distinctive melodic configurations. One has the sense that here the harmony, which we have now examined in much detail, constitutes a governing scheme in the relations between voice and piano.

Example 5.20a is a reduction of the voice melody in measures 3–9 viewed as centering on the dissonant C̲-sharp (ninth of the protracted V), and in its antecedent and consequent units fundamentally embracing the dissonance and its step-descending resolution. This is one aspect of the earlier point regarding the prominence of C-sharp in this introductory segment. In another sense it looks ahead to important occurrences of C-sharp in the tonal motions of stanza 2 (ex. 5.18), in the recurring structure of the fundamental primary V, and in structures of I (as six-five) at such key points as measures 20 and 46–47. In still another aspect, the structure revealed in ex. 5.20a has been characterized as an underlying reflection of the prevalent step descent as a motivic derivative.

Ex. 5.20a

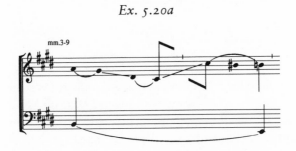

In measures 11–18 the voice, tightly interdependent in relation to the piano's chords, articulates a whole-tone pitch-class "ascent" (ex. 5.20b) culminating in a singular, tonally clarifying semitonal motion to D-sharp, the whole thus linking E:3 (in I) and E:7 (in V) through a process of passing tonal detachment followed by decisive functionality. This is one of the voice's more declamatory, quasi-recitando passages, the compositional and performance details of which rest heavily on textual interpretation, as well as on tonal implications detailed here and in ex. 5.16.[14]

Ex. 5.20b

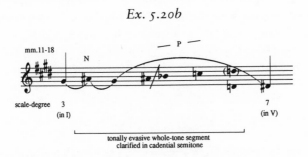

The voice melody of measures 20–27 in one important sense prolongs the underlying G-sharp represented in ex. 5.20c. This pitch class, manifest in two registers, undergoes a tonally critical shift through G to F-sharp (ex. 5.20c), thus reflecting the prevailing condition of chromatic tonal fluctuation. The voice's initiating E:3 and culminating D:3 circumscribe the process.

Ex. 5.20c

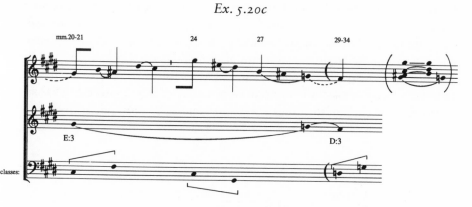

An element in the relatively quiescent textual content at measures 28–34, and in the musical content, which is oriented toward D, is the voice's axial, structural F-sharp (as D:3) within a delimiting octave C-sharp; it thus articulates an F-sharp (-minor) triad both a part of the recurring D:I and texturally disjoined from it (ex. 5.20d). The lower C-sharp (c-sharp₁) can be heard in a vital linear relation to the piano's registrally equivalent sforzato C at measure 36, which signals and prepares tonal return in stanza 3.

Ex. 5.20d

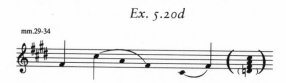

As a final illustration in the present series, ex. 5.20e surveys the voice melody of stanza 3: its framing V linearizations, its relation to the hierarchy of structural and auxiliary harmonies, its functional dissonance content (in the tonally detached harmony based on G) precisely at the stage of predominating climactic progression, and its fundamental contour of ascent to and subsequent descent

Ex. 5.20e

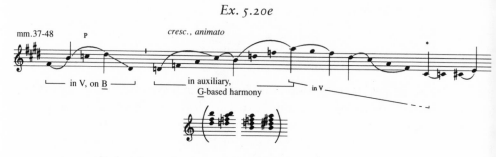

*The C-sharp, dissonant ninth in V, is "suspended" into I.

from a_2, the voice melody's highest pitch, strategically a semitone above that of stanza 2.

General principles of relation of the voice melody to harmonic structure

The analyses confirm that the voice melody is, as in tonal music by and large, tightly allied to immediate harmonic context: in its underlying or surface arpeggiations, or in discretely projecting one or more notes of the harmony in relief.

But a sign of the voice melody's expression of mobility, dissonance of varying degree, and limited independence is that it doubles the harmonic root in only a few instances: at measure 41, in an auxiliary thirteenth chord based on C-sharp;[15] at primary cadential approaches (decisively at measure 17, as a passing tone at 32–33) and at the final cadential arrival; and in the corresponding triadic outlines at measures 16 and 39, of which the latter continues and underscores the dominant harmony reestablished at measure 37. In the last instance, the close (parallel-octave) alliance of voice and piano bass serves too in striking contrast to textural counteractions that follow.

On the other hand, the voice melody in distinct relief in relation to immediate harmonic environment is accordingly especially significant: at measures 20–21, where the voice isolates the factor {C-sharp,G-sharp} from the complex I + VI as an impetus for tonal actions that ensue directly and to which it points; and at the comparable measures 29–34, where the component {F-sharp,C-sharp} is linearized within a settled tonal condition otherwise based in D (ex. 5.20d). Example 5.21 depicts variant implications of F-sharp and C-sharp in this segment. In all of these the quasi-independent triadic component compromises the sense of tonal stability.

Ex. 5.21

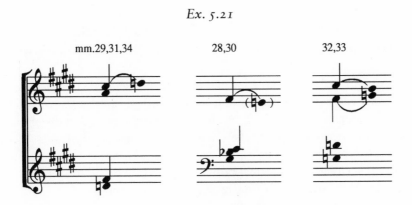

A very summary view of cadential pitches of the voice melody is given as ex. 5.22. The significance of the formal and tonal interrelation of the three focal points is at once evident. And the note to the illustration is important in that it calls attention to the ultimate arrival, on $\underline{E}$ and e_1, as being unique for the entire voice melody of stanza 3 and exceptional for the song as a whole, hence extremely persuasive in its resolutive effect.

Ex. 5.22

stanza cadences as to E:I and voice's e_1

Singular occurrence of the pitch class $\underline{E}$ in the voice of stanza 3, and in the voice melody overall except for four metrically weak and tonally subsidiary occurrences in stanzas 1 and 2 only; thus of markedly conclusive effect.

Some Interpretive Implications of Tonal, Harmonic, and Melodic Pitch and Pitch-Class Structures

The performers' reflective pondering of the events that delineate Debussy's tonal structure affords, with experimentation and directed rehearsal, a framework for interpretive judgments of many kinds. Ideally, these are evident in the ultimate refinements of performance. At the same time, whether areas of tonal focus, arrival, clarification or reclarification want underscoring or understatement depends on such factors as formal position, status in a broad tonal hierarchy, and the extent of established or intrinsic clarity and emphasis.

To take a particular case in the consideration of tonal factors and interpretation, if one compares varying occurrences of the primary V it is clear that measures 1–8 have durational emphasis not paralleled elsewhere, suggesting (as does the requisite musical and poetic atmosphere) an approach of tentative emergence, restrained execution, even understatement. The occurrence at measures 18–19, which is exposed cadentially and in motivic statement akin to that of the song's beginning, requires with its punctuative role an interpretive attitude of ongoing. Of those of measures 37 and 39, and 44–45, the former is a tentative occurrence, the provisional basis for progressive actions following directly, the latter climactic on many counts, and of expansive and ultimately decisive redirection in the tonal structure.

One can to similar ends compare occurrences of I at measures 9–10 (in a crucial but tentative resolution, formal punctuation, and motivic statement, moving directly into protraction of the same harmony out of measure 11; exx. 5.4a, b) with that of measures 46–48 (the voice's decisive, ultimate arrival, yet deferring to the piano's subsequent, conclusive elaboration; exx. 5.4f, g). The first tonic arrival (measure 9), which is an object of diminuendo and preliminary tonal recession, and a well-marked cadence, is negotiated importantly yet with an appreciation of its function in preparing forthcoming motions in the poetic and musical structures.

Interpretation of the opening period as a basis for tonal and other departures suggests other interventions: modest dynamic inflections; extremely cautious dynamic shading of the motive (its initiating appoggiatura accorded perhaps slightly more attention at the second statement, measure 5); and a sense within this controlled scale of action of portentous but preliminary, superficial harmonic fluctuation in measures 7–8. Here the voice's dissonant C-sharp is cautiously projected in Debussy's crescendo and, in measure 8, conceivably lengthened slightly, with supportive actions in the piano (see ex. 5.4a), including a delicate marking of the bass's triadic arpeggiation.

The special importance of the first occurrence of E:I at measure 9 is obvious. It is also the first significant departure from the sound of the major ninth, and takes place well into the piece. The tonic at measure 9, however tentative, is an occasion for a common performance technique: a prudent underscoring or projection, more in clarity and warmth of color than by any intervention so overt and direct as relative dynamic intensity or enhanced duration. The entry of I, which reflects change in both harmonic function and sonority, is thus the occasion for keenly cognizant interpretive address: it should not be louder, not longer, perhaps enhanced by the slightest hesitation between measures 8 and 9, surely by observing strictly the exposing rest in the piano part of measure 9, and by a deliberate effort of impeccably clear articulation of the low, isolated tonic root. Although the fundamentally overreaching E:I is here a necessary vehicle of onward motion, it is one of only two triadic occurrences of the tonic harmony.

Examples 5.4a, b make these points in addition to indicating the dynamic shaping of the primary motive's reentry, pointing inexorably to the advancing tempo of the following subsection. In the upcoming segment, where the established tonic is sustained, a cautious but deliberate action of interpretive thrust is required (and specified in the composer's un poco mosso, and the indicated articulations of the chords, pochissimo marcato).

Example 5.23 makes another point regarding measure 9, a factor further conditioning its qualities of articulation and exposure: this is its entry into the structure's deepest register, a region of pitch exploited uniquely in the song's three primary cadences. Here is yet another bass symmetry, now registrally as well as intervallically consistent, fortifying the sense of an ultimately overreaching tonal and linear framework of E-D-E. The sensitive pianist is likely to treat these pitches with a deliberate richness of sonority, within a carefully calibrated, controlled scheme of relations.

Ex. 5.23

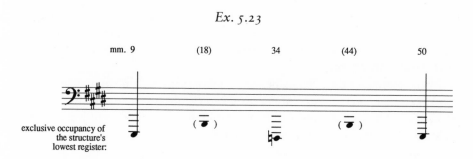

Tonal content in measures 11–18 suggests many possibilities of interpretive decision. These bars reflect modest tonal deviance in which I, initially retained, yields to a structural V. The critical juncture in the process is measure 15, which signals departure in the poem as well, and where the composer has indicated certain special articulations (see ex. 5.26). A striking factor here is the bass's E-flat, an object of crescendo by which it is emphasized in relation to the three other, durationally superior, notes of a symmetrical ordering (ex. 5.16). The pianist who has a sense of whole in this tentatively mobile passage, and who wishes to outline an interpretive etching of the bass, may well subordinate measures 13–14 in their redundant relation to 11–12 and as a further means of drawing attention to the textual and tonal significance at measure 15, the point of most severe tonal severance. The voice's notated, stressed syncopation is a pertinent, active element, as is its crescendo in measure 15, imitating the piano's into that bar. At measures 16–18, in a context of renewed functionality in tonal structure and of textual focus on the image that will prevail in stanza 2 (*le chœur* ...), the piano defers to distinctive articulations in the voice. The piano's articulations, of a mode now well established, are accordingly tempered, yielding to the voice (which signals renewed functionality at measure 17 by breaking the whole-tone succession), and looking ahead in a restored tempo to the more lyric phrases that follow. The piano's cadential harmony and motivic entry at measure 18 are brought directly to the fore (see ex. 5.4*b*).

Tonal structure suggests a fundamental guiding principle for performance in stanza 2: that of going with decisive fluctuations, one critical element of which is the judgment that the tempo of measure 18 is assuredly not that of measure 1. Expansion of the dynamic range to an inferred mezzo piano is associated with a perspective of active progression (ex. 5.4*c*). The question of immediate harmonic and motivic repetitions at the foreground (as at measure 25) can be answered with respect to a general principle of withdrawal in the second statement or, where relevant, as contributing to continuing intensification (for example, through measure 23): context is the determinant, and a penetrating evaluation of context is the only basis for decision.

Example 5.4*c* represents important performance issues following the focal measures 24–25, and especially into measure 27 and its critical, final sixteenth-note articulation, a dramatic interruption in the voice's chromatic descent (1-1-3) and in prevailing references to diatonically related tonal elements. Here, in a moment's tonal ambiguity to be enunciated unerringly, G̲ (assigned uniquely to the voice) abruptly dislodges the stanza's prolonged G̲-sharp. This extreme of diminishing intensity (molto diminuendo) and pivotal harmonic complex must be unmistakably clear. Intelligibility is aided by the suggested slight punctuation between measures 27 and 28 (exx. 5.4*c*, *d*), exposing a momentary tonal hiatus as well as the forthcoming D̲-related harmony, and allowing an instant of reverberation time for the preceding, crucial motion from G̲-sharp (piano's right-hand thumb) to the voice's G̲. In connection with ex. 5.31 we deal with a question to which the score gives no explicit clue. Where and how should the tempo animato end?

Prevalent tonal elements in measures 28–34 are those of interim resolution: the voice's melodic plateau around f-sharp$_1$; and the piano's pitch-class descent (G̲–F-sharp–E̲–D̲), centered in the tenor register, first articulated into measure 29, and fulfilled in the deeper register of measure 34 (ex. 5.4*d*). The fitting interpretive attitude here is calmato, and the motivic statements are to be played pianissimo but misurato and treated as inactive reverberations of the climactic chromatic variant (*ressemble au cri*), particularly in immediate repetitions within a governing recessive process (measure 30, measure 33). Yet there is subsidiary, residually active implication in the contradirectional motions of the piano's doublings at measures 32 and 33 (ex. 5.4*d*), to be brought out very circumspectly.

Looking over stanza 2 with respect to the performance implications of tonal structure, one can identify as examples certain specific questions of interpretive choice. Thus ex. 5.18 reveals a number of potentially applicable, overreaching pitch-class successions delineating various conceivable unities, and posing different requirements of interpretive articulation. These include the linear motion encircling the goal D̲ (E̲–C̲-sharp–D̲), apparent in ex. 5.18*b*. Another is that of an intervallically symmetrical bass, brought out with attention to relevant individual successions, through pitches embodying registral continuities (that is, the C̲-sharp of measure 24 rather than that of measure 22); this can be heard to relate to the analogous organization of bass segments elsewhere (see ex. 5.18*c*).

A number of points in stanza 3 that are integral to the tonal structure warrant consideration in performance, whether or not they prompt particular interventions. Measure 36 is such a point of impulse in the structure: its C̲-natural, marked sforzato, signals a thrust toward the functional restoration of B̲. The idea of diminuendo in the bar preceding (see ex. 5.4*e*) is one manner of exposing the dissonance, as is the cautious movement of tempo at measure 36, suggested in ex. 5.4*e*. Again immediate repetition (in measures 38–39) suggests subordination of the second occurrence in performance, a view confirmed by the analysis of context, for slight withdrawal here provides a basis for the forthcoming intensifying progression (see also ex. 5.39 and the attendant commentary).

Measures 40–43 are an area of mobility in a number of elements: there is a more radical severance of tonal functionality than in the expansive modulations of stanza 2,[16] and the important juncture in tonal structure requires discreet punctuation between measures 39 and 40 (exx. 5.4*e, f*), with the B̲ of measure 37 taking precedence over that of measure 39 in the broad, symmetrical bass succession B̲–G̲–C̲-sharp–G̲–B̲. A different, potentially convincing approach could be that of consistent crescendo through the bass, reaching a culmination at the climactic and tonally decisive restoration of B̲ at measure 44.

The E:V of measures 44–45 is a critical point for interpretation in a number of respects, of which its decisive tonal function is only one. The voice's crescendo into measure 44 is on a_2, its overall apex and the pitch class linking the consecutive ninth chords on G̲ and B̲. The slight temporal stretching of this note (un poco allargando) indicated in ex. 5.4*f* seems fitting on all counts, as does the piano's abundant articulation of the harmony (its root in particular) at measure 44, and the sustained crescendo into measure 45 overlapping the voice's peak.

Example 5.4*f* draws attention to the recession toward tentative tonic arrival at measure 46, and its ultimate confirmation in the piano's concluding harmonic and motivic statements. Of the song's conclusion, a primary point of performance in the matter of tonal structure is a gradual cadence-in-process culminating at measure 50 in the structure's first pure tonic triad since measures 9–10, and in the restored deepest register of pitch so selectively reserved over the piece as a whole (ex. 5.23), to be played warmly and sonorously though at the most subdued dynamic level. Examples 5.4*f, g* set forth a number of details of performance following from an awareness of phased cadential process.

Indeed, the above paragraphs embody many representative interpretive possibilities and choices issuing from the analysis of essentials, unities, interrelations, expressive fluctuations, and relations of mobility and stability (as well as degrees to which these attributes apply) in the tonal structure. Suggestions and conclusions about performance posited above will be confirmed in further consideration of the poem and its enhancement in Debussy's setting.

Thematic Content in a Generalized Summation

Example 5.24 is a generalized summation of the composition's distinctive elements of rhythm, harmony, melody, tempo, motive, dynamic shading, and poetic imagery, and of the principal midlevel events by which each is realized and delineated. Some relations are shown in registral displacement, according to their component pitch classes, to clarify constructions of essential voice leading. Much of the content is represented in sketched notation, but principal, integral melodic-rhythmic identities of motivic content are shown as are key segments of the text and its setting.

Many foreground specifications of articulation, tempo, and dynamic nuance are left out of this generalized image, while precedent and basic tendencies are given, and the metric placement and content of integral motivic entries are clarified by occasional barlines. The whole can be read, played, and heard as a kind of under-surface improvisation on Debussy's song.

The composition's fundamental thematic essence is thus grasped through filters that catch the essentials of its structural and expressive substance. The purpose is akin to that of exx. 3.5 and 4.30, although details of method differ appropriately with disparate vocabularies. All three are in a sense composed abstractions, each a creative exercise suggesting a framework within which the piece's ultimate details of compositional refinement interplay. And each is a map of principal tonal and thematic events, a digest of focal points of content by which interpretation may in one sense be guided.

Such a representation is itself an interpretation, a thoughtful perspective for the realization and projection of interpreted salient events, here in both music and text. It can serve to inform and reinforce decisions of performance about essentials of expressive nuance and exposure, as adduced in the analysis of basic directions and tendencies of all cofunctioning elements.

Ex. 5.24

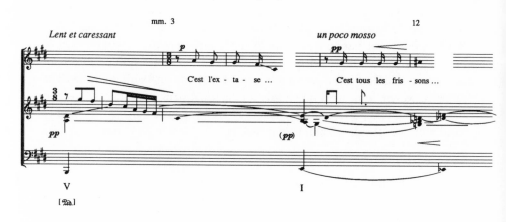

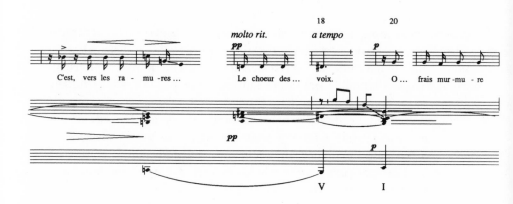

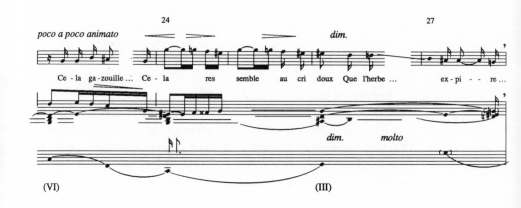

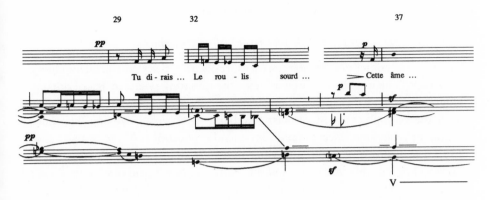

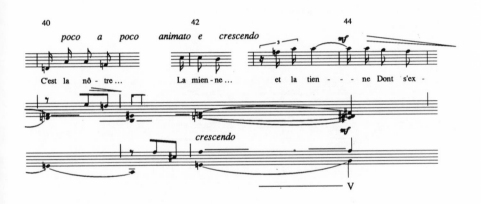

Text in Music: Reflections of Poetic Content in the Textures and Other Musical Elements

Stanza 1: Text, texture, and further issues of performance

An aspect of content in the first ten measures, earlier discussed as introductory in Debussy's setting, has to do with text: the initiating poetic image of dreamy languor. Associated elements of musical structure are the song's slowest tempo until the reminiscences of the last few bars; a restricted dynamic intensity; prevalent recurring descents (and diminuendo inflections) of the primary motive;[17] separations of piano and voice entries (measures 1, 3, 5), consequent distances of leisurely imitation, and the relative textural void of measures 3–4; harmonic inertia in the protracted ninth chord through eight bars of loose nonresolution (with melodic protraction of the dissonant C-sharp); and overall pitch and pitch-class descents of C-sharp (to B) and B (to E). Some of these factors are schematically represented in ex. 5.25.

Ex. 5.25

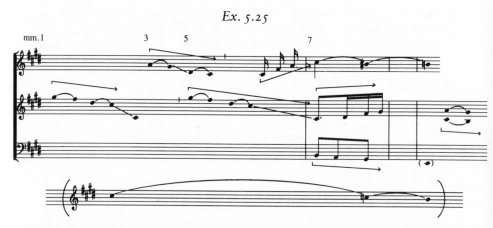

The descending inflections can be conceived as analogous to a yawning exhalation, in contrast to the comparative mobility of the second phrase. Moreover, the virtually lethargic motivic descents in measures 1–5 and 9, spaced at leisurely intervals, can suggest token gestures of recollection, of reference to a passionate state which, now subsided, precedes and is the basis for the poem's beginning. The composer's instructions *caressant* and *rêveusement* are of course of the essence in denoting prevalent attitude in this first segment.

The second phrase and second line of poetry reveal that the dreamy, languid ecstasy is that of love's exhaustion: *la fatigue amoureuse*. Within a general condition of preliminary restraint (*langoureuse, amoureuse*), and scaled to that perspective, the second phrase embodies certain elements of tentative mobility.

It evokes the emerging condition of awakening in the languorous aftermath of embrace, as from a dream. One vital factor of mobility is the coactivity of piano and voice in restricted, local, contradirectional motions (measures 7–8) sketched in ex. 5.25, in contrast with their agreement in this respect at the outset and in a deeper implication of underlying descent. Example 5.4a suggests as a case in point the pianist's discreet actions of crescendo, merely from pianissimo to piano and of local import, in measure 7 and (less) in measure 8. These actions are a means of carefully underscoring incipient, superficial textural oppositions and harmonic motions (the foreground tonicization of the protracted C-sharp). In this suggestive atmosphere of awakening, there is a virtual metaphoric image (of stretch) in the voice's moderate crescendo into measure 8 and within it, supported by the piano's inflections, with the phrase sloped in diminuendo toward measure 9.

Example 5.4a deals with the bridging motivic entry at measure 9, molded characteristically in dynamic nuances. The noted articulation (un poco hesitando) and slight punctuation at the middle of measure 10 are an occasion for a hint of metric diversity; a chance to delineate the sixteenth-note motivic derivative (ex. 5.13), which emerges critically in stanza 2 and recalls measure 6 (voice) and measures 7–8 (piano); a means of projecting the foreground I-arpeggiation of sixteenths (a diminution of the deeper, bass arpeggiation preceding); and a way of subtly yet overtly enforcing the role of the motive as a link into measure 11, interpreting it with respect to implications of anacrusis at two levels.

The pace established at measure 11 is crucial as a matter of reference for the song's ensuing tempi. Yet a slight advance in metronomic tempo (un poco mosso) is qualified by certain intrinsic elements of motion appropriate to the poem's outward turn (les frissons des bois, brises, petites voix): dynamic inflections;[18] accompanimental syncopations (including the recurring second-beat accent of the piano's tenor voice, reflecting in augmentation the right hand's syncopation); the voice's declamatory repeated notes and increased rate of attack; the notated articulative stresses in both instruments (with a requisite cohering effect of the piano pedal, the dot denoting slight separations of impulses); directional oppositions, to be etched in performance, between the piano's upper voices and the voice melody; and superficial harmonic fluctuations within the controlling I-V.

Notwithstanding these activating tendencies, the dynamic condition remains essentially pianissimo with some indicated nuances. The general perspective is one of gently unfolding activity, in a line of gradual development pointing toward its further course in stanza 2, for which measures 1–11 set a basis of precedent tempo and poetic imagery.

Example 5.26 affords attention to particular problems of performance in measure 15.

Ex. 5.26

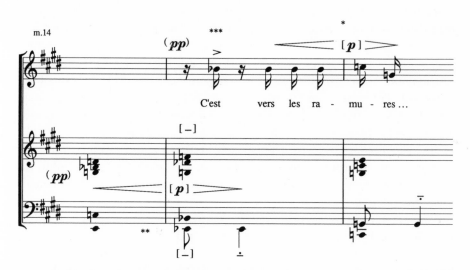

*Decisive, crescendo ascent in voice (vers les ramures), culminating the whole-tone succession.
**Striking chromatic inflection preparing the poetic "turn" and voice syncopation.
***Attention-marking (and voice's first) off-beat entry, directed toward central poetic image of (les) petites voix.

If measures 11–18, as postulated, constitute a phase of poetic redirection marked by the evocation of new images, measure 15 is a precise point of focus in this process: *C'est, vers les ramures, le chœur.* The voice's first off-beat attack is enhanced by stressed articulation and by the harmony's striking chromatic departure, the latter underscored by crescendo (the pianist's leaning) into measure 15. This crescendo is in turn exposed and heightened by slight withdrawal to a lesser dynamic condition (*pp*−) at measures 13–14, the content of which repeats literally that of 11–12. Moreover, the physical image of looking up (*vers les ramures*) and for the first time into the scene that has been drawn is reflected in the voice melody's decisive ascent into measure 16 (toward which it has tended since measure 11), and in the crescendo supporting the ascent.

The next bars (ex. 5.4b) have been viewed as critical to the poetic and musical structures. They are also precarious in performance: the reference to sounds of birds (*le chœur*), variously interpreted by the poetic speaker, are a central focus for most of the remainder of the text. The singer's declamation is here slowed, even to the point of slight tenuto at the end of measure 17 (logically and particularly at the stressed syllable—*pe-ti-tes*). A slight elongation here (as a factor in the ritardando declamation) exposes the key word *voix* by delay, and with it the reaffirmed E:V. In lieu of later, specific attention to tempo, it can be noted that the pace at measure 18 has to be regarded in a context of developing momentum overall, the reentering motive thus un poco mosso, rather in the tempo of measure 11 than that of measure 1. Further, the motive's unobtrusively quickened presentation (al tempo secondo) better serves to bridge the cadence, and to prepare the animate processes of stanza 2 (see ex. 5.4*b*).

This may be a suitable point at which to interject some observations regarding the realizations of poetic prosody in the musical setting, which in a few cases are problematic. The singer whose analysis of the poem includes a study of its natural metric inflections, as well as spoken rehearsal of its organization around stressed syllables and, more broadly, in relation to central focal images, will discover the extent of Debussy's remarkable allegiance to the poetry, including its meters, in a scale of musical accents reckoned in accord with poetic structure. A number of instances have been noted.

In measures 11–18, the words *frissons, brises, ramures,* and *voix* are set with impeccable fidelity to requisite prosodic inflection, musical accents realized by dynamic intensities, ascents in pitch (applicable to all four cases), and durations (agogic accents). But in other instances—very few in the song as a whole—the singer may well find that the setting allows or even wants modest liberties of execution to adjust musical setting to the needs of poetic prosody. Two such cases occur in measures 11–18.

Ex. 5.27

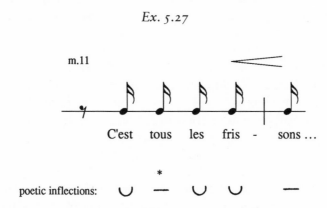

*Piano attack and cessation on dotted eighth-note.

Example 5.27 cautions among other things against misplaced musical accent in the line *C'est tous les frissons des bois,* where at the surface of the music's metric structure *C'est* occurs on the beat and *tous* after the beat, in opposition to the natural prosody. The singer can counter this by the slightest durational or articulative attention to *tous,* realizing that the result not only obviates any distortion of necessary poetic inflection, but may in fact delicately support the subtle variance of meter suggested in the piano articulations (ex. 5.27) and even be an extremely mild factor in the thrust of tempo at measure 11.

A second case is that of the apparent neglect of *chœur* in the text setting at measure 17, where the article *Le* occurs curiously on the first beat, which the singer may well understate in favor of the noun, especially in view of the latter's focal significance in poetic imagery. A minute lengthening of *chœur* can be used to initiate the ritardando as well as to moderate this discrepancy of setting.

Stanza 2

All elements of content signify at the entry of stanza 2 a quality of renewed progression. The voice, singing again after the quasi-recitando that concludes stanza 1, carries everything in its sweep, and its off-beat entry can have a propulsive effect. Its pitch classes (C-sharp, G-sharp), over E:I, represent a basis for tonal fluctuation in the next phrases.

Central poetic images are extensions of that just introduced (*le chœur des petites voix*): initially *frêle et frais* (adjectives which also denote the resurgent character of the first phrase of stanza 2), then poignantly and climactically (*le*) *cri doux de l'herbe agitée,* and ultimately the lethargic movements of pebbles under water (*le roulis sourd des cailloux*). These few images perfectly describe the course of expressive contour in stanza 2, shaped toward a tentative peak of intensity, then receding into the quiescent conditions of measures 28–34.

The following is a summary of musical elements by which the poem's development in stanza 2, oriented toward the focal image *cri,* is realized: (1) the voice's broad, lyric ascent through an underlying G-sharp-minor triad (measures 22–24), extending its range by a fifth; (2) prevalent wide leaps in the voice melody; (3) registral expansion (voice up, piano down); (4) shifting position of the dissonance in the appoggiatura motive (traced in ex. 5.12); (5) crescendo at measures 24–25, and likely before (ex. 5.4c); (6) changes of dynamic intensity in every bar; (7) the structure's most extreme tonal fluctuation (exx. 5.18a, 5.19); (8) motivic concentrations and increased rate of motivic entry in both instruments after measures 20–21; (9) textural oppositions (traced in connection with ex. 5.29); (10) tempo: poco a poco animato; (11) gradual evolution of the motivic derivative toward its ultimate chromatic contraction, as traced in ex. 5.13; and (12) a subtle factor of metric acceleration in foreground units of 2/8 articulated by agogic accents in the voice's second phrase (ex. 5.28).

A comparable survey of musical elements of recession, following the climactic measures 24–25, would be as follows: (1) registral descents and a relative

Ex. 5.28

plateau of registral locus in both voice (around f-sharp$_1$ following measure 29, ex. 5.20d) and piano (from measure 31), including the cadential descent, paralleling that of the other stanzas, into the voice's deepest register; (2) diminuendo; (3) ritardando (not explicit in the score; see the later discussion of tempo); (4) textural resimplifications from measure 28; (5) the voice's return to more declamatory content, quasi-recitando, from measure 29; (6) relative tonal stability (with reference to D̲ and the protracted D:I as a major seventh chord), measures 28–36;[19] and (7) relevant factors of motivic variation (from directionally opposed statements in measures 24–25, to a slowing extension in measures 25–27, to spaced reminiscent entries at fixed pitch-class levels and in largely homodirectional doublings); with rhythmic smoothing into regular sixteenth-note values, the climactic *cri* motive becomes the resigned setting for *le roulis sourd.*

Debussy's interpretation of *(le) cri* as a focus for interim climactic development is indeed apt, and this development is expressed in all the controlled element-structures detailed above, as a vehicle of poignant though not melodramatic reference. In the recession to cadence (a basis for renewed development), the lyric, restrained (dolcissimo) setting of *vire* is notable: it is not a churning, but rather an idle shifting of water under the surface of which the mute pebbles roll, their silent movement marking for stanza 2 the final reference to a central image reinterpreted variously by Verlaine.

Principal events of textural structuring, measures 22–27

Perhaps no musical element is more susceptible to purposive control in performance than that of texture, and consideration of its role in musical development and poetic realization in stanza 2 can be a further basis for interpretive approaches.

Measures 22–23 are the first point of significant motivic divergence between piano and voice, this in itself an activating factor (ex. 5.29). Although from measure 24 the two are allied in motivic content, the factors of directional

opposition (exceptional for the context) and dissonance are intensifying textural properties (ex. 5.29, measure 24). The opposed directions of surface
motion are moreover reflected in a comparable, midlevel counteraction in
measures 22–24 (piano descending, voice ascending).

Ex. 5.29

A look at the score reveals that functional contradirectional relation (for
which a tentative precedent was set in measures 7–8) pertains also to measures
25–27, the voice descending and the piano ascending through motivic extension (ex. 5.30). In these measures, recessive and progressive tendencies overlap:
diminuendo in both instruments, and the voice's descent against the piano's rise
in pitch and sustained, intense dissonance content (ex. 5.30), to be resolved in
relative pitch-class agreement in the following, D-oriented segment. In the
illustration, the circled areas are those of unusual textural compression, which
is itself a factor of intensity in the pivotal balance.

Ex. 5.30

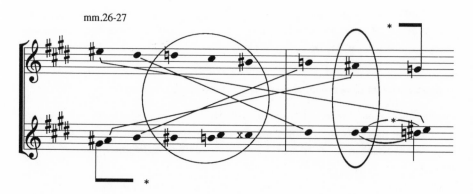

Chromatic successions toward F-sharp of the forthcoming D-rooted harmony.

Texture also has a role in the recessive tendency toward cadential resolution, already manifest in measures 25–27. The following textural conditions comple-ment processes of tonal resolution and relative harmonic simplicity: (1) motivic content concentrated in the piano, except where doubling occurs; (2) release of the dense compressions of measures 26–27, marked in ex. 5.30; (3) without the aforementioned crowding, occupancy by piano and voice of, generally, the same registral space, in contrast with the climactic phase in the preceding development;[20] (4) largely literal doublings at measures 33–34, where there is however a superficial residual implication of mobility in the contradirectional motions of the second half of each bar; and (5) the ultimately simple outcome at measure 34 and, concurrent with a modest restoration of activity, measure 35.

Details of performance in stanza 2

With its progressive developments in text and music, the second stanza is clearly climactic in relation to the first, while tentatively so in relation to the third, notably in tempo and dynamic intensity but also in a number of vital comple-mentary actions that have been identified. Its atmosphere of development is intimated at the outset. With these general presuppositions, one can suggest a number of vital interpretive details in stanza 2 that follow from textual and musical analysis:

1. The reservedly mosso motivic entry at measure 18 must convey a necessary sense of importance as initiating forthcoming development and as the piano's last statement—no longer *langoureuse,* yet *caressant* and molded dynamically as before.

2. The piano chord at measure 20—an interim, ambivalent tonic—is pianissimo *ma deciso,* setting off the voice's new phrase *(frêle et frais).* The piano of measures 20–21 yields to the voice and is thus diminuendo; its momentary withdrawal is also a factor in preparing the development which follows.

3. A slight comma between measures 21 and 22 frames the piano's motivic entries and the structure's emerging textural diversification (ex. 5.4c). It also denotes a new phrase and new phase in development and is a comment on *(les) petites voix: gazouille, susurre, ressemble au cri.*

4. The motivic statements of both parts are shaped dynamically in a context of progressive animato and crescendo. If the expressive shape is to be realized, the performers must be aware of such functional elements as registral opposition, tonal movements, implicit metric variance in the voice (ex. 5.28), motivic concentration and interactions (ex. 5.29), and other factors in a gradual process.

5. There is a felt tension in motivic directional oppositions between the instruments at the climactic measures 24–25 (exx. 5.4*c*, 5.29), and a determined but not exaggerated sonorous solidity in the C-sharp of measure 24, the significance of which is adumbrated earlier (exx. 5.18*a*, *b*).

6. The voice's dynamic inflection is crescendo and diminuendo—an aspect of (*le*) *cri*—during its g-sharp$_2$; the crescendo is slightly reduced the second time as the peak is passed (unless a case is to be made for measure 25 as the peak of development).

7. Everything in the progression from measure 20 to measure 25, especially a guiding tempo, is scaled in a context of comprehended poetic and musical elements; here as always the performers should be keenly aware of the difference between unmotivated tempo and a sense of urgency induced by musical and poetic meaning.

8. Measures 26–27 are a distinct turning, a point of the most difficult, fragile balance in which musical and textual recession predominates. Both parts are diminuendo, the piano especially because of its ascent crossing the voice melody.

9. The expressive dissonances must be impeccably clear (B̲ + B̲-sharp, B̲ + A̲-sharp, finally G̲ + G̲-sharp); they are reflectively *agitée* in the recessive context.

10. The especially vital last sixteenth-note of measure 27, emphasized earlier as a point of tonal redirection (ex. 5.19), is exposed in part by slight punctuation following measure 27 (exx. 5.4*c*, *d*).

11. The piano's syncopations in measure 27 recall and restore the prevalent accompanimental figure, and serve to arrest tempo (unspecified in the score). The tempo is distributed to allow breathing space for the descending voice (*expire*), and its pace is adjusted toward deliberate articulation of the measure's crucial final harmony (ex. 5.4*c*).

12. The D̲-sharp of measure 27 poses a very particular problem: sustained by the finger through the harmonic shift and coinciding with the D̲-natural of the final sixteenth-note (ex. 5.31), it blurs this critical, D̲-oriented harmony, which is clarified in the D:V that follows at measure 28. Here too, dissonance is appropriate to the textual image (*l'herbe agitée*).

13. The motivic recollections following measure 28 include the two-note fragment in measures 29 and 31 (the latter marking a diatonic descent toward D̲). These are typically molded in foreground diminuendo within an overreaching decline spanning this second segment of stanza 2. The motives are rendered dolcissimo, paler reflections of preceding intense statements, in an atmosphere distinctly calmato and calmando (for example, measure 30 with respect to 28, 31 as compared with 29; ex. 5.4*d*).

Ex. 5.31

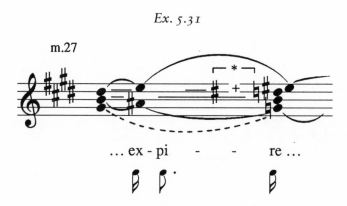

m.27

... ex - pi   -   -   re ...

__D__-sharp and __D__-natural sounding together in the same register.

14. The performers should be aware of settled tonal content in the final bars, marked by a restored tempo secondo that is perhaps gradually un pochissimo meno at measure 33. A clue is the slow turning from the voice's focal f-sharp$_1$ and back to it (*l'eau qui vire*), which takes place in an atmosphere of interim resolution.

15. There are some actions of residual intensity even at the penultimate phase of cadential recession (ex. 5.4*d*): for example, the most cautious foreground crescendo in the piano's late ascents against the voice's descents (measure 32 and conceivably but to a lesser degree at measure 33); and steady articulations in the same bars (misurato, calmato) of the sixteenth-notes and rich plagal harmonic elaborations.

Three problems of prosody in stanza 2

One might speak of an implicit crescendo of dramatic connotation in the poetic succession *frêle, frais, gazouille, susurre, ressemble au cri,* and the final series of sibilants may be interpreted as a factor in its realization. Curiously, the crucial word *cri* is in Debussy's setting neglected even in relation to the preceding word (an elided preposition and article) and the adjective *doux: cri* occurs at the last sixteenth of measure 25, within descent and at the extreme of a foreground diminuendo. A slight hesitation appears indicated, un poco tenuto, in exposure of this noun and image; indeed, such an intervention can also be a discreet factor in arresting the developed animato (see ex. 5.32).

A second problematic case that is comparable is the setting of *l'herbe,* perhaps less critical yet easily garbled in the singing. Here too a carefully moderated emphasis—probably just the time it takes fully to enunciate the word—can counterbalance its rhythmic subordination and prove functional as before in

Ex. 5.32

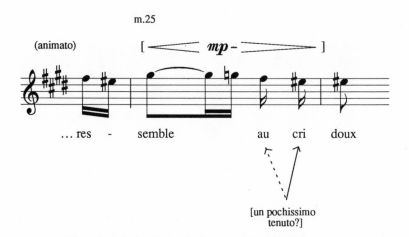

arresting tempo.[21] Of course, after each such slight intervention the tempo is resumed within the scaled recession of elements detailed earlier.

A third anomaly is in the setting of *le roulis sourd*, where the metric placement of the article at the head of the motive is problematic and must be understated. The singer aims toward the important image *sourd* and gives preference in measure 32 to the noun *roulis* (ex. 5.33).

Ex. 5.33

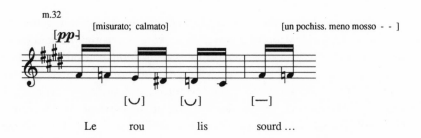

The entry into stanza 3

Example 5.5 reveals that related turning points in the poem's outer stanzas correspond in Debussy's setting in important respects of pitch, intervallic content, and melodic contour. That is, the first poetic reference to the sound (initially bird songs) that is the central image for stanza 2—*le chœur,* and its immediate approaches—is distinctly related in musical setting to stanza 3's decisive *C'est la nôtre,* and its direct approach. Thus two critical poetic junctures are clearly related in musical setting and overreach the song's interior; it is at these junctures that the voices are first sensed, and at which they are finally accorded climactic personal significance.

Measures 34–35, a momentary void with regard to motivic content, effect one of only three purely triadic resolutions while accompanimental syncopations, prevalent in stanza 3, sustain a modest ongoing momentum enhanced in the registral ascent at measure 35 (even as texture is thinned).

Measure 36 warrants particular attention in performance: it is the site of renewed mobility following tentative tonal and other resolutions late in stanza 2. The vital dissonance, motivic resumption, and marked dynamic intensity of measure 36 are crucial, as is the stressed $\underline{C}$ in a pitch-class "descent" linking the preceding $\underline{D}$ to the forthcoming structural $\underline{B}$ (E: 5).[22] The derivative descending-step motive reintroduced in measure 36 becomes a virtual ostinato in stanza 3; and its registral exposure assures its projection. Yet cautious stress on the dissonant higher note, however subordinate to the left-hand $\underline{C}$ in dynamic intensity, is appropriate and characteristic, and its off-beat entry, dissonance, and status of ultimate motivic fragmentation contribute to its propulsive effect (ex. 5.4*e*).[23] Everything indicates a tempo modestly yet deliberately moved at measure 36, as noted in ex. 5.4*e*.

Elements of progression, measures 40–45

My analysis of Verlaine's poem points to the intensely personal references of the third stanza as an objective of comprehensive development, and to the analogous content of stanza 2 as an interim stage. That Debussy's realization accords with this reading of the poem may be substantiated in review of a number of intensifying elements in his approach to the core of stanza 3:

1. significant textural interactions and interchanges, and a renewed motivic concentration, traced below (ex. 5.38);
2. the acceleration of tempo, *poco a poco animato;*
3. the piano's *sforzato* articulations (within a subdued dynamic state) at measures 36, 37, 38, and 39, prefacing the forthcoming, motivating crescendo;
4. the crescendo, *poco a poco,* from *piano* and *pianissimo* to *mezzo forte* and (presumably) *forte* (measures 44–45), an extreme of dynamic intensity for the structure as a whole;

5. within an essential basis of V-I underlying the process of progressive development (ex. 5.17a), a marked tonal severance in auxiliary chromatic harmony (ex. 5.17b): the dominant seventh chord yields to a characteristic major ninth chord on G̲, which yields in turn to a tritone-related further auxiliary linked in three common pitch classes (ex. 5.34);

Ex. 5.34

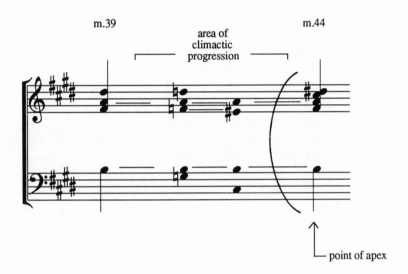

6. the dramatic, expansive reassertion of tonal functionality at measure 44, in a potent, final occurrence of E:V allied with the restored primary motive: *la mienne, . . . la tienne*;
7. ascent of the voice melody through notes of the G̲-based auxiliary harmony (ex. 5.35);

Ex. 5.35

8. the achievement by the ascent noted above of an apogee of pitch for the entire voice melody, with stanza 3 embodying both its registral extremes (ex. 5.36);

Ex. 5.36

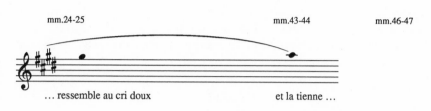

9. an impetuous, quasi-recitando setting of text (measures 41–43), in an exceptional concentration of off-beat entries and breathless, short utterances, especially at the climactic *dis, et la tienne*;
10. renewed accompanimental syncopations in measures 39–43, contributing to progressive development;
11. metrically dissonant second-beat accents in the voice melody (measures 40, 41, 43; ex. 5.37), out of synchronization with harmonic and bass rhythms, and an acceleration toward measure 42 (the indicated 2-unit), followed by the holding effect of longer 4-units and 5-units at the melodic apex, where a complementary slight broadening brings an end to the tempo animato.

Ex. 5.37

Processes of textural development, measures 36–45

In addition to the elements functioning in the structural progression as summarized above, texture must be regarded against the perspective of relatively uncomplicated conditions in measures 37–39, where tentative motivic entries, the sforzato stresses, and continued (but lessened) accompanimental syncopation suggest forthcoming, renewed development.

Example 5.38 portrays interacting motives and motivic derivatives, often entering in dissonance, along a line of increased frequency and, notably in measures 41–43, increased overlapping, or stretto.

Ex. 5.38

(area of most intense interaction and directional opposition)

A striking textural event at the apex of development is the determined opposition of piano and voice (measures 44–45), where the piano's statement is a contradirectional imitation of the voice's expansive presentation of the song's initiating, generative motive. The two dramatically interacting lines also effect a potent diatonic and chromatic arpeggiation of the final, structural E:V.

The musical-poetic resolution

The poem's resolution is a concluding reference to the languorous, amorous state evoked at its outset (*ce tiède soir*). Identifiable musical elements convey a concordant sense of recession after the song's late climactic progression. These elements are as follows:

1. a quick descent, and consequent registral agreement of the two instruments;
2. the retardation of tempo, unspecified but clearly occurring in advance of the voice's final cadence;
3. the morendo and molto ritardando tendencies of the piano's last bars;
4. gradual diminuendo;

5. a consonant relation between piano and voice (measures 46–48), confirmed in the perfect agreement of pitch-class content;

6. against the precedent of its just-concluded dramatic sweep, the voice's quasi-recitando articulations (*murmuré*; compare measures 17–18) within greatly simplified melodic content;

7. a tonic harmony, albeit impure, at measures 46–47, and at measure 48 the voice's first $\underline{E}$ in stanza 3 and the first metrically prominent $\underline{E}$ anywhere;

8. the encircling, tentative pitches of the voice's two preceding principal cadences (measure 18, d-sharp$_1$; measure 34, f-sharp$_1$) consummated in the voice's arrival at e_1, measure 48 (ex. 5.22);

9. the elaboration of E:I, left mainly to the piano's codetta, measures 48–52;

10. on components of the elaborated tonic, subdued reminiscences of the chief motives of stanza 3 (measures 48–49) and stanza 2 (measures 46–47);

11. corresponding to the musical reminiscences, textual references of recalled scene and image: *ce tiède soir* (stanza 1), and *l'humble antienne* (stanzas 2 and 3).

Details of performance in stanza 3

Interpretation of Debussy's moving, eloquent setting presupposes a keen understanding of form, structural process, and myriad details of intimately allied poetic imagery and particulars of musical content. In stanza 3, where the gradual inwardness of poetic reference is associated with a mounting exuberance of musical setting, a particular challenge is the very late crest of development, leaving only the voice's five measures and the piano's nine for resolution to a condition of recaptured tranquility. Insights into all coactive elements and problematic circumstances must condition both general approaches and fine points of nuance, examples of which follow.

Allowing a slightly hesitant, deliberate articulation in measure 33 in recognition of cadence and poetic meaning, measure 34 requires renewed thrust over a solid but pianissimo $\underline{D}$. The pure triad of interim arrival is richly sustained by the pedal through measure 34. The restored accompanimental syncopation and notated marcato articulations are motivating elements, yet the active sense of resumed tempo (mosso) is a further imperative (see exx. 5.4*d, e*).

The simplification of texture and thinning of sonority at measures 34–35 are both cadential and a preparation for events to follow. In particular, the registral locus of the vital sforzato c_1 of measure 36 is opened in measure 35. Diminuendo, suggested earlier for measure 35, complements textural simplification, whereas registral ascent and continued syncopations are motivating factors.

With the abrupt, animating, sforzato dissonance of measure 36, a corresponding thrust of tempo (un pochissimo più mosso; ex. 5.4e) functions appropriately against a partial withdrawal of accompanimental syncopations (measures 36–39), to be reset at measure 40. The piano's diminuendo inflections (measures 36, 38) accord with established, characteristic motivic content, and expose the energizing appoggiatura dissonances. The two-note motivic derivative, to be prevalent in stanza 3, is established at measure 36 in an exposed register, where its off-beat entry is a further factor of thrust. The motive will undergo changes of intensity according to prevailing tendencies of midlevel crescendo and diminuendo.

Debussy's articulative stresses on the pitch classes C and F-sharp in measures 36–39 are a striking detail (ex. 5.39): they bear an explicit relation to the forthcoming, elaborative G-based harmony, linearize the dissonant component of the established D-rooted neighbor to E:V, and compromise the restored, understated E:V of measures 37 and 39 in deference to its expansive, cadential occurrence later. The pianist must understand that the sforzato articulation applies to these notes in particular, in (with measures 24–25) one of the structure's two most active rhythms of dynamic inflection, and in a context of piano and pianissimo.

Ex. 5.39

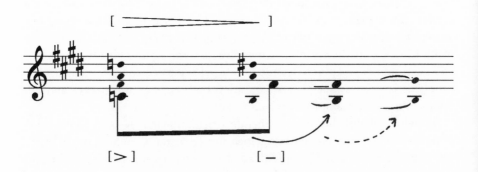

Notwithstanding these tentatively animating tendencies, measures 37–39 have an essential implication of preparatory neutrality, and are approached with a sense of reserve and expectancy. The singer's first phrase (*cette âme, cette plainte*) resets the central image as a further point of departure, articulating three times the rhythmic unit of an eighth-note and four sixteenths against pitch-class doublings of the piano that linearize the dominant, all in a context of restraint.

As is so often the case in the song, consideration must be given to the treatment of material immediately repeated—in measures 36–37 and 38–39. The principle of modest change in the repetition again applies. In recognition of these four bars as prefatory to active progression, the second occurrence in each case may well be dynamically inferior, complementing the voice melody's descent (*dormante*) and the piano's diminuendo and descent, where accompanimental figuration may easily impede the voice in a vulnerable register (measure 39).

Example 5.4e calls for a slight punctuation following measure 39: this will mark the descent in the bass's symmetrical sequence, facilitate and set off the strikingly deviant, chromatic harmonic change, establish an impression of poise before the animato, and announce a critical turn in the poetry.

In the measures that follow, the interpretive gauging of tempo is exceedingly problematic: the extent of the animato and the manner of restoring stability in a markedly brief time. This is a topic of special focus later. As for the crescendo to measures 44–45, it may be assumed that for both instruments it surpasses that of stanza 2, and is staged from pianissimo (in the piano part) and something between piano and pianissimo (in the voice) at measure 40, a point of latent intensity, through mezzo piano at measure 42, to a culminating mezzo forte and forte, as indicated in ex. 5.4f. The voice's final crescendo concurs with its pitch apex (*la tienne*), supported by the crescendo of the piano's left-hand part. During this development, the piano's reiterated two-note motives maintain their accustomed dynamic shape, but their stressed, initiating impulse advances in intensity with the prevailing crescendo; especially urgent is that of measure 43, where octave doubling is abandoned to clear the voice's register. Example 5.38 drew attention to a number of motivic imitations to be projected clearly in this segment, some of which (for example, the piano's left-hand part of measure 41 in relation to the voice's corresponding thirds in measures 40–41) are easily neglected in denial of an intrinsic textural vitality.

Some further caveats of interpretation pertain to the voice's critical, breathless, short utterances during the climactic progression. The triplets at measures 41 and 43 mark the voice's most independent rhythmic assertions anywhere, and are to be brought out deliberately and precisely; the composer's articulation signs in measure 41 appear directed to this end of rhythmic and textual clarity, where the first C-sharp (*n'est-ce pas?*) is vulnerable to loss. And the off-beat sixteenth-note at the end of measure 42 (*dis*) does much to motivate and propel. Beyond the ideal accuracy of rhythm and intonation, the singer's enunciations through these affecting words and melodic fragments must of course convey a sense of drive, continuity, and spontaneity toward the peak of progression at measures 43–44.

Of all the poetic and musical properties of special import in measures 44–45, the primary harmonic function, significant for the whole structure, warrants a deliberate expansiveness of interpretive approach: a held tempo (allargando in measure 43); a sonorous octave B̲ in the piano, left hand; a crescendo to forte in the piano's ascent;[24] the piano's culminating leap, emphasized at arrival, rushed and impetuous (measure 45—presumably this explains Debussy's notational irregularity);[25] and in the latter part of measure 45, the voice un poco deliberato, an intervention justified on grounds of textual clarity, imperative motivic statement, and further holding of tempo after the climactic peak (see ex. 5.4f). Moreover, stretching the time of measure 45's last three sixteenth-notes facilitates the voice's extreme diminuendo (mezzo forte to pianissimo, murmuré), which must be effected largely in this brief time.

A breath before the second beat of measure 44 is appropriate to the text (in the voice, not in the piano, where the motivic statement demands legato continuity), can be used as a dramatic gesture, and sets off the descending motive from g-sharp$_2$, vividly and precisely recalling its initial occurrence in measures 1–3.

However tempo is broadened after measure 43, its animato drive will inevitably spill into measure 46, which is thus moved somewhat more than its immediate repetition. A sense of onward motion is also appropriate at measures 46–47 to the tentativeness of inconclusive tonic arrival, which nevertheless requires deliberate enunciation in the piano, set off by a brief rest at the end of measure 45. At the same time, the voice's measured articulations, quasi-recitando, serve to control the tempo, as do the piano's recollective motivic statements, now passive (in contrast with their origin in stanza 2) and legatissimo, with measure 47 softer and slower than measure 46 in the context of cadential recession.

The voice's arrival on the tonic degree, measure 48, must be conceived in performance as inconclusive although tonally significant, an interim point in the phased series of cadential events, yielding to the piano's codetta. Here are the singer's final utterances, in a context of resignation against the perspective of fulsome, late, climactic intensity. The last notes, more declamatory than sung, have full rhythmic value in a slowing tempo, as the piano moves on with decisively conclusive materials. In pitch doublings, the piano defers to the voice, and to the imperative of poetic enunciation: l'humble antienne, ce tiède soir.

Examples 5.4f, g reflect all of the above, indicating a restored tempo primo at measure 48 (even slightly hesitant), and pointing to a number of details of interpretation in the last five bars. The sense of movement into measure 48 is in part a basis for concluding, confirming interpretive restoration of the character of the beginning (langoureuse, caressant), in keeping with the poem's final,

reflective image. The tempo is slowed beyond the original *lent,* and the diminuendo governing the piano's passive, reminiscent motives is brought to a condition of near inaudibility, as suggested in ex. 5.4g. To this end, the pianist can use
the syncopations as halting (they have elsewhere had impulsive effect), and can
bring out the descent of the richly doubled bass toward the ultimate, warmly
sonorous triadic consonance and functionally evened rhythms of measure 50.

Of the pure triad, uncontested in the last three bars, it is interesting to note
that E:I has in the course of the structure occurred in three forms (ex. 5.40),
which strongly suggest departure, development, and resolution. And of the four
occurrences illustrated in ex. 5.40, the first is preliminary, the two interior
chords active, and the fourth ultimately conclusive; this in itself tells much
about their interrelations and their fitting treatment in interpretation.

Ex. 5.40

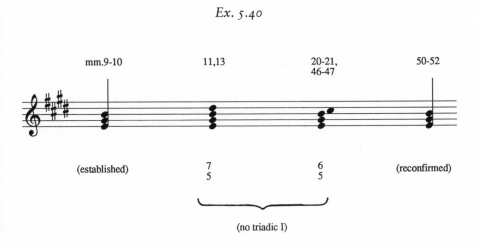

Problems and Indicators of Tempo

As a first step, one may inquire into factors that suggest a fundamental metronomic perspective, as well as changes in tempo as the structure unfolds. Some of
these point toward restraint:

1. the directions *lent et caressant* and *rêveusement,* and such poetic images
   as *langoureuse, la fatigue, l'eau qui vire* (especially as set), *le roulis
   sourd, cette plainte dormante, ce tiède soir;*
2. notated increases in tempo at measures 11, 22, and 40, requiring a stable basis for development;
3. a prevalent sixteenth-note attack rate, at times marcato in both instruments, signifying deliberate, unhurried articulations;

4. interior textural concentrations of motivic activity, demanding reasonable temporal latitude for the ideal clarity of interacting voices;
5. especially in animato segments, text setting requiring time for enunciation, predominantly at the rate of a syllable to each sixteenth-note, and critically at measures 25–26;
6. prevalent foreground accompanimental syncopation requiring a stable, referential basic pulse.[26]

One can assemble a comparable list of factors arguing against a tempo that is too slow, or pointing toward a tempo mosso at certain points:

1. segments in the song governed by relevant images in a poetic structure of gradually emergent vitality, where movement is indicated: *les frissons, (les) brises, frêle et frais, gazouille et susurre, ressemble au cri, l'herbe agitée,* and the fervent *la nôtre, la mienne, la tienne* of stanza 3;
2. in the musical structure, a beginning harmonic unit of dominant ninth chord over six measures without surface change, and over eight measures almost without change;
3. frequent two-measure harmonic units;
4. rare harmonic change within the measure (except, as in measures 7–8 and 46–47, superficial auxiliary harmonic change on the measure's third beat);
5. text setting admitting a faster tempo in the second animato progression than in the first;
6. the final molto ritardando, which requires a basic point of departure not exaggeratedly slow.

A *fundamental perspective*

The initial qualities of inertia, a palpable (and rapturous) drowsiness, have been documented in poetic and musical elements: the initiating motive's yawning implication, suggestive in its metaphoric descent and harmonic immobility. One might argue that it is virtually impossible to render it too slowly; yet continuity can be impaired by a tempo that is too slow, and the motivic statement must hang together as a unit, with each of the first two vocal phrases manageable in one breath.

Thus a slow tempo must be gauged that effects an ideal balance of leisurely ease with a grasp of motivic wholeness and a sense of progress and continuity. It must also be a tempo from which one can both accelerate (at three critical stages) and make a final, extreme slackening (at measures 48–52). One can identify tempi that are ponderously slow (say, $\flat$ = 42) and others so fast that the pace of textual enunciation at such points as measure 11 and measure 22 would be trivializing (say, $\flat$ = 66). A judicious determination might be a basic, initiating pulse at $\flat$ = 46 or 50, conceived flexibly (see ex. 5.4*a*).

The tempo structure as an aspect of rhythm

Like any coherent structure in which tempo undergoes functional modulations (such as that of the Berg), Debussy's music articulates within the singular element of tempo a vital, cogently apprehensible shape and continuity. Here there is a broad progression through measure 42 (with giving and taking inflections at the foreground within this overreaching tendency), followed by a phased slowing that achieves in a very short time a state of lassitude surpassing that of the beginning.

As in the Berg, the property of broadly advancing, then receding, tempo is a critical dimension of rhythmic articulation, exactly paralleling the poetic structure as interpreted in the analysis. Given a systematically reasoned initiating pace, it offers a conceptual framework for calibrating relations among basic tempo, decisive changes (as at measure 11), measured advances and withdrawals (as in the two animato developments), and subtle inflections of the absolute surface, as suggested in ex. 5.4 in a number of instances. The concept of an inclusive tempo contour thus affords a guiding perspective for functional changes in the course of the piece, as does any analytically determined sense of whole.

Some representative details of decision about tempo

The last three sixteenth-notes of measure 10 may for several reasons be rendered with slight hesitation (ex. 5.4*a*): because they are a poised anacrustic preparation of vital textual and musical changes, because they delineate the motivic derivative to be prominent in stanza 2 (ex. 5.13), and perhaps to savor the first pure tonic triad (and the last until measure 50). Another example of tempo modulation conceivable in the song's first segment is in measure 7 (ex. 5.4*a*), where an impatient, slightly pressando execution of the piano's sixteenths adds to a moderate, preliminary expressive focus, complementing the surface crescendo, projecting the word *amoureuse,* and effecting a trace of activity in the context of slow tempo and relative immobility of structural content.

Measure 11 is critical as the musical and poetic awakening from the state denoted by Debussy's *rêveusement.* Yet the tempo mosso must be conceived as to its place in a gradual progression overall, and in recognition of the singer's deliberate enunciation of text. Further, the inception of accompanimental syncopation is itself motivating, and the new metronomic tempo is to be a basis for the accelerative events of stanza 2 (see ex. 5.4*b*).

Critical elements noted in connection with ex. 5.26 may well imply correlative, minute inflections of tempo: a slight hesitation before the striking harmonic change and emphatic entry of the voice at measure 15 (drawing attention to it); and in measure 15, in keeping with the turning in poetic imagery and locally culminating ascent (with crescendo) in the voice melody, a careful pressing of tempo toward measure 16.

The tempo ritardando of measure 17 (ex. 5.4b), judged in light of textual significance and prosodic requirements of declamation (le chœur des petites voix), is a foreground process likely initiated in the tempo of measure 16. Late, slight hesitation on the second syllable of petites serves the ritardando inflection, and is a factor in exposing the image voix as well as the chromatic, cadential restoration of E:V.

I have dwelled at length on vital processive changes in measures 22–29, and of all cofunctioning elements here tempo is probably the most decisive and the most readily appreciable. There are important reasons to assume that the tempo of measure 11 is resumed at measure 18: it is unlikely that the broadly advancing tempo structure described above will here be reversed, and the tempo mosso at measure 20 must be prepared (it is signaled by the foreground rhythms—including the voice's impulsive, off-beat entry, and by the dissonant tonic and the text; it is confirmed in the subsequent lyric sweep).

In general, the gradual phasing of the animato is controlled by the rhythm of harmonic change (♩ ♪) in measures 22–23, and the animato advances to the point of the voice's melodic apex, where the requirements of clear enunciation in Debussy's problematic setting (ex. 5.32) contribute to arresting the developed tempo. Complementary actions are the motive's extension, the diminuendo, melodic descent, and dense chromaticism (which by its very nature limits tempo). The element of pronounced, complementary diminuendo especially supports the controlled slowing of tempo; indeed, it in itself conveys an illusion of slowing.

The imperative ritardando of measures 26–28, which is not notated, must in performance seem natural, inevitable, almost imperceptibly an element of recession. It is oriented presumably toward a restored tempo secondo, that of measures 11 and 20, again in recognition of the overall rhythmic implication in a structure shaped by tempo changes. The change of tempo is wrought in a brief time and requires extreme control, not least in the critical articulations of measure 27; there the retardative rhythms of both instruments can function complementarily in the tempo change.

The ritardando process may well extend through measure 28, achieving a stability that coincides with tonal and harmonic arrival at measure 29. Thus, the recalled cri motive of measure 28 still reflects the preceding climactic drive, and is in its tonal implication a pivot preparing the forthcoming, calmato events conditioned especially by elements of text, tonality, and register (see ex. 5.4d).

A prudent, further holding of tempo at the approach to measure 34 (exx. 5.4d, 5.33) has been discussed in connection with cadence, texture, text, and other factors, as has the vital necessity of renewal at measure 34 by way of resumed accompanimental syncopation through the interim, triadic resolution, and the slight thrust of tempo at measure 36, which in so many ways signals further development (ex. 5.4e).

In light of overall tempo structure and poetic contour, the animato of stanza 3 surpasses that of stanza 2, a circumstance which tells the performers something crucial about both progressions. Paradoxically, accompanimental rhythms again both impel and restrain, whereas the voice's melody, of simple intervals and short utterances, facilitates the build-up of tempo.

The arrival at an apex of pitch in the voice melody (now at a_2, also the voice's longest note), is both an aim of progression and a pivot for reversing the tendency of acceleration, as is the case in stanza 2. Here allargando and crescendo interventions intensify the goal of climactic drive (exx. 5.4e, f), and set a basis for the gradual restabilization of tempo through melodic descent and extreme diminuendo in the next four bars (poco a poco meno mosso al tempo primo), again a severe redirection to be achieved convincingly over a very short time. This adjustment at measures 43–44 also emphasizes the structural E:V, and enhances the voice's expansive, recapitulative presentation of the primary motive.

The ensuing ritardando change (ex. 5.4f) is complemented by cited textural simplifications (albeit in a context of bigger sonorities), the abandonment of accompanimental syncopations, the piano's absence in most of measure 45, and deliberate enunciation of the text leading into measure 46 (dont s'exhale l'humble antienne—a final reference to the poem's central image).

The slowing can logically continue through measures 46–47, where tentative harmonic arrival occurs as the voice melody approaches, in its deepest register, its final resolution. The setting of text, returning to the declamatory articulations of slightly détaché individual impulses, is instrumental in the phased ritardando. The harmonic rhythm (♩ ♪) of these bars functions similarly under the passively recalled cri motive sounded within a prevalently recessive tendency requiring a slowing tempo.

Notwithstanding the lack of notational specification measure 48 is presumably the point of tempo primo, moving into the final codetta by way of a restored, slowing accompanimental syncopation.[27] The piano's right-hand motivic reminiscences are clearly to be conveyed as dim echoes of past events, the second slower than the first in the context of a final tempo molto ritardando.

The final five-bar slowing is part of the phased process that begins in measure 43, and applies through measures 51–52. The poised, evened attack rhythms of the triadic E:I of measure 50 express resolution in all intrinsic elements. In this context, the surface motions of measures 48–49 are passive gestures—the slightest opposition to subsiding currents, merely suggesting retrospectively the materials of past, interior developments. The final tempo is of course even slower than that of the languorous beginning, and no sensitive performer will fail to regard measure 52 as a part of the conclusive process, and its eighth-rests as a commensurately elongated interval of silence through which the structure dissolves. Many of these suggestions of interpretive detail are illustrated in ex. 5.48.

Chapter Six

POINTS OF SUMMATION

Whatever conceptual images it seeks to represent, truly illuminating musical performance is richly informed by analysis, the indispensable, pragmatic basis for resolving problematic decisions of interpretation. Searching, genuinely comprehensive analysis leads to a shaping, conditioning concept that is distilled from many kinds of inquiry into all elements of structure, and that concerns the ways in which structural and expressive elements articulate continuities to be elucidated and rendered convincingly in performance. Most decisions regarding performance and most realms of interpretive decision making involve analysis in the perspectives of a particular composition rather than on any basis of abstracted common principles.

A derived conceptual image motivating interpretation is often the ultimate convergence of initially divergent constructs—once they have been considered, reflected on, reconsidered, weighed against the implications of cofunctioning compositional elements, and finally absorbed through conscious study to a level of guiding, postcognitive, seemingly intuitive impulse. The means of proceeding from conceptualization to realization in performance are those of doing and those of not doing: that is, bringing out certain elements (after seeking in arduous rehearsal the precariously measured degree of intervention that is neither too little nor too great), and on the other hand exercising care to avoid obscuring or distorting important, integral elements.

Regarding most compositions, the sensitive musician acknowledges a necessary diversity of reasonable and enlightening views, recognizing that varying interpretive approaches or even major reconsiderations borne of analytical review will often obtain from one performance to another: the interpreter may adopt one conceived path through the piece today, another as the result of subsequent reflections and in differing circumstances.

The purely spontaneous, unknowing and unquestioned impulse is not enough to inspire convincing performance, and surely not enough to resolve the uncertainties with which the performer is so often faced. Although the interpreter's impulsive response to the score can fortuitously hit on convincing approaches through a developed (if often unreasoned) sense of appropriateness, the purely intuitive is unlikely to afford a necessary grasp of—or of place in— the comprehended whole. In any event intuition is inadequate to solving dilemmas or providing justification that can be articulated.

There is also risk in an analysis that penetrates deeply and expansively, then stops short of deliberate discrimination, leaving the performer's consciousness burdened with conflicting images. This is what I mean when I suggest that the analysis that ultimately guides performance is distilled: it is a selective determination among inferred lines of structure that are a basis for the reasoned, reasonable unity to which analytical inquiry ideally leads, and which in turn is expressed in illumined, illuminating performance.

The twelve issues and questions posed in this book's second chapter have, with the exception of the problem of disputed readings of the notes, arisen again in the major analyses undertaken in chapters 3, 4, and 5. As for ambiguities of notation, it must be concluded that conflicts of the sort cited in exx. 2.1 and 2.2 probably often resist final settlement, whatever documentary evidence can be convincingly adduced. This is true especially because analysis is itself largely an interpretation of structural and expressive functions. But it is in any event obvious that no performer can reach a persuasive judgment in such cases with only inarticulate preference: any choice must be constructively substantiated.

With respect to the interpretive realization of motivic content, all three major examples demonstrate that some motives and motivic occurrences are self-evidently explicit, requiring no intervention, while others have a relatively covert presence that demands interpretive attention, or at least an avoidance of contradictory intrusions. And at times a motivic statement is considered to be surpassed by some element of superior import and is thus subordinated to it. These are questions of structure that performers commonly heed, but it is by no means universally recognized that any decision to bring out a motive (or to leave it alone on the ground that it is explicit and well established) demands a clear cognizance of its every manifestation, of the degree of its basis in precedent occurrences, and of the place of each occurrence in a comprehended total context. I have also suggested that the performer must be conscious of unifying recurrences apart from those of a motive in its usual sense: particular sonorities and other kinds of groupings may have quasi-motivic significance. Their prevalence often suggests understatement in accord with subsidiary status or, on the contrary, some marked attention to formulations of surface rhythm, harmony, or figural pattern that are exceptions to a piece's normative content or that function critically in a discerned, vital structural tendency.

Dynamic intensity and inflection are a constant concern in interpretation, especially in more fluctuant later styles, but also in literatures in which specific notational indications and nuances of the foreground are not given or are stipulated minimally. These studies have shown how inflectional modulations of calculated dynamic intensity relate to the coincident processes of other elements, at times supportively (usually so, with respect to a prevalent tendency), at other times in counteraction (as when harmonic content is relatively immobile and action is rather of dynamic intensities and other elements). The analysis of the processive conditions of coactive elements is an imperative basis for deciding whether to make a corroborative or counteractive dynamic inflection, and certainly for considering its appropriateness, precise placement, and extent, especially where no such intervention is indicated. Analysis instructs the performer to ask at every turn in preparing a performance: In the light of structural context, why am I doing what I am doing?

Voice-leading connections must be inferred and evaluated before the performer can consider which might, or will, be enforced. And will they be made across a formal division? Across registral space? Across a middleground segment? This problem has been much in evidence in the foregoing studies; it is particularly acute where an overt effort of voice-leading connection might impair or distract from some other element of primary structural consequence.

Factors of function and place in the formal narrative and in formal process can often be a basis for decision about attitude and detail in interpretation. Does the material occur in a context of introduction? Of closure? Of fluctuant transition? In a working out of materials otherwise exposed? In a climactic development? In reexposition, perhaps in a new guise, and in an environment of relative stability? The analysis of prevailing formal content and process is never irrelevant to performance, and will often suggest a perspective in which particular interpretive approaches, even those of radical expressive impact, such as phased or precipitate interventions of tempo and dynamic intensity, can be weighed. Equally, the path to resolving a dilemma concerning a problematic passage often lies in assessment of the role and position of the passage in the formal scheme.

A fundamental, primary, often perplexing problem of performance is that which takes in such questions as the following: What events are most effectively and appropriately grouped together? According to what principles and elements of association are the events of the piece best interconnected? And if there are divergent possibilities, as is often the case, on what rational basis do I justify a particular judgment about grouping? Any decision about the linking of materials (asserted in performance by enforced continuities, consistencies of articulation, avoidance of punctuative separation, and other means) has its proper basis in some construct of formal process, motive (or other formal unit), harmonic unity, metric ordering, structural tendency, or relation to focal points

determined in analysis. And the expressive modulations of elements in intensifying or resolving directions, a matter of syntactic organization and a topic of
fundamental concern in the foregoing studies, are a further, vital implication of
musical organization to be grasped in analysis and meaningfully conveyed in
performance.

The analysis undertaken as a basis for shaping interpretation and reinforcing
interpretive decisions and choices engages also the examination of texture—its
properties of action and cohesion, its functional, organic changes. Imitative and
other interactions in musical texture, as constituent factors of formal unity and
structural vitality, are invariably important to the performer, even if they are
often so explicit as to require no direct intervention, but only the assurance of
clarity and the avoidance of obscuring actions. Texture has been considered in
all three of this book's principal inquiries, and it has been seen to be a critical
element of processive fluctuation and directed activity; indeed it is commonly
one of the most readily experienced. Of particular concern in performance is the
relatively covert textural interchange, in which cross-referring relations of substance are reasonably inferrable and implicit but not direct and verbatim, and
may require illuminating exposure by compatible articulations. However textural properties are finally disposed in performance, they are always pertinent as
a comprehended factor of interpretive consciousness. Of course this is especially
crucial where texture is a primary motivating element, as in the area of harmonic inertia in Berg's piece.

The justification of tempo in its fundamental aspect and in surface modulations is a predominant issue of analysis and performance. It is reckoned not only
as the governing rate of referential pulsation (metronomic tempo), but also in
relation to the volume and distribution of aggregate rhythmic activity of the
absolute surface. In one frame of reference, tempo has been regarded critically
in terms of its balancing (parallel or counteractive) relations to the actions of
other elements. Decisions concerning tempo—how fast, how slow, how much
acceleration or deceleration—must thus be logically defensible and demonstrable through an analysis of the correlated processes against which tempo is
calibrated. Changes of metronomic tempo in the course of a work may denote a
broadly paced, overall rhythmic configuration that is clearly functional and
powerfully expressive, as they do in the pieces by Berg and Debussy. Perhaps no
interpretive choices more urgently demand analytical study and justification
than those of tempo, for no musical element bears more profoundly and decisively on expressive shape and character.

Directed, dynamic, broadly gestural lines of action to and from points of
orientation in musical structures are critically important and of fundamental
expressive effect. Often these lines are oriented around a single such point
having overreaching implication; this is evident in each of the three examples

studied. Such a concept of dynamic structure, based on an understanding of interrelated, cofunctioning lines of action and directed processes of musical elements, can in many contexts guide a performance's motivations and articulate continuities in a special, persuasive sense, whether viewed as expansively metric or otherwise. This is one necessary aspect of wholeness in the musical organism, quite probably that most susceptible to interpretive molding. A distilled overview of distinctive content, sketched as a thematic essence, is another: a synoptic perspective in which the performer can capture a work's essential thematic basis and generalized directions, and achieve insight into them. The summation of a piece's distinctive, midlevel individuating materials is considered in either sense to be an interpreted construct, capable of realization in performance and appreciable in experience, and distinct from the generic, deep harmonic bases that tonal compositions often widely share.

The analysis of tonal structure, particularly at forelevel and midlevels, is an imperative basis for distinguishing interpretively between the essential and the auxiliary conditions of specific tonal materials. This is a sharply posed issue in the Debussy, critical also in the Brahms, and not irrelevant to the Berg. The performer who merely negotiates the notes of the score reveals nothing more tellingly than a lack of awareness of the distinction between central constituents in the tonal framework and elaborative ones, and this is especially critical for the midlevels of phrase and phrase groupings. By no means is this to say that primary tonal elements necessarily want deliberate exposure: to the contrary, tonally primary events usually have intrinsic prominence, and often prevail without overt emphasis at the relatively quiescent stages of departure and resolution, whereas structural phases marked by elaborative tonal deviance and mobility (that is, dissonance) are often the scene of dynamic process and the basis for compelling interpretive intervention. The analytical identification and assessment of tonal elements in all domains of melodic and harmonic action are thus an imperative precondition for many kinds of interpretive choice.

Out of searching review and reflection, the interpreter derives in analysis a governing sense of what the piece is "about," its scope of potential utterance, its expressive message and character, beyond the understanding of objective materials of structure. We all know that a performer's approaches to a composition, in physical deportment but especially in the interpretive strokes of realization, can reflect a discernible attitude toward the music, appropriate or not, insightful or indifferent, convincing or bewildering; and this attitude colors the subtle and manifold inflections and expressive effects that are woven into and are consequences of the intricacies of musical structure.

The special, often profoundly affecting (if at times too blatant) import of descriptive connotation in music is relevant to much performance, frequently and perhaps most sublimely in alliance with poetic text and textual image. This book includes an early reference to specific musical depictions of poetic imagery in one of Hugo Wolf's consummate achievements, and in chapter 5 a full-length exploration of very different qualities of poetic reflection in Debussy.

Finally, in all the foregoing analytical contexts, not least in connection with musical reflections of suggestive poetic content, it is assumed that the interpreter's taste and discretion are the only safeguards against exaggerated intervention, against crossing those parlous lines between too little, enough, and too much in the projection of any intended interpretive flow of ideas following from analytical penetration and resulting insight.

It bears reemphasizing that analysis can often tell the performer not to intervene overtly in the interest of one thing only to obscure another, latent value; not to magnify in representation the self-evident and thoroughly established; not to impair expression of the character of a piece, recognized as the sum of its cofunctioning parts, by any violation of its discerned atmosphere; not to overstate what is assessed as subsidiary in some chosen perspective, at the risk of confusing by distraction and dilution what has been found to be of the immediate or overreaching essence. A satisfying performance illuminates its subject according to the interpreter's full understanding and appreciation, achieved in arduous, ultimately exhilarating, thought and effort. It is a portrayal of coacting and interacting musical elements profoundly apprehended to the level of apparently spontaneous realization. In the best sense it is a dramatic representation, in which every event is tempered in relation to a re-created, holistically assimilated structure embodying the potential for expressive effect and affect.

In conclusion, I restate a rhetorical query that I have posed elsewhere:

Does it matter whether the performer is aware of the (often subtle and at times tenuous) interrelations and materials of musical form and structure? My answer is unequivocal. Certainly no justifiable decision respecting the manifold possibilities of tempo and articulation, of intervention or the lack of it, can be made without the underpinning of that systematic analytical discovery which yields a reasoned, justifiable determination among conceivable possibilities of portrayal in the illusion of spontaneous rebirth each time a piece is heard.

The intuitive impulse, fed by experience yet too often unverified and adventitious as to the elements of a particular context, may indeed "hit it right"; but the thoughtful interpreter, stirred by intellectual curiosity no less than by untempered feeling, will seek the reassurances of corroborative rationale, in the analytical exploration of putative, alternative conceptions. And the analysis which informs interpretation affords a basis—the only

basis—for resolving the hard questions both of general interpretive de-
meanor and of those elusive refinements of detail which make for performance which is both moving and illuminating.[1]

Again, the striving for an analytical perspective in which to regard interpretive choices does not signify for a given composition some singular resultant
outlet inflexibly embraced and mechanistically reproduced. Rather, the sensitive, imaginative, inquiring performer reflects on the derived sense of a piece,
considering and reconsidering its always tentative realization, in response to
evolving attitudes and varying circumstances. Each renewal of a composition's
transient and uncertain existence thus seeks to portray comprehended interrelations in commensurate qualities of sound, the indispensable substance of truly
interpretive musical representation.

Notes

CHAPTER ONE. POINTS OF DEPARTURE

1. Edward Cone, *Musical Form and Musical Performance* (New York: W. W. Norton, 1968).

2. Edward Cone, "*Musical Form and Musical Performance* Reconsidered," *Music Theory Spectrum* 7 (1985): 149–58.

3. Joel Lester, *Harmony in Tonal Music* (New York: Alfred A. Knopf, 1982).

4. Janet Schmalfeldt, "On the Relation of Analysis to Performance: Beethoven's Bagatelles Op. 126, Nos. 2 and 5," *Journal of Music Theory* 29, no. 1 (1985): 1–31.

5. Wallace Berry, *Structural Functions in Music* (Englewood Cliffs, N.J.: Prentice-Hall, 1976; reprint, New York: Dover, 1987). Certain of the book's fundamental points, including that of prevalent expressive tendencies of progression and recession in music, are stated in its introduction, pp. 1–26.

CHAPTER TWO. THE RELATIONS OF ANALYSIS TO PERFORMANCE

1. Wallace Berry, "Formal Process and Performance in the 'Eroica' Introductions," *Music Theory Spectrum* 10 (1988): 3.

2. Edward Cone, *Musical Form and Musical Performance* (New York: W. W. Norton, 1968), pp. 38–39.

3. See my review of Cone's signal study, in *Perspectives of New Music* 9, no. 2, and 10, no. 1 (double issue; 1971): 290.

4. Heinrich Schenker, "The Largo of J. S. Bach's Sonata No. 3 for Unaccompanied Violin [BWV 1005]," trans. John Rothgeb, *Music Forum* 4 (1976): 158. Schenker's assertions of a relation between dissonance and dynamic intensity reflect an eighteenth-century tradition of performance theory.

5. Heinrich Schenker, "The Sarabande of J. S. Bach's Suite No. 3 for Unaccompanied Violoncello [BWV 1009]," trans. Hedi Siegel, *Music Forum* 2 (1970): 282.

6. Berry, "Formal Process and Performance," p. 3.

7. Wallace Berry, "Sense and Sensibility: What Can We Know about Music? What Do We Want to Know?" in *Fact and Value in Contemporary Musical Scholarship* (Boulder, Colo.: College Music Society, 1986), pp. 9–14.

8. Janet Schmalfeldt, "On the Relation of Analysis to Performance: Beethoven's Bagatelles Op. 126, Nos. 2 and 5," *Journal of Music Theory* 29, no. 1 (1985): 28.

9. Berry, "Formal Process and Performance," p. 3.

10. Schmalfeldt, p. 18.

11. There is a distinction between a "motive" and a "motivic" item, as will be clear in succeeding chapters.

12. Schenker, "Largo of J. S. Bach's Sonata No. 3," p. 158 and accompanying graphs.

13. Schenker, "Sarabande of J. S. Bach's Suite No. 3," p. 282 and accompanying graphs.

14. Ibid., p. 282.

15. Schmalfeldt, p. 27.

16. It is helpful to think of form in terms of specific processes by which it is expressed: preparation, expository statement and restatement, transition, development, and closure, although any given segment may of course reflect more than one of these fundamental tendencies. See chapter 1.

17. Examples 2.11 and 2.12 and their accompanying comments are borrowed from Berry, "Formal Process and Performance," pp. 4–7.

18. Developmental acceleration is explored in Wallace Berry, "Rhythmic Accelerations in Beethoven," *Journal of Music Theory* 22 (1978): 177–240.

19. There is a discussion of rhythmic elements of this piece in Wallace Berry, "Dialogue and Monologue in the Professional Community," *College Music Symposium* 21, no. 2 (1981): 92–99.

20. See Wallace Berry, "Metric and Rhythmic Articulation in Music," *Music Theory Spectrum* 7 (1985): 21–30, concerning groupings in Prelude No. 1 of Bach's *Well-Tempered Clavier,* book 1, and other examples.

21. Cone, p. 35. Some lines are omitted. Cone goes on to suggest that "such choices need not be permanent," that "they ought not to be," and that a particular interpretation "may become boring through repetition."

22. Heinrich Schenker, *Free Composition (Der freie Satz),* trans. Ernst Oster (New York: Longman, 1979), p. 120 and fig. 138, 3.

23. See Berry, *Structural Functions in Music* (Englewood Cliffs, N.J.: Prentice-Hall, 1976; reprint, New York: Dover, 1987); idem, "Metric and Rhythmic Articulation."

24. Berry, "Metric and Rhythmic Articulation," pp. 11–12.

25. Wallace Berry, *Structural Functions in Music,* pp. 365–71.

26. Berry, "Metric and Rhythmic Articulation," pp. 20–21, 25–30.

27. Cone, p. 23.

28. Berry, *Structural Functions in Music,* pp. 4–13 and passim. See also my other writings, including "Apostrophe," *Perspectives of New Music* 14, no. 2, and 15, no. 1 (1976), as well as chapter 1 of this volume. The function of an event is conceived here as generally in my published work: that is, in terms of its processive role in an identified directed tendency.

29. See the analysis by Schenker cited in notes 5 and 13, and Schenker's examples 1c and 1d.

30. Certain of my other writings consider conceptual problems of broad tonal structures: the complicating factors of angled and intersecting lines of association, and

"multilateral" relations. See *Structural Functions in Music*, chap. 1, and especially "On Structural Levels in Music," *Music Theory Spectrum* 2 (1980): 19–45.

CHAPTER THREE. FIRST CASE: BRAHMS

1. Discussions of accompanimental rhythms in Debussy's song considered in chapter 5 will be found parallel in implication.

2. It may be seen in ex. 3.7 that the arpeggiation of the minor subdominant by metric accents coincides with that of a dominant ninth on G-flat by weak-beat attacks and interim resolutions of the exposed, active appoggiaturas. This is symptomatic of the dual or even multiple meanings of harmony in this passage.

3. For my concepts of meter and metric process see *Structural Functions in Music* (Englewood Cliffs, N.J.: Prentice-Hall, 1976; reprint, New York: Dover, 1987), chap. 3, and more recently "Metric and Rhythmic Articulation in Music," *Music Theory Spectrum* 7 (1985): 7–33. The present discussion is restricted to an impression of partitioning in the Intermezzo, of the grouping of events in relation to accents of the near-foreground, a palpably experienced rhythmic punctuation which I consider to be "metric."

4. However problematic it may be to evaluate some of the cited accentual relations, there is no question of the superiority of the barline accent of measure 21 to that of measure 22, nor of those of measures 25–26, the area of acceleration, to that of measure 24.

5. There is a useful study of the Intermezzo's harmonic structure and voice leading in Felix Salzer and Carl Schachter, *Counterpoint in Composition* (New York: McGraw-Hill, 1969), pp. 458–59.

6. The techniques of representation not discussed in the text are self-evident, or so common as to require no explanation.

7. To what extent Brahms's direction of stringendo applies is problematic; no doubt some would take literally its apparent restriction in the notation to measures 13–14. Yet it seems unlikely that the intervention of overt forward thrust will not also apply in a lesser degree to the parallel motivic substance of measures 15–16 and 17–18, as a declining tendency in the predominantly recessive, comparatively immobile context of closure.

8. It was suggested earlier that for these reasons mezzo forte seems appropriate at the approach to measure 27, and as an outer limit for the piece's dynamic range overall.

CHAPTER FOUR. SECOND CASE: BERG

1. Intervals are, as commonly, referred to by the number of semitones between component pitches: the semitone is 1, the tritone 6, and so on. I use the term "chord" in its common sense, to refer to a simultaneity of three or more pitch classes.

In my illustrations of structural elements in the Berg, the natural sign is not used where in conventional notation it would be assumed, in contrast with the composer's practice.

2. Some readers will recognize this structure as a distinctive term in Berg's music, and as the "Wir arme Leut'!" motive of his opera *Wozzeck*.

3. Also of demonstrable motivic significance, but less pervasive, are the diminished triad and to a lesser extent the diminished seventh chord, both discussed later in this study. The former applies specifically to a broad underlying unity in the clarinet part: A–C–E-flat (measures 1–2); E–G–B-flat (measures 2–3, mirrored in the descending piano bass); and B–D–F (measure 5 and measures 10–13).

4. The appoggiatura motive is a stylistic term recurrent in much tonal music, and notably in later nineteenth-century literatures, as is evident in the analyses of Brahms and Debussy. This fundamental, expressive term in music, a sign of Berg's immediate heritage, is a compelling topic for another study.

5. An important further study of tonal implication in the Berg piece is Christopher Lewis's "Tonal Focus in Atonal Music: Berg's Op. 5/3," *Music Theory Spectrum* 3 (1981): 84–97. My views on tonality in later styles and in general are treated extensively in Wallace Berry, *Structural Functions in Music* (Englewood Cliffs, N.J.: Prentice-Hall, 1976; reprint, New York: Dover, 1987), chap. 1.

6. Later examination of D-references entails consideration of measure 1's tritone {G, C-sharp/D-flat}, prominent by virtue of recurrence and, in the immediate context of the motive, its longer notes.

7. Articulation represented by Berg's symbol "–" (denoting a cautious, slightly leaning, stress) is functional in the chords, yet potentially contradictory of their anacrustic role if overdone. (The composer's placement of the symbol for the chord in measure 4 is of course an anomaly, but the intent is clear.)

8. In the terms of Hindemith's "best interval," B would be the "root" of the harmonic complex with which the piano enters at measure 5. Indeed, the B is vital as the root of the only perfect fifth, and in its leading-tone relation to the clarinet's interim goal, C (ex. 4.7c). My analysis of the harmony in question gives primacy to G by virtue of its persistence as a lowest-voice pedal, and what I regard as Berg's "V"–"I" interplay between the thirds {G,B} and {C,E} of the piano and clarinet.

9. A further staged diminuendo at the second half of section (B) is essential in subordinating the sense of subsequently shifted tonal reference toward D, a fluctuation to be compared with that of the piece's final section.

10. Not including the descending chromatic line, the section has nine pitch classes. Until the point of harmonic shift at measure 12 it lacks the A and D-sharp/E-flat of the cadence at measure 8, as well as C.

11. A residual, registrally unified E-flat triad will be considered in connection with conceivable D-references, the chord's outermost pitch classes (D and F-sharp), and the clarinet's reiterated, registrally consistent arpeggiation D–F–B-flat–A-flat in the preceding measures (ex. 4.15).

12. The D-orientations of the final section, initiated in the symmetrical wedged motions of measure 15 (ex. 4.9), are detailed in the upcoming segment of this study.

13. The third (Ḇ,Ḏ,F̱,A̱-flat) emerges prominently as a reference to C̱ at measures 9–12.

14. The experience in such a case of one expressive tendency or another (of release, of intensification) no doubt depends on factors of timbre, dynamic intensity, and other elements beyond those reviewed here. Yet, although little is known of the perceptual and cognitive import of such a process of textural content, it seems likely that opening expresses relaxation (that is, what I have characterized as recession). In the chords that begin section (B) a process of textural opening and release is functional in preparing the slower pacing and relative harmonic immobility that follow, much as relative concentrations of intervallic distribution at measures 5–8 support the sense of active dissonance.

15. I refer here to specific intervals rather than classes, and distinguish between, for example, the third and tenth, because the point is one of a profile delineated in a graduated succession of specific interval sizes. The intervals are articulated directly—that is, between pitches in direct succession in a particular voice.

16. With the original dotted quarter note at 72, the original quarter would be equivalently at 108, more than twice the 42–46 of section (C). Another way to regard the tempo relations is to compare the original eighth-note pulse (at 216) with the triplet eighth-note of measure 9 (at 118, a bit less than half as fast).

17. There is an anomaly of notation in the published score, where the second half of measure 14 restores the normative duple division of the eighth; the final bracketed duple grouping includes the Ḏ, and must be placed before the eighth-rest.

18. Where there is risk of losing an integral element, as at the very beginning, perfectly clear execution is paramount. Of the stream of thirds, the registrally shifted {Ḇ-flat,Ḏ} is an object of repetition and dynamic inflection in measures 9–11, whereas this dyad and the succeeding {Ḇ,Ḏ-sharp} are heard in the long sonority of measure 13 (though the preceding {A̱,C̱-sharp} and later {C̱,E} notably are not).

19. Because the notated mensural organization of barlines has been abandoned in ex. 4.30a the alignment of notes is approximate, yet important to the image of the piece as depicted. The procedure of generalization applies to tempi and dynamic intensities as it does to other elements. Parentheses denote implied or subsidiary items, and subsidiary ones are also represented by unstemmed notes. Beams are used to group notes according to construed structural unities, especially of form, motive, melody, and harmony.

CHAPTER FIVE. THIRD CASE: DEBUSSY

1. Consider in comparison elaborative chromatic streams of tonally detached harmonies in many eighteenth-century fantasy pieces, or in Chopin, as examples of earlier, analogous practice. With respect to Debussy's idiom and related ones, the distinction can often usefully be drawn among such intensely chromatic linear techniques of semitonal association used in Chopin and German styles contemporaneous with Debussy, a more pronounced sense of tonal detachment in whole-tone linear associations (in some re-

spects evident in Debussy's song), and other distinctively idiomatic linear relations, such as that of the tritonal pair {G,C-sharp} at measures 40–42 in the Debussy.

2. See my discussion of harmonic structure in the closing bars of the third song of Debussy's "Ariettes oubliées," in Wallace Berry, *Structural Functions in Music* (Englewood Cliffs, N.J.: Prentice-Hall, 1976; reprint, New York: Dover, 1987), pp. 105–7. Also discussed is the tonal structure of one of Ravel's "Histoires naturelles" (*Le Martin-Pêcheur*); see pp. 142–47, which treat the concept of predominantly linear functions of surface components over underlying tonal reference to F-sharp, and to diatonically related secondary tonics.

3. This particular sonority (the primary V in ex. 5.1 and a subordinate auxiliary in ex. 5.2) is a quasi-motivic, favored element in the song as a whole, as in much of Debussy.

4. As a pitch class it joins the tonic triad at key points (measures 20 and 46–47), not to mention its sheer prominence in measures 1–8 in the voice melody and as a factor in the characteristic dominant ninth.

5. The components of neither are topically interdependent. The collection *Romances sans paroles* (1874) by Paul Verlaine (1844–96) includes the "Ariettes oubliées." Of the latter, Debussy's collection under the same title, published in 1903, incorporates the first ("C'est l'extase langoureuse"), the third ("Il pleure dans mon cœur"), and the ninth and last ("L'ombre des arbres"), and also includes other poems from *Romances sans paroles:* one from "Paysages belges" ("Chevaux de bois") and two from "Aquarelles" ("Green" and "Spleen").

6. "Yet such poetry is, by its very nature, more or less untranslatable. . . . the poetry of impressions, of suggestion, of subtle musical effects." From Cecily Mackworth, ed., *A Mirror for French Poetry: 1840–1940* (Miami: Royale House, 1947), p. x. From the same source, on the reader's role: "To seize on a suggestion, to capture this fluid and effervescent element which hovers behind thought, implies a real effort of sensibility."

7. *C'est l'ex-tase lan-gou-reuse*, for example; but *La mienne, dis, et la tienne*. I do not presume to deal with the complexities of French poetic scansion, but a few inescapable, intriguing anomalies in Debussy's alignment of musical prosody to poetic prosody will be found to require consideration in the singer's performance and cautious adjustments of articulation.

8. That is, a line's final *-e* or *-es* is sounded when sung, a rhythmic factor inapplicable to every third line of Verlaine's poem.

9. The appropriateness of these and other tempo changes to poetic content is considered in full detail later.

10. The bass of measure 7 may well be conceived as an imitation, in augmentation of the directly preceding descending steps of the piano's right-hand part, supporting the notion of the primary motive as a generative resource.

11. That this active, spatial configuration is so important in all three works analyzed in this book says something about its virtual universality as an expressive term in music.

12. Some of the terminology here, especially the references to "reactive" and "anticipative" metric impulses, is set forth in Berry, *Structural Functions in Music,* chap. 3. But it is assumed that the implications of these terms and concepts are, in the present limited context, self-evident.

13. The harmony rooted on D̲, although it is a midlevel tonal goal tonicized over a considerable span, conceivable even as IV of IV, seems to me to have primarily linear significance: locally in its association with V (measures 17–18 and 36–37) and broadly in its quasi-modal pitch and pitch-class relation to E̲ (ex. 5.23). It affords a good example of the tonal-linear functional duality considered early in this chapter.

14. My reference to quasi-recitando setting in the voice has to do with a relative confinement of melodic undulations of the foreground, an attribute most clearly evident in the measures examined here, which have repeated notes often in regular rhythms. (The recitando aspect has less to do with note-per-syllable setting, the rule through by far the greater part of Debussy's adaptation of Verlaine's poem.) Measures 29–34 have something of a comparable recitando quality, in part because of the striking contrast with the soaring melodic flights that directly precede. And in measures 41–43, in the course of sweeping melodic ascent, the rhythmic setting is fragmented and so specifically allied to poetic prosody that one has in another sense the impression of a declamatory implication. The factors of lyric and declamatory contrast will come up again with respect to issues of interpretion.

15. Recall the significance of C̲-sharp in the structure as a whole.

16. The ambiguous tritone {G̲,C̲-sharp} can be associated with the chromatically related, prominent {F̲-sharp,C̲} of measures 36–39.

17. A factor that has been cited in the motive's dynamic molding is a very cautious articulative stress on its first, highest, most dissonant note (to which corresponds Debussy's slight, *caressant* emphasis on the voice's first note in measure 4: *l'ex-ta̲-se*). The voice's first two phrases reflect perfect fidelity to the poetic lines' natural prosody, realized in the coincidence of principal musical accents of dissonance, pitch, and duration.

18. The voice's crescendo on the word *frissons* is an instance of controlled surge at this point; it can be used also to enunciate and project, in tremulous excitement, the allusive word itself. Example 5.4*b* suggests a corresponding urgency and controlled intensity in the piano.

19. An aspect of local process is the reiterated recessive succession from an intense dominant structure (measures 28, 30) to the purely triadic D:I (measures 29, 31, 34–35), by way of the interim, D̲-rooted major seventh chord (measures 29, 31) and plagal elaborations of measures 32–33.

20. The implicit assumption is that both textural extremes—wide registral variance and severe crowding—may, paradoxically, contribute to active phases of development where other factors are commensurate, in that both are departures from normal occurrence.

21. This can also have a provocative effect of local metric deviance in the voice's resulting implication of 6/16: *doux / Que l'herbe agitée.* (Compare measure 11 as discussed in connection with ex. 5.27.)

22. The alert performer will also see that there is a registrally consistent pitch descent bridging the two stanzas: d_1 (measures 29, 31)–c-sharp$_1$ (measures 32–33)–c$_1$ (measures 36, 38)–b (measures 37, 39). The pianist may well choose to accord some attention in performance to this line of functional succession.

23. This motivic derivative has been discussed as extracted from the primary motive of measures 1–4 (that is, from measure 1), but also as a diatonic variant of the chromatic *cri* motive central to the preceding stanza. It is interesting that in measures 36–43 the motive's upper note is first B̲, then E̲, the structure's primary tonal degrees having in stanza 3 essentially dissonant function even in the voice melody's final arrival at measure 48, where the E̲ awaits consonant implication in the piano's ultimate resolution.

24. But the crescendo is restricted in the interest of the descending voice, easily covered at the beginning of measure 45. The piano's second attack in that bar, forte, is however rhythmically placed so as not to impede the voice.

25. In ex. 5.4*f*, there is an editorial emendation at measure 45.

26. The surface accompanimental rhythm of one eighth-note and four sixteenths (or a dotted eighth and three sixteenths) is, like the recurring syncopations, potentially instrumental in either accelerative or retardative tendencies, depending on context.

27. As a device for gauging the original tempo, the pianist may well associate the sixteenth-notes of measure 48 with those of measure 2.

CHAPTER SIX. POINTS OF SUMMATION

1. Wallace Berry, "Formal Process and Performance in the 'Eroica' Introductions," *Music Theory Spectrum* 10 (1988): 18.

Index

Cross-references to *individual elements* pertain to the headings Dynamic inflection; Melodic structure; Metric structure; Register; Tempo; Texture; and Tonal structure. A page number in italic refers to a relevant musical excerpt or analytical illustration.